RIGHT
ON THE
MONEY

Other Books by Doug Casey

International Man (1978, 1979, 1981)
Crisis Investing (1979, 1980/1981, 1983)
  New York Times Bestseller for 29 consecutive weeks
Strategic Investing (1982)
  New York Times Bestseller for 5 weeks
Crisis Investing for the Rest of the '90s (1993, 1995)
Totally Incorrect (2012)

RIGHT
ON THE
MONEY

**Doug Casey on Economics,
Investing, and the Ways of the
Real World with Louis James**

Doug Casey

Cover Design: Wiley
Cover Image: Casey Research

Published by John Wiley & Sons, Inc., Hoboken, New Jersey.
Published simultaneously in Canada.

For general information on our other products and services or for technical support, please contact our Customer Care Department within the United States at (800) 762-2974, outside the United States at (317) 572-3993 or fax (317) 572-4002.

Wiley publishes in a variety of print and electronic formats and by print-on-demand. Some material included with standard print versions of this book may not be included in e-books or in print-on-demand. If this book refers to media such as a CD or DVD that is not included in the version you purchased, you may download this material at http://booksupport.wiley.com. For more information about Wiley products, visit www.wiley.com.

ISBN 978-1-118-85622-2 (Paperback)
ISBN 978-1-118-85620-8 (ePDF)
ISBN 978-1-118-85618-5 (ePub)

Printed in the United States of America.
10 9 8 7 6 5 4 3 2 1

Contents

Part Three: A Moral Minority

Part Four: You and Me and the Other 8 Billion

Part Five: Wrestling for Countries

Preface

Dear Reader:

This book may look like a sequel, or perhaps a punch line, but it's much, much more than that. What you hold in your hands is a set of keys to a potential fortune available to contrarians who are brave enough to use them during a time of unprecedented chaos and volatility gripping our world. These key concepts, set out and elaborated in these pages, will enable you to turn Doug Casey's essential philosophical (if unabashedly irreverent) views of economics, politics, and life itself into actionable investment ideas. This book is nothing less than a speculator's guide to profiting from the Greater Depression.

Many readers have commented on how brash, amusing, and refreshing *Totally Incorrect* is. That's great; Doug and I are pleased to have gotten so many people thinking about important things. But in *Right on the Money*, we want to show readers the path from basic ideas to actionable steps that can make a huge difference in one's finances, and life itself. This is the "so what" to our last book.

We hope readers will take it seriously, and act upon what Doug says in these pages, because it could make all the difference in the shape of those lives in the years ahead.

The following conversations were originally published online and were peppered with hyperlinks to additional material we believed readers would want to reach. In this print edition of *Right on the Money*, we've retained the hyperlinks in ghost fashion. Don't try clicking on your book; it won't work. But you can follow any link that interests you by visiting www.rightonthemoneybook.com. There you'll find all the online links that the book refers to, laid out conversation by conversation, just as they appear in the book.

Sincerely,
Terry Coxon

Acknowledgments

There are always more people to thank at the birth of a new book than can be named, so let me start with a blanket thank you to everyone who contributed.

Special thanks go to my wife, Ancha Casey, for suggesting, guiding, correcting, prodding, and motivating me on these conversations, throughout the years of their creation. My partners, David Galland and Olivier Garret, also deserve special thanks for their work and support making it happen.

Terry Coxon, economist and editor extraordinaire—also former editor of Harry Browne, whose books contributed so much to my developments as a person and as an investor—I thank profusely for jumping on this project and getting it done so quickly and completely. The production staff at Casey Research deserves great thanks as well, for all their work proofing, tweaking, posting, fixing, etc., these conversations over the years.

Finally, I'm not sure how to thank my friend and brother in arms, Lobo Tiggre (Louis James), whose uncanny ability to almost read my mind made these conversations what they are. It is he, the indefatigable "L," who saddles up with me every week for our intellectual excursions and makes sure they get published on time for our readers.

I do hope you enjoy reading about the ideas as much as we enjoyed conversing about them.

Sincerely,
DRC

Part One

AN ECONOMY IN TROUBLE

Chapter 1

Doug Casey on Bernanke: Be Afraid, Be Very Afraid (Part One)

December 8, 2010

Louis: Thanks for the link to the "historic" <u>Ben Bernanke interview</u>*. It was breathtaking to hear the man who didn't see the crash of 2008 coming say he's "100 percent confident" he can control the U.S. economy. What do you make of that—is it hubris or stupidity?

---

* The following conversations were originally published online and were peppered with hyperlinks to additional material we believed readers would want to reach. In this print edition of *Right on the Money*, we've retained the hyperlinks in ghost fashion. You can follow any link that interests you by visiting www.rightonthemoneybook.com. There you'll find all the online links that the book refers to, laid out conversation by conversation, just as they appear in the book.

Doug: As *60 Minutes* pointed out, it's rare for a Fed chairman to give an interview; this was only Bernanke's second—here's a link to his first. It's such an unusual thing that I think it's a sign that the Powers That Be are really quite worried. As they should be. His last interview was at the height of the crisis in early 2009.

L: Bernanke himself looked worried. I was amazed, actually, watching the interview, by just how nervous and stressed he appeared. He stuttered, his lip quivered continuously, and that pulsing vein on his forehead really stood out throughout the interview. He looked like he was flat-out lying and doubted anyone would believe him, but had no choice but to keep lying. It was almost like a cartoon of a liar caught red-handed. It's a shocker that the Powers That Be would let such an interview be aired—it would seem to be the opposite of reassuring, to me.

D: I know. It'd be nice to run that interview through a voice stress analyzer and see what it says. It's a question of whether he's a knave or a fool—neither answer is bullish for the U.S. economy. He'd be wonderful to play poker against.

He's not a skilled or enthusiastic liar, but he is certainly becoming more practiced at it, which is, of course, par for the course of being Fed chairman. That aside, the interview is really interesting, because there are several times in the interview when he really comes across as being scared and warning people: the way he stressed how close to the edge of a precipice the economy was, and how troubled it remains.

L: Well, that was the reason given for the interview. He says the critics of his latest $600 billion shot in the economy's arm don't understand how serious things are, how dangerous the high unemployment rate is.

D: Yes, of course he'd say that. You know my argument is that "doing something" is a mistake, if it's based on incorrect economics. Everything they are doing is not just the wrong thing, it's the opposite of the right thing.

L: So, do you believe Bernanke was actually lying? Or was he just highly stressed, because he's the one in the hot seat, and he knows that just because the *Titanic* didn't sink the moment it hit the iceberg, that doesn't mean it's out of danger?

D: Perhaps it's a bit like Hitler in the bunker, who was under great stress, and really wasn't lying when he insisted that the Third Reich could still win the war. In fact, I can't wait to see if someone does one of those "Hitler in the bunker" spoofs, based on this interview.

L: I wouldn't be surprised to see one posted on YouTube tomorrow. Meantime, Jon Stewart skewers Bernanke admirably in a recent skit on his show.

D: Actually, someone just did one of those "Hitler in the bunker" spoofs on manipulation of the silver market—which, incidentally, I don't believe is a reality. But it mentions our redoubt at La Estancia de Cafayate. There's a lot of very rich and colorful language, which some people won't like, but it's very funny.

L: Warning to readers: That video is not family-friendly. So, lying aside, let's look at some of the things he said. The first and foremost thing that jumps out at me is that he says the Fed is "not printing money" and that the Fed's actions have no significant impact on money supply. How can he imagine they can inject liquidity into the economy, and that it won't have any impact on money supply?

D: I think he knows better than that. Look, what the Fed has been doing is buying securities. And the way they do that is to credit the account of the seller with dollars. So, of course it creates money. That's why they call it "quantitative easing"—because they're increasing the number of Federal Reserve units in circulation. I really love that term, QE, because it's so cynically dishonest, like the whole monetary system itself. And it's amazing that nobody even challenges it. They just accept it instead of calling it what it is—printing money. It's Orwellian.

In any event, creating more currency units by buying government bonds serves several purposes, from their point of view. It raises the prices of bonds, and therefore pushes interest rates down—and they want lower rates because it makes it easier to finance the staggering amount of debt out there that threatens to collapse the system. And they want more currency units out there because that makes people feel richer, consume more, and that props up preexisting economic conditions—which are actually unsustainable. The crash prompted them to buy toxic paper from banks for a while, to keep them from going under. Now they're buying U.S. treasuries again, with the latest $600 billion.

Bernanke is taking desperate measures to solve an acute problem. But their consequences will be disastrous—much, much more damaging than if he'd done nothing. Of course if he did nothing, the system would collapse through a deflation: bonds would default, banks would close. What will now happen is the currency itself is going to be destroyed, which is much worse. But since it's put off a bit further in the future, that's the course he's taking.

L: Agreed. In spite of what Bernanke says, whatever the sellers of the securities do with the new dollars deposited to their accounts—even if they leave them on deposit with the Fed because the Fed is now paying interest for excess reserves—it still frees up other money the sellers can now use for other purposes. And because of the fractional reserve system, there's a multiplier effect on the added liquidity. Bernanke says that all he's doing is keeping interest rates down to stimulate the economy, but the way he's doing it adds to the money supply.

D: Exactly. We're beyond the time when you have to cut down trees to print up hundred dollar bills. It's just a keystroke, now. But playing with the amount of currency doesn't create new wealth—it actually makes real wealth creation much harder.

So as the situation gets more serious in the months and years to come, you can expect ever more ad-hoc measures from the government. They'll probably try capital controls, to keep people from transferring wealth outside the U.S. Those will be popular because only "unpatriotic" people would do such a thing, as well as rich people—and it's now time to eat the rich. They'll likely require all pension plans to buy a certain amount of government securities. They'll have restrictions on the amount you can spend on foreign travel. They'll probably even try price controls, like Nixon did in the early 1970s. They'll increasingly limit what can be done with cash—like the new requirement that all transactions of any type above $600 must be reported on 1099s—because digital money is much easier to control. New government bureaucracies will be set up to enforce all these things, and many more.

L: Scary. Does it mean anything for Bernanke to say that the $600 billion came from the Fed's "own reserves"? Where would the Fed's reserves come from, if not from electronic dollars newly created at the stroke of a computer key?

D: No. That's a cynical lie. I think what he was trying to stress was that the money was not coming directly from taxes. The Federal Reserve is a misnomer. There is no reserve, as there was in the days when the gold at Fort Knox backed the dollar. Now, the dollar isn't backed by anything, so there's nothing to reserve—they can and do create as many dollars as they want, as ledger entries, which they can and do use to pay banks and others, who can and do use them to pay others, and so forth.

It's not a "reserve," and it's not "federal." Although the Fed is a creature of the government, it's not, technically speaking, part of it. It's really controlled by the large banks, who benefit primarily through "fractional reserve" banking. In the past, when banks were just ordinary businesses that warehoused money and acted as brokers for loans made with savings, keeping a fractional reserve was a fraudulent practice that would eventually result in bankruptcy, followed by criminal charges. The creation of central banks, like the Fed, facilitated it as common practice; in effect, debt became a form of money. This isn't the forum to explain the subject in detail; I've done that in my books. But we've now reached the inevitable consequence of the system, which is a financial cataclysm. Bernanke is trying to forestall the inevitable, and in the process is making it worse. As Louis XV correctly observed, "Après moi, le déluge."

L: Deluge indeed. You can see the out of control growth of what they are doing in any M2 money supply chart.

Ancha Casey [Doug's wife]:   Mfmmmf mmmfmf.

L: Hi Ancha—I didn't catch that.

Ancha [Leaning closer to Doug's mic]: Hi Lobo. That growth of money supply erodes purchasing power. One peso here in Argentina today is worth one trillionth—literally—of its value at the beginning of the twentieth century.

D: Yes. It really amounts to an indirect form of taxation: As more dollars are created, they dilute the purchasing power of the dollars already in existence—though we call it inflation. The first organizations and people to get those dollars are able to spend them at their old value. And, of course, the government—which is not the country or the people, but a group with its own identity and interests—gets to spend as many as it wants on what it wants. And now the numbers are moving into the trillions. Obama may soon have to ask his science advisor what comes after "trillion." It's all a charade.

L: Inflation is taxation through dilution. But most modern economists don't think inflation is the result of excess at the printing press, so whether Bernanke is lying, or just doesn't see the danger of what he's doing, it doesn't look good.

D: That's right. Most economists blame inflation on the butcher, the baker, or the candlestick maker raising their prices for other reasons than the loss of purchasing power of the currency. They attribute inflation to "greed" on the part of producers and workers.

The problem is a totally fallacious basic theory of economics. Almost all the "economists" coming out of school today aren't actually economists. An economist is someone who describes the way the world works. But these people—Bernanke being a perfect example—aren't interested in describing the way it works. Rather, they want to *prescribe* the way they want it to work, and then get the state to enforce their views on society. The state, of course, welcomes such advice when it serves its agenda.

Bernanke has a high IQ, but he's just an uninteresting and unoriginal suit. He grew up with the reigning orthodoxy, got his PhD in it, taught it, and has been rewarded with the leadership of the world's largest central bank. But he's not an economist. He's a political apologist. And, I suspect, he's now a very confused and scared one. Perhaps he can see that the ridiculous theories he's grown up believing in are more phony than a Federal Reserve note. But he doesn't dare admit it.

L: Maybe we could buy one of the thousands of mirrors in Mugabe's house in Zimbabwe and send it to Bernanke, as a gift. To look at himself, and perhaps see where the problem lies.

D: It won't help. The fundamental problem we have is an unsound money system, and no amount of fiddling with it will make it work well over any extended period of time. All fiat currencies follow one of two paths. One is when they keep printing more money to keep the ball rolling, which is what Bernanke's doing. Or they stop printing money, in which case banks go bust, insurance companies go bust, and all sorts of corporations go bust, throwing the economy into a catastrophic deflation. The latter is the better alternative, sad to say.

There's no painless way out of this, at this point. Bernanke is caught between the Scylla of deflation, which would liquidate the inefficient part of the economy, and the Charybdis of inflation. He's chosen Charybdis—the whirlpool—which will take the whole economy down.

L: Bernanke did specifically say in his interview that the Fed had to take action because there was a serious threat of deflation, which was the problem with the Great Depression.

D: Bernanke is afraid of deflation, because at this late stage, it would be extremely dramatic and immediate. In a free-market economy, neither monetary inflation or deflation are realistic problems, because gold is used as money, and the supply typically rises by only a small amount every year—and it almost never declines. But deflation is actually a good thing. Deflation may cause some wealth to change ownership, as any change can, but deflation does not destroy wealth, as inflation does. And deflation can be a very good thing because when dollars are worth more over time, it encourages people to save—and one of our big problems is that nobody's saving. People don't save because today's artificially low interest rates are beneath the actual inflation rate, so of course nobody wants to save. But the only way to become wealthy is to produce more than you consume and save the difference. Banks can't make loans unless, first, there are savings. This makes deflation's reward to savers a very important positive.

L: Bernanke says that falling prices would lead to lower wages, which would send the whole economy into decline.

D: That's an old fallacy. If all prices fall, including the price of labor, so does the cost of living, and no one is worse off. The price of labor would have to fall faster than the price of food, rent, et cetera for people to be hurt, and it does not follow automatically that this would be the case. If the butcher doesn't have to spend so much for bread, maybe he doesn't have to charge the baker so much, and both might be able to put aside a little more to save up for new goods from the candlestick maker, or to invest, or to create new businesses, and hire more people, which could actually drive wages up.

L: Wages may be influenced by inflation or deflation, but are not really set by them. What determines wages is productivity; how much value does the laborer create, and what can he or she trade for that value?

D: Exactly. And you get increases in productivity from capital creation, which arises from saving and investment. What this all boils down to is that you can't create wealth by printing money. That just debases wealth and distorts the economy.

L: Seems hard to believe Bernanke can't understand such a simple thing.

D: Well, the whole system is so precarious at this point that it may be quite accurate to label the Fed's actions as "panic." [Bernanke] said several times in the interview that he had to act—"aggressively" and "proactively"—to save the system. But you can't save a system that's built on quicksand—a fiat currency. The whole thing ought to be flushed away, along with the whole crazy-quilt work of Keynsian economics that most students are educated in. It's strange. It took the catastrophic collapse of the USSR and other socialist states to prove to all but the most dogmatic ideologues that Marxism was a sociopathic scam. It may take the collapse of the United States and the Western world to put the lie to Keynes. If so, then the sooner the better.

L: A lot of people would go down with that ship.

D: Yes. The whole business of the United States, its "consumer economy," has really become banking and finance. Everyone is buying and selling and trading electronic ghosts in between institutions, derivatives piled on derivatives, all magnified by the fractional reserve system. Or they provide services to those who do, paid for with meaningless accounting fictions that go back to the banks to pay for maxed-out credit cards. Nobody's thinking of actually producing things of value. The whole thing is a completely ridiculous house of financial cards.

People have forgotten the basics of banking, which are that a bank was a place where you deposited real money—mostly gold. There were time deposits (savings) and demand deposits (checking). The banks paid you some small amount when you deposited savings for some agreed upon period of time, typically about 3 percent, and made money lending it out at 6 percent. And banks charged you a small fee for the service of keeping your demand deposits liquid and paying them out to you or to whomever you gave your bank notes, or checks. That was it; banking was and should be no more exotic than a pawn shop.

But nobody believes this is the way things should be anymore; there's no way back without hitting the reset button. That's why I think the whole system has to—and will—collapse.

L: So you're not buying Bernanke's line that they are simply lowering interest rates to stimulate economic growth?

D: No. Aside from the fact that paying for this stimulation increases the money supply, stimulating growth through artificially low interest rates is the opposite of what they should be doing. It encourages debt and spending—living beyond your means, which is what the whole country has been doing for decades. They shouldn't be in a position to do anything—the Fed should be abolished. But, if anything, they should be raising interest rates to encourage savings. That's how wealth is accumulated, and wealth is what's needed to invest in new businesses and technologies, not to mention keeping yourself alive.

L: And unfortunately, in lowering rates to stimulate the economy, Bernanke is simply following the recipes of mainstream economists, so there seems to be little chance that he or anyone in power will realize the disastrous course they are on.

D: The chances are Slim and None, and Slim's out of town. The trouble with mainstream economics, the way it's taught in most colleges today, is that it's like sociology, or English literature, or gender studies: It's based on theoretical castles built in the air—no reality whatsoever. And [this is] of negative value in the real world. But, fortunately, the education system we suffer with today will also likely be washed away in the deluge.

L: That reminds me of the part of the interview in which Bernanke was asked if the Fed would be able to rein inflation in, should it appear. It was one of two questions he jumped on without hesitation, saying that inflation was not a problem. He could raise interest rates in 15 minutes, if necessary, and that would quash inflation. Made me wonder what planet he was living on, to imagine that after he's gone down the path of Mugabe, simply raising interest rates would restore purchasing power to the dollar. Even in recent memory in the United States, we've had high inflation *and* high interest rates—we call it *stagflation.* How could he not know this?

D: It just goes to show what a bad economist Bernanke is. The whole science of economics is not about seeing the immediate, direct, and obvious effects of any given economic policy—a smart six-year-old can do that. It's about seeing the indirect, hidden, and long-term effects of that policy. If the Fed goes into the bond market and buys a trillion dollars' worth of bonds, the short-term and fairly straight-forward effect will be for bond prices to go up and interest rates to go down. But the indirect and delayed effects from the creation of a trillion more currency units are inflationary, and eventually it will force even the interest rates back up again, because people won't lend unless they can charge a rate that will more than make up for the lost purchasing power of the inflated currency.

L: The seen and the unseen. Is it possible that Professor Bernanke has never read Bastiat?

D: [Laughs] Don't make me laugh. That's old-fashioned stuff, Lobo. The Great Depression disproved classical economics, don't you know? Now we have new economics—all built on quicksand, as I say, and that means the whole house of cards is doomed.

Chapter 2

Doug Casey on Bernanke: Be Afraid, Be Very Afraid (Part Two)

December 15, 2010

Louis: Quicksand, if not lies. That Jon Stewart link I provided last time shows that Bernanke himself called quantitative easing "printing money" in his previous *60 Minutes* interview, even though he denied the very same thing in this new one. Throughout the whole interview, aside from the quivering lip and the quavering voice, he seemed to be speaking out of both sides of his mouth, in terms of content. On one hand, he repeatedly sounded his warning that the economy is not out of the woods, and that's why printing more money was necessary; but on the other, he said the risk of a double-dip recession was very low.

Doug: I find it amazing that anyone pays any attention at all to what the man says. Except for a brief time waiting tables in school, he has zero experience in the real world. His whole life has been reading abstruse books written by people like himself, and doing complicated math formulas that are supposed to describe economic phenomena, but have absolutely nothing to do with the study of human action. He's a character who should appear in *Alice in Wonderland*, or *Through the Looking Glass*.

For instance, he claimed that another leg down for the economy was very unlikely because "cyclical" elements, like housing, were already very weak.

L: He actually said they couldn't get much weaker!

D: He's either a knave or a fool—possibly both. But the odds are he's just an educated fool, an archetypical, clinical example of one. Either way, it's bad news for the U.S. and global economies. Of course, there's really nothing that anyone could do, at this point, to avoid a huge amount of economic, political, and social turmoil. There are only two choices for a central bank: One is to keep printing money, and hope that magic happens; two is stop printing money, and let the existing structure collapse. Neither is a pleasant prospect, and there's no third alternative, in my view. It might have been possible to negotiate a relatively soft landing some years ago, but I believe that time has passed.

Of course, things will eventually bottom, and then get better. But in the meantime things can get worse—much worse—and, in fact, they are worse than the government is admitting. They don't admit it because they think confidence is important. It's not. If an economy rests on confidence, then you're in real trouble. Confidence can blow away like a pile of feathers in a hurricane. A big reason things will deteriorate is because the people in power are under the illusion that all is well as long as people keep spending.

L: Spending money they don't have.

D: Right. I keep coming back to basics: to accumulate wealth, you have to produce more than you consume and save the difference. In time, that savings can be invested in new ventures and new technologies that create prosperity. You simply cannot spend and consume your way into prosperity, either as an individual or as a society. Worse, all the debt in the world is an indication that many people are, in effect, living out of future production. This is why I keep saying that what they are doing is not only the wrong thing, but the exact opposite of the right thing. I'm not just being rhetorical—it's the literal truth. Real, sustainable economic recovery and growth depend on abandoning the old, uneconomic patterns of production and consumption that punish saving.

L: Brings to mind the strongly negative association most people have to the words "I'm from the government, and I'm here to help." And yet people seem willing to let the government do just about anything, from printing massive amounts of money to trampling the Constitution in the name of the War on Terror. How can people be so foolish as to trust an institution they know is untrustworthy?

D: Just goes to show how degraded society has become. This is a primary reason why I believe things must and will get worse before they get better. The average person in the United States doesn't much believe in the virtue of productive work, or saving. Instead, they believe they have a natural right to spend and consume with virtually no limit. Americans have come to believe they should maintain a higher standard of living than the rest of the world. They don't understand that the world is full of people willing to work harder and longer, doing equivalent work or better, for less pay. Things have changed. The old model is broken, and things are not going back to the *status quo ante*, no matter how hard they try to "stimulate" economic activity by printing up money.

Europe is no better off, and neither is Japan. The old way of things is bankrupt, and we're in the endgame now, during which we'll see more and more violent fluctuations as the system disintegrates.

L: "All the king's horses and all the king's men couldn't put Humpty Dumpty back together again."

D: No. But, frankly, Humpty had it coming. An egg had no business trying to balance on top of a wall. Anyone living in what is now called a first-world economy should be afraid—very afraid.

L: Hm. Well, does Bernanke get any brownie points for saying that the United States is going to have to tackle its budget deficit? He said that in 15 to 20 years, almost all of the government's budget would be taken up just by Medicare, Medicaid, Social Security, and interest on the national debt, leaving none for even the military.

D: No, no credit at all, unless you get points for mouthing idiotic platitudes. He said that while reining in spending is important, it should not be done now. He said the United States should not take any actions that would cut spending this year, and slow the so-called recovery. This is exactly how you set your feet on the path to Zimbabwe. Good theoretical intentions for some indefinite but faraway future.

Central bankers don't think of themselves as deciding to destroy their currencies; they think of themselves as taking emergency measures necessary to keep things going today. Tomorrow, they'll get back to doing things properly, after the emergency passes. And of course, every time tomorrow dawns, there's some new urgent need to keep emergency measures in place, or to take even stronger emergency measures, leaving the harsh medicine for yet another tomorrow.

L: What about Bernanke's call to simplify the tax code and lower tax rates? That sounds like a push in the right direction.

D: Sure. But it's way too little, too late. Cutting taxes is always good for any economy, and so is minimizing red tape, with the U.S. tax code being among the worst masses of red tape in existence. But the kind of seismic shifts needed—like eliminating capital gains taxes entirely, and income taxes as well—are not politically viable. It does no good to make marginal improvements to a system that is fundamentally flawed and broken. Bernanke is proposing a band-aid where amputation is needed.

L: How do you know Bernanke doesn't mean really deep tax cuts?

D: He's not a closet anarcho-capitalist secretly out to reform the entire system. He's a mainstream academic economist, and a bureaucrat who believes he can fiddle with the economy and control it. Remember what he said about being able to stop inflation, simply by raising interest rates, in 15 minutes? And remember his evasive answer to the question about how the Fed missed the impending crisis? He said that "large parts of the financial system were not adequately covered by the regulatory oversight."

L: He specifically cites AIG and Lehman Brothers as being examples of financial institutions that were essentially unregulated. That's total nonsense, of course; they may not have been regulated by the Fed, but they sure as heck were regulated by other federal agencies. And it's a misdirection. The Fed's theoretical responsibility is the economy, not individual banks and insurance companies that might be taking excessive risks. To say that he and his colleagues at the Fed didn't see the crisis coming because of lack of regulation shows a complete lack of understanding of what their task is. Besides, any observer with any sense could see what was happening then. We certainly did.

D: He may just have a complete lack of honesty. And absolutely a complete lack of understanding of economics, finance, history, and monetary theory—a shameful but perhaps predictable state for someone who's lived his whole life in an ivory tower. The man has been wrong about everything he's ever said about the U.S. economy.

L: Another sign of his worldview being a problem was his answer to the question about the "income gap" between the rich and the poor in the United States being a product of education. He cited as evidence in support of this idea that unemployment for college grads is half that of high school grads.

D: Of course, as a professor, he'd see it that way. And that was true 50 years ago, maybe even 25 years ago. But he's out of touch. Even if it were true today, it has nothing to do with the fact that college grads have stupidly misallocated four years and $200,000 having their heads filled with politically correct nostrums, getting worthless degrees in stuff like English, psychology, sociology, art history, education, and gender studies. But education is not the problem. The great income disparity between Mugabe and his cronies and poor Zimbabweans isn't due to the superior education of the Zimbabwe rich. American history is full of examples of people with little education making it big. What's needed is an entrepreneurial spirit and the freedom to pursue it, not a college degree. (For more on this, readers should see our conversation on education.)

Bernanke also said that increasing income disparity is a very dangerous development that is creating two societies. Even when Bernanke is right, he misses the actual point. The rich have always had their own society, even in the most egalitarian cultures. But what's happening is there's a growing perception of "us versus them" between the diminishing middle class and the rich, and it is indeed very serious—because of *the way in which* many people are getting rich. People can see bankers being paid gigantic bonuses with government money, and it justifiably makes them angry. The pot of envy and jealousy is being stirred up big time, and the implications for anyone with any amount of wealth are potentially dire. It doesn't take much to turn widespread resentment into a wave of violence.

As I said, it's time to eat the rich, and these days, anyone who isn't poor is considered rich.

This is why, since the crisis, my mantra has been to not just diversify one's assets and financial risks, but to diversify political risk. Political risk is actually greater than financial risk today. It may not be time to get out of Dodge quite yet. But if you don't want to be left with grabbing a backpack and heading for the hills as your only option, it is absolutely time to be setting up second residences in places you'd enjoy going for an extended vacation while the global economy works through the coming liquidation of decades of stupid government economic policies.

It's going to get really, *really* ugly, and if you don't prepare now, you're going to get hurt.

L: We've talked before about diversifying to protect your assets, diversifying to minimize political risk, where you think it's best to do so, and how to invest during the crisis. I'd guess that as far as protecting your assets goes, especially with currency controls already ramping up, you'd say that's gone beyond urgent. If any readers have not taken action yet, they need to do so immediately. What about physical security? I can imagine angry mobs on Main Street at some point, but probably not tomorrow. How much time do you think we have to set up alternative residency in safer jurisdictions?

D: A society can fall from grace with amazing speed. Yugoslavia was a relatively rich European country that went from peace to chaos and violence in a matter of weeks. I suppose that in terms of actual social disorder, there will be increasingly obvious signs, and even in the event of a breakdown in social order, some days of transition. But at that point, it's too late to set anything up—if the borders are even still open.

L: And the way various U.S. authorities have taken the term "lockdown" from prison use and applied it to airports and even schools, it's not hard to imagine the entire country being put on lockdown for the duration.

D: Indeed. It's high time to set up residences in places where you'd like to weather the storm, and see to the legalities of extended stays.

L: What about those who can't leave, because of family members who refuse to move, or because they have jobs they can't work from afar?

D: Better start educating those family members and looking for work not tied to a specific office or place. If you're really stuck, at least getting out of the big cities and setting up base in a rural community, even if it means long commutes, is probably a good idea.

L: Pretty grim, Doug.

D: That's the way I see it. I don't make the rules, I just play the game. But just because it's going to be tough for most people doesn't mean it has to be tough for you. Most of the real wealth in the world is still going to be here; it's just going to change ownership. And since there are more scientists and engineers alive now than have ever lived before in all of history, new wealth will continue to be created. There's plenty of cause for optimism, long term.

L: What about an investment update: What's your guru sense telling you today?

D: Nothing new to regular readers, but I am feeling that the mania phase of the current bull market for precious metals is coming closer. Gold is not cheap, compared to 10 years ago, but it's definitely the one asset most certain to retain value throughout the unfolding crisis. Putting a significant amount of your savings or net worth into gold is no speculation at this stage, but positively the safest thing you can do with your money. It's what I'm doing.

That's for surviving the coming Greater Depression. Your best bet at thriving is to speculate on gold stocks, especially the kind of junior exploration companies working on discovering new deposits, such as you focus on in the *International Speculator.*

All these trillions of currency units that governments around the world are creating will result in other asset bubbles. That's bad news for society, but good news for speculators like us. This will probably help equities in general, as they represent ownership companies that presumably are worth something. But gold is going to be the hottest asset throughout this crisis, and gold stocks will offer leverage to that heat. I think we're going to see a spectacular mania in these things. It's such a small market sector that even a small shift of interest from mainstream stocks will be like trying to siphon the contents of the Hoover Dam through a garden hose—the better ones are going to go absolutely ballistic.

L: Well, I'm not going to argue with that, but I'd add silver to the mix. Anything else?

D: Agriculture, in certain areas, is good. Energy, in certain areas, is good. Betting on rising interest rates is as close to a sure thing as I can see in mainstream investments today. But the main thing is to take seriously our calls to diversify political risk. The crisis is *not* over; we're just in the eye of the storm. It *is* going to get worse, and those caught unprepared are *really* going to regret it.

L: And if people do buy gold, speculate in great stocks, set up second residences in Argentina, Panama, or wherever . . . that won't hurt them if the old world order does not come to an end, as you're predicting. Those investments and allocations can always be unwound. Better to prepare for the worst and hope for the best.

D: Just so.

L: Thanks, Doug. 'Til next time.

D: My pleasure. We'll talk soon; the passing parade is getting more interesting, day by day.

Chapter 3

Doug Casey on the Collapse of the Euro and the EU

January 25, 2012

Louis: So Doug, a lot of readers are concerned about what's going on in Europe. Is this the beginning of the proverbial "it"? Or can the Eurozone be saved?

Doug: In brief, the answers are "yes," then "no," and a "good riddance" to both the Eurozone and the euro. But most people think the old order should be maintained at almost any cost. That would include George Soros, who recently penned an article called "Does the Euro Have a Future?"

Now, I don't normally look to Soros for economic commentary, despite the fact that he's one of the shrewdest and most successful speculators in the world. He does, however, represent the way the Davos people, Eurocrats, and the ruling classes in general think. But just because he's made a lot of money doesn't make him an expert in economics, any more than financial success is proof that Ted Turner, Bill Gates, or Warren Buffett know anything about economics. They're all idiot savants, a bit like Dustin Hoffman's character in *Rain Man*. But that's another subject.

Soros writes: "The political will to create a common European treasury was absent in the first place, and since the time the euro was created the political cohesion of the European Union has greatly deteriorated." He's absolutely right about that and goes on to say that to create a common European treasury, the EU would have to have the power to tax. So, he's saying that the euro should be preserved, and that to do that, it should be backed by wealth extracted by force from the average person in Europe.

But that's the problem with every currency in the world today; they're not backed by a commodity, but only by the ability of government to steal from the people. And the euro doesn't even have that going for it.

L: And the power to tax is an essential, defining characteristic of the nation-state. It's the thing that empowers it to exist and separates it from voluntary organizations. To create that power in Europe would really be to turn the place into one single country. It wouldn't be long before they had a European army.

D: Exactly. Right now the Eurocrats in Brussels really only have the power to regulate, which is bad enough. But if the European Union had the power to tax, it would become an actual empire. Especially if they then created a European army—there's no telling what kind of mischief they'd get into.

On the bright side, they can't really afford an army. That's the bright side of all these governments being bankrupt: They spend way too much on welfare and debt service to afford much warfare; I guess that makes welfare and debt good things, in a perverse way.

Anyway, Soros went on to observe: "The euro crisis could endanger the political cohesion of the European Union." That's true too, of course. The EU is a completely artificial union. The Swedes are very different from the Sicilians, and the Portuguese very different from the Austrians. These people have little in common besides a history of fighting with each other. Force them together into a phony union, and they'll become mutually resentful, the way the Germans and the

Greeks now are. The EU was put together partly to avoid future wars, but it may turn out to be a war incubator. It makes no sense for there to be a European Union at all.

Incidentally, people think of these countries—Italy, France, Germany, and so on—as though they are fixtures in the cosmos, but they aren't. In their current forms, they're all newcomers on the stage of history.

L: You mean the gods didn't affix them to the celestial spheres, up there with the stars? I could have sworn Jupiter told me he did.

D: No. The average person doesn't realize that the country we know as Italy today was only created in 1861, a consolidation of many completely independent and very different entities that had been separate states since the collapse of the Roman empire. Germany was only unified in 1871, out of scores of principalities, dukedoms, and whatnot. Both unifications were very bad ideas. Even today, there are separatist movements in big Western European countries, like the Basques in Spain, or those in the United Kingdom who wish it weren't quite so united.

L: So what's the alternative?

D: Of course, the ideal would be for there to be seven billion little countries on the planet—each one a sovereign individual. But I'll take what I can get in the meantime, and would rather see smaller states competing for citizens as customers, although I don't really like that analogy because states are not voluntary organizations, nor do they provide much in the way of useful services. Anyway, a more cohesive European Union is a step in the direction of Orwell's Oceania, which was in constant warfare with Eurasia and Eastasia. It's odd how the world is becoming much more like *Nineteen Eighty-Four* in some ways at the same time that the nation-state itself is collapsing.

What would have made sense is for Europe to have become a free-trade and free-travel zone. No customs duties and no need for work permits or passports. A free-enterprise union, created simply by dropping barriers, would have facilitated all sorts of business and job creation. Instead, idiotically, the Europeans just created yet another layer of government in Brussels. Which is rather ironic in that Belgium is itself a non-country, created out of two very different societies—Flanders and Wallonia. Now there's a wannabe mega-government bent on finding new ways to regulate enterprise out of existence. And if people like Soros are heeded, it will have the right to tax in addition, in order to give value to its essentially worthless currency.

All this would be a non-problem if they simply used gold, which is what, as I've long predicted, is happening, starting with the gold-for-oil trade between India and Iran.

People talk about the EU as being a way to avoid new wars in Europe. But they forget that in the nineteenth century, Europe had fewer wars than ever before or since. At that time, *mark, lira, franc*, and *pound* were all just names for specific amounts of gold. It worked very well. And to paraphrase Ludwig Von Mises: When goods cross borders freely, soldiers don't—or at least are less likely to.

All the gyrations and machinations these Eurocrats are desperately rushing into place to try to save the unnecessary and counterproductive euro are . . .

L: "Not just the wrong thing, but the exact opposite of the right thing."

D: Just so. Back to Soros. He has a prescription for preventing a meltdown, of course. He advises: "First, bank deposits have to be protected." In other words, to discourage people from bailing out of unsound banks and destabilizing a corrupt banking system, all bank deposits should be guaranteed. That's a catastrophic idea. It would further encourage all sorts of bad lending by incompetent bankers while sucking hundreds of billions of capital from productive parts of the economy. He also asserts that some banks in defaulting countries have to be kept functioning, in order to keep the economy from crashing entirely. That's another ridiculous idea, plundering the prudent and productive to pay for the profligate.

If banks were run according to sound banking principles, with a clear division between demand deposits and time deposits and no fractional reserve banking, we wouldn't have to worry about any of these issues.

But instead, Soros goes on to write that the European banking system should be recapitalized and put under EU supervision. I want to know how this recapitalization would be done—all those governments are bankrupt. All that Soros is suggesting is to make a bunch of national problems into one big continental problem. For all anyone knows, the Fed is planning on creating trillions of dollars to give to the EU. The only thing that's really clear is that we're moving out of the eye of the hurricane and back into the storm. But it will be much, much fiercer than what we saw in 2008.

Soros also states that government bonds have to be protected from "contagion." Whatever that means, the implication is more central control and throwing more taxpayer money at the insoluble government problems. The bankrupt banks will have to lend the bankrupt governments money, so they can pay their bonds off, while at the same time the same bankrupt governments lend the bankrupt banks money, so they don't go under. It's all just a ridiculous shell game.

L: It all sounds like a call for creating more unbacked currency units. If their only answer is just to run the printing presses, it'll be Weimar hyperinflation all over again.

D: Yes. Soros's bottom line is: "There's no alternative but to give birth to the missing ingredient: A European treasury with the power to tax and borrow." This, he claims, is "the only way to forestall a possible financial meltdown and another great depression." Forestalling the depression is impossible. All that can be done is to make it less severe, by doing exactly the opposite of what Soros recommends.

L: And that would be?

D: My view, as you well know, is that they shouldn't forestall the meltdown, but should let the market correct past mistakes and get on with building real economic growth for the future. Nietzsche was right when he said, "That which is about to fall deserves to be pushed." But it really doesn't matter what these fools do; we're in the early stages of the Greater Depression. It's going to have a life of its own.

Soros's solutions are counterproductive band-aids. But since he's got to offer solutions, I'm going to offer some too. For starters, the national debts of all these countries should be defaulted on, including the United States. Those debts constitute an unethical mortgage without consent on the next two or three generations of people as yet unborn as a result of the excess consumption of their parents and grandparents. The government debt should also be defaulted on to punish the people stupid enough, or unethical enough, to lend these states the money they've used to do all the destructive things they do.

Second, central banks should be abolished and thereby fractional reserve banking as well. That would force banks to run on sound, classical terms, and depositors would be induced to seek out the most sound and secure banks.

Third, there shouldn't be national currencies. Commodities—with gold most likely the popular choice—would again be used as money.

Fourth, most financial regulations and taxes, especially income taxes, should be radically reduced or eliminated. At the same time, government spending should be cut even more radically. These governments, if their existence is to be tolerated at all, should be strictly limited to doing nothing more than protecting people from overt force and fraud.

L: Sounds good to me, but you know that's not gonna happen. So, tune in your guru-vision for a moment and tell us what you think is most likely to happen. Does Soros get his wish and we see a new European superstate emerge? Or does the EU disintegrate?

D: There's not a snowball's chance in hell that the EU will turn into a superstate. The chances are much, *much* better that it will fragment. If these countries have breakaway movements within them, how could they possibly succeed in peacefully joining together?

If you think about it, the Soviet Union was a sort of Eastern European Union, and it disintegrated. Yugoslavia also showed what happens to artificial European unions, as did Czechoslovakia. These are all straws that show which way the wind is blowing in Europe.

That's quite apart from the fact that trying to compact all of these different ethnicities, languages, religions, cultures, and so forth together into one giant nation-state is illogical, counterproductive, dangerous, and pointless.

L: So, how long do you give the EU before it breaks up? And the euro?

D: Well, as you know, one should never predict both an event and the time it will take place. But I've long said that, "While the U.S. dollar is an 'IOU nothing,' the euro is a 'who owes you nothing.'" So I think the euro will reach its intrinsic value long before the dollar does. The euro—in anything like its present form—will cease to exist within two to three years at the outside. If I had a lot of my wealth in euros, I would get it out ASAP. My favorite alternative for protecting wealth, of course, is the precious metals: gold and silver. If you want to speculate for gains on this trend, I think there will be a bubble in the mining stocks, many of which are cheap right now.

L: For new readers, Doug's notion of the intrinsic value of the euro, the dollar, or any unbacked fiat currency is zero. They are literally worthless and only useful as long as people imagine otherwise. So much for the euro, but what about the EU itself?

D: Centripetal force will eventually tear it apart, with the EU as a whole disintegrating long before its individual parts—France, Italy, Germany, the UK, et cetera—fall apart.

L: How long is "eventually"? Can the EU itself last long after such a crushing setback as the collapse of the euro?

D: Probably not—they'll likely go in close succession. Europe is just in a world of trouble; the continent reminds me of that cruise ship that sank off the coast of Italy recently. They are dying financially, with all the debt bankrupting governments, businesses, and individuals. They are economically in a lot of trouble, with stifling regulations and taxes. They are demographically in a lot of trouble, with birth rates far below replacement in general, except among African and Muslim immigrants who are not integrating. Europe has long been a hotbed of religious, ethnic, and race wars; quite frankly I see the next one building up right now.

L: What about Eastern Europe? They have different problems—like endemic corruption and other Soviet legacies—but they tend to be very pragmatic and willing to work hard.

D: Yes, there's a dichotomy. The bad news is the Soviet legacy hanging over them, but the good news is that they've experienced naked socialism, and they know what it's really like. A lot of thinking people there are experiencing shock therapy and leaning much more toward free markets than people in the West. I'm definitely more optimistic about Eastern Europe than Western Europe. However, the general decline of Europe, which started with World War I, is going to continue. I only hope Europe just declines in relative terms, not absolute terms.

The fact of the matter is that I'm most optimistic about the Orient. That's where the action has been and is going to be. I'm also favorably inclined toward Latin America, which has huge problems but is, at least, mostly out of harm's way from the evolving Forever War.

L: Doug, you're on record as saying that China is in a bubble and that it's going to pop. How does that square with your being optimistic about the Orient? You can't be thinking Japan will take the lead again.

D: No, certainly not. I do think China is ripe for a fall, but it's a matter of the short versus the long run. I'm very bearish on China in the short term, but after the current system washes out, I think it's going to be the place to be—or at least, that area. I think China is another country that has excellent chances of breaking up into five or more separate countries.

L: Wow, okay. More investment implications, besides getting out of the euro?

D: Buy gold and silver. Don't be fooled into thinking the dollar is strong just because the euro is weaker.

L: Very well; thank you for your thoughts.

D: My pleasure. I've got some other things on my mind, so we'll talk soon.

L: Looking forward to it. Have a great evening, Tatich.

D: You too, Lobo.

Chapter 4

Doug Casey on Labor Unions

March 2, 2011

Louis: Doug, last week we talked about turmoil arising from the clash between labor unions clinging to wages from the fat years and bankrupt governments facing lean-year budgets. You saw that as a sign of more imminent chaos—a warning worth giving—but we didn't really get into the subject of labor unions themselves. Knowing your philosophical bent, I'd bet your views on them might surprise many people.

Doug: My take is that there's nothing inherently wrong with unions, as long as they are voluntary associations of people; they're just associations working in certain trades or in certain places. It's natural. Sure, why not?

But there are problems with the way unions exist in reality today, particularly when membership is made mandatory. That's a violation of the human right to work. When you can't work unless you join the union, and union membership is limited—often to people with political connections or family relations with union officials—it's clear that the union is not a defender of the little guy, but a kind of protection racket. It's a fraud.

That doesn't just harm the individual worker who may wish to enter a unionized field; it has broad economic consequences. When only union members can work, the union can set wages at whatever level they want. That makes the product or service in question more expensive for everyone in society. In other words, unions don't help the average working man; they only help those who can get into the unions. They hurt everybody else: non-union workers, employers, and consumers at large. And it gives union bosses extraordinary power.

L: Always a dangerous thing. As a matter of principle, whenever unions get politicians to write their wishes into law, what they do ceases to be collective bargaining and becomes naked coercion. And of course the politicians pander to the big unions; unions are big blocks of voters. How could it be otherwise?

But Doug, you're the capitalist's capitalist, the world's most unabashed defender of wealth accumulation. Aren't you supposed to hate labor unions? Don't you risk being kicked out of the cigar club for The Evil Exploiters of the Masses?

D: First off, there's no way I'm giving up my cigars—especially those from Cuba. But how could I object to voluntary associations of people? If unions were more like the Lions Club or Rotary Club—both of which simply encourage people to get together and act in unison—I'd have no beef with any of them. But the fact of the matter is that labor unions, guilds, and so forth are not truly voluntary associations. And that's entirely apart from the corruption that the union movement is riddled with—not just in the United States, but everywhere in the world.

The good news, however, is that coercive unions are on the way out. They're anachronisms. They're leftovers from the time when people were like interchangeable parts in the giant factories they worked in. People were so replaceable that one person was little better or worse than another, because they were basically biological robots. In the early industrial era, labor was in over-supply, society was poor, and conditions were harsh everywhere. It's understandable why workers felt they had to band together for self-protection. But the industrial era is gone. The assembly line with thousands of workers is totally outmoded. In the global information age, trying to extort high wages for manual labor is pointless. Soon robots will be doing almost everything, then nanomachines will replace the robots. People will only be doing work that requires thought, judgment, and individuality. Those aren't things that can be unionized.

L: I've long thought that Big Labor was a rational market response to Big Business, a lot of which relied on rote behaviors back then. If you were just one little guy on the assembly line and your supervisor didn't like you, what chance did you stand without the backing and solidarity of your fellow laborers? Unfortunately, huge industrial concerns were highly vulnerable to sabotage; it's hard, for example, to police thousands of miles of railroad tracks. I believe that weakness in the soft underbelly of tight-fisted business owners proved too tempting a target for many workers. And that sort of thuggery prompted management to hire thugs as well, to intimidate workers. I can't really say who started it, but tit for tat brutalized the whole dialogue—and both sides scrambled to secure politicians in a sort of labor-relations arms race. "Labor" and "management" have been at odds—sometimes violent odds—ever since. It's no surprise to me that Marx and Engels, products of the early industrial era, saw everything in terms of class conflict.

Absent government coercion to be used as a weapon by one side or the other, organized labor and management would have worked out their differences in a very different way. If one union bargained collectively for a high wage for their members, another union could bargain for a lower wage for their members and get the jobs. Or the company could decide to hire non-union employees and take on the extra burden of dealing with each employee individually. It would be a normal market process that would discover the right price for reliable labor at any given time and place.

As with so many things, it's the state and its coercive power that's the problem, not the unions. Nor management.

D: Exactly. It was also a time in history when society was changing from an agricultural base to an industrial one, so of course there was turmoil. Just like today.

Suppose some Mexicans or Salvadorans living in Detroit got together today and formed a union for Hispanic people and offered to build cars for half the wages the current unions are getting. They could even allow non-Hispanics to join the union—to try to defuse the inevitable accusation of racism—but the deal would be that you join to get steady work in exchange for willingness to work cheap. Would the mouthpieces of Big Labor stand up to defend them? I doubt it.

And as for Big Business, the fact is that a lot of it got that way through collusion with the state. They get special favors, such as regulatory barriers that impede the competition. This has allowed businesses to become unnaturally large. In a true free-market society, you could only get big by making a product the consumers love. In a fascist society, you get big through political favors.

Everyone is constantly trying to improve their lot in life, which is wonderful. The problem is when you add institutionalized coercion—the state—to the picture. Coercion leads to conflict, and conflict raises costs and destroys wealth. But even if the economic effect of coercion was neutral, it would still be unethical. And unnecessary. That's the bottom line. Big Business and Big Labor are both unnatural. And they're both corrupt, because they're creatures of the state.

L: Agreed: Big Business is no more pure than Big Labor. I remember researching some early industrialists back in college, after reading Ayn Rand's books, hoping to find heroic captains of industry in history. Instead, I found that no sooner had Robert Fulton invented the steamboat than he applied to the government for a steamboat monopoly. And the first transcontinental railroad in America was not built by a Nat Taggart, but by a bunch of political hacks who went bankrupt within three years. (But the guy who was the historical model for Nat Taggart did exist: His name was James Jerome Hill, and he and his Great Northern Railroad overcame stiff political opposition to become the second transcontinental railroad—and this time, at a profit.)

D: Too bad no one pointed you at Robert Fulsom's *The Myth of the Robber Barons* then. But the takeaway point for this conversation is that labor unions are dead men walking. They're dinosaurs.

The figures show that in spite of the millions of jobs that have been exported from the United States to China over the past few decades, which was largely caused by the success of U.S. labor unions at artificially raising wages and benefits, U.S. production has stayed about level. You go to most car factories these days, and they're not full of workers; they are full of machines. Labor itself is disappearing, as computer-controlled machines grow more and more capable of doing physical work better and cheaper than humans can. Work, in the future, will be something you do with your mind. People are going to have to adapt to that, or suffer the consequences. Labor unions are absolutely on their way out.

But, if it's any consolation to those who love labor unions, Big Business is on its way out too. With the technologies we already see developing, most manufacturing will be done on the individual level. You can already order cargo containers with everything you need to set up almost any sort of factory you want; you don't need giant factories anymore. And as nanotechnology advances, manufacturing will simply be a function of telling your software assistant what you want made and feeding your machines the raw materials. In the near future, 3-D fax machines will enable you to build almost any physical object, layer by layer, right in your own garage. It will be a bit as described in A. E. Van Vogt's sci-fi classic, *The Weapon Shops of Isher*. You won't have to hope Walmart has something you need; your 3-D fax will make exactly what you want, right now.

More broadly, small, swift, new competitors are going to devour the big old dinosaurs like a school of piranhas—and any new business that gets too big and bureaucratic, as well. The whole world is in the early stages of downsizing.

L: I've thought about that—about the evolution of labor and business in the information age. Isn't it possible that just as businesses are forced to become smaller, leaner, and faster, labor unions could evolve to provide value to intellectual workers? "Programmers of the world, unite!"

D: No, I don't think that makes any sense, any more than the laughable old Soviet idea of writers' and artists' unions. You can't regiment and standardize creativity. And there is no such thing as "job security," which was always a stupid and parasitic notion. Your job is secure as long as you're productive and creative, and your company is profitable. Unique products provide job security to those creative enough to make them; great art, for example, can't be produced by a piece-work assembler on an assembly line.

L: But there *are* writers' and artists' unions. It seems to me that the Hollywood TV writers' union delayed the fall TV season a while back, by going on strike.

D: That's true, although I don't know how they would fairly compensate a Shakespeare and a hack if they were both union members with the same seniority. On the other hand, big broadcast TV is disappearing too, for the same reasons we've been discussing. When some kid with a webcam in Egypt, Libya, or even Belarus can produce a live documentary that's more riveting and costs nothing compared to professional TV news coverage, you know that the business model of major news networks is on its way out. Anyway, kids today don't watch TV, where you just absorb what you're fed. They watch a million channels on YouTube, and get what they individually want and need on millions of websites. Broadcast, network, TV—with its arrogant executives, and feather-bedding union workers—is on its way out.

It's funny how perception always lags reality. Even as people were moaning and wringing their hands about children wasting endless hours in front of the TV, it turns out that kids today spend vastly more time interacting on their computers.

The world is changing. Trying to use the coercive power of the state to maintain the status quo is a doomed effort. It's like trying to carry water in your hands for an entire marathon.

L: I heard that during the last Super Bowl, the Doritos commercial made for a pittance by some guy tied for first place as the most popular ad.

D: Yes, there are a lot of rice bowls that are going to be broken over the next decade. The good news is that the post-industrial world will be one of true marvels. Bringing production down to the individual level, at very low cost, will create the most prosperous society the world has ever seen. The same forces are advancing medicine, and that will make our descendants the healthiest and most long-lived people the world has ever seen. And the individual nature of value creation should make it the freest culture the world has ever seen. That's why I'm an optimist; I'm looking forward to a true renaissance, a golden age. The Greater Depression is just going to be a period of readjustment on the way up.

L: Not coincidentally, that golden age should see the return of a gold standard, as well. But first we'll have to go through a bloodbath.

D: I'm afraid so. The old world order will have to be washed away, and it won't want to go quietly. But it will go, one way or another. As the tyrants in the Middle East are showing, you can only resist history for so long. Incidentally, I believe everything there will be for the best, as long as the U.S. government doesn't invade yet another Muslim country.

L: Investment implications?

D: I can't emphasize enough the sort of things I've been saying all along, and that we mentioned again last week: Rig for stormy weather. But, more specifically, these changes are why we created *Casey's Extraordinary Technology*. Granted, it's in my interest to drum up subscriptions, but I still think it's the best source of ideas in this area. As the trends develop, CET is where we'll be going into detail on how best to profit from them.

L: Fair enough. Thanks for the thoughts, Doug. I'll have to take some more time to think about them.

D: My pleasure. Until next week.

Chapter 5

Doug Casey on the Tightening Noose

July 11, 2013

Louis: Hola, Doug. It's been a busy month, full of interesting events. Where do we start?

Doug: Well, almost everything on the news is disturbing these days, of course, but let's start with the dog.

L: Ah. I saw that "Cops shoot dog" story come across the wire and didn't think that much of it at the time—not because it's okay, but because it's by far less egregious than other things cops have done. Now the thing is really causing a stir.

D: The footage is truly disgusting. The police are making a bust, and many people are seen taking pictures or shooting video. This one black man is doing the same while peacefully walking his dog. He is no different from others, except maybe a little closer, so the police say something to him. Recognizing the potential for trouble, the man puts his dog in his car, then goes to speak with the police. His behavior is in no way aggressive. He cooperates completely, even turning around and assuming "the position"—hands behind his back, so the cops can cuff him. The dog starts barking. The cops start roughing the guy up, then the dog jumps out of the car and runs over, barking, and one of the cops shoots the dog.

L: It is bad, but par for the current course, no? I mean, the siege at Ruby Ridge started when the cops who were sneaking up on the cabin shot the dog. As I recall the story, Randy Weaver's son, Sammy, was outside and saw what looked like home invaders shoot his dog, so he started shooting back. The Feds shot Vicky Weaver in the head, through a glass door, while she held her baby in her arms. Later, there was the Waco tragedy, where both sides claim the other started shooting first, but the Feds shot the dogs when they jumped out of their concealed positions to storm the church, which I think prompted those inside to start shooting back. It's SOP for cops to shoot dogs because they won't respect an arrest warrant as their owners might.

D: I think you're exactly right about that; it's probably a standard operating procedure cops just don't like to talk about. And police brutality is hardly new, but there seems to be quite a spate of it lately, and I believe that it's symptomatic of what's happening throughout the United States.

Same as with what's happening in schools, where a five-year-old girl can be labeled a terrorist for bringing a bubble "gun" to class, or a six-year-old boy can be suspended for pointing his finger like a gun and saying "pow!" The latest government-induced hysteria, with its so-called War on Terror, has insinuated itself into society at large. To the degree that the average U.S. citizen has accepted this insanity, it seems like society is actually going crazy.

That's bad enough, but there's evidence of a particularly malignant twist to all this, such as the latest meme circulating among government types: "Officer safety is paramount." That means that the top priority is no longer stopping a crime in progress or catching the bad guys, but making sure no cop is ever endangered. What happens to the "mundanes" doesn't matter. Cops have always lived in a world of their own, but it's increasingly the case.

L: This "us versus them" thinking would explain why, when there's a hostage situation or school shooting, the cops set up a perimeter en masse and wait for the shooting to stop. Doesn't matter how many kids trapped inside get shot—can't endanger an officer!

D: No, no, perish the thought. These are not the days of Andy Griffith. Or even Dick Tracy. People need to understand that cops are not their friends. The last thing you want to do is have any contact with them at all. They have always tended to be the sort of people who drew an extra Y-chromosome. Now, with most new cops being ex-military who've picked up all kinds of bad habits and nightmare experiences during senseless U.S. military adventures abroad, you have to worry about what kinds of mental aberrations and illnesses anyone in uniform might be suffering from.

So, I expect we'll see more and more stories of cops losing restraint, with more and more lethal consequences. Get a load of these stories; there are scores more just in the last week:

- Police arrest family for refusing to let them use their home to stake out suspects.
- Cops shoot and kill unarmed man.
- Cops shoot unarmed man 11 times.

L: Very disturbing.

D: Yes, and it gets worse; military indoctrination results in these people absolutely following orders and doing what they're told. In addition, they are loyal first and foremost to each other, then to their employers, and only remotely, if at all, to the people they are supposed to serve. One thing I like about the French Foreign Legion is that they swear an oath to the legion and not to France—at least they are honest about their priorities. You put people like that in the employ of unscrupulous politicians, and it can get really ugly. In the United States, the stage is being set for genuine atrocities in the not-too-distant future, right here on American soil.

Sadly, I don't see anything that can stop this trend. Trends in motion tend to stay in motion until they hit a crisis. This is yet another sign of the United States That Is ramming the America That Was, heading for an epic crisis.

L: That brings to mind the latest in the ongoing Edward Snowden saga. If politicians were angels, I might not worry too much if they trained their minions to act like demons. Or if they were mere mortals, but highly principled ones who upheld the Constitution and served the public, I might think the danger of abuse of power was slight. But the things Snowden revealed, and now similar revelations in France, show that these governments are corrupt, hypocritical, and rife from top to bottom with people who think the law does not apply to them. It's just a tool for manipulating and subduing the masses.

D: Yes. Snowden's revelations were not news to me, but he is a real hero for making the general public aware that they are being spied on. It's not just every e-mail and phone call, but also every piece of postal mail—about 160 billion pieces annually—that is being photographed and stored as well. (That will keep a lot of Postal Union folks employed, instead of being fired, since snail mail is increasingly anachronistic.) And that's not to mention credit card transactions, passport and other ID scans, and surveillance cameras with facial recognition software sprouting around the world like mushrooms. More and more of every person's daily life is being monitored and recorded. If some government official points a finger at you, all that information is accessed, and almost everyone you communicate with may get dragged into an investigation.

It's one reason why you likely won't see any more politicians like Ron Paul. Everybody has secrets. And a message from a spook will ensure that none of them will do or say anything that's not deemed in the interest of the State. You'd better be a good little lamb.

L: Chinese friends tell me that the famous "ancient Chinese curse" is usually given only in part. It's not just, "May you live in interesting times," but "May you live in interesting times and come to the attention of important people."

D: That sums up what I'm saying precisely. We are rapidly approaching a world in which, as David Galland has taken to saying, Big Brother has won. Where is "V" when we need him?

L: I understand, and I'm no fan of Leviathan, but I have to say, the average Western citizen does not fear the midnight knock the way, say, comrades in the old Soviet Union used to.

D: That's true. But I'm not saying we're living in Orwell's *Nineteen Eighty-Four*, just that we're headed that way—and, once again, that trends in motion tend to stay in motion.

Another thing I've said before, but that's worth new emphasis, is that when conditions are right, the sociopaths who normally hide behind masks, have families and dogs, and play baseball on the weekends start coming out of the woodwork. They gravitate to positions of power where they have sanction to coerce others, which is to say, the police for the petty ones and politics for the ambitious ones. When enough of them fill positions in related institutions, they tend to drive out the good people who might have worked for them, which results in whole organizations suddenly taking a turn for the worse—the vicious and nasty kind of worse.

L: I agree with you, but for those who don't, I'd point out that giving the state such far-reaching powers, such as the ability to spy on everyone all the time without even the need to get a warrant, lends itself to abuse even without sociopaths taking control. For example, say you're a member of a religious majority that gives the government the power to persecute a minority, and then demographics change and your religion becomes a minority. It's too late; you've created the tools for oppression, and now they are in the hands of your opponents, perhaps the very ones you once oppressed.

D: Exactly. That's why I think Julian Assange and Bradley Manning are heroes for doing what they did; it took immense courage, given the huge personal risk to themselves. I would definitely put Edward Snowden in the same class. And I'm using the word *hero* in a precise and accurate way when I refer to them and Snowden: A hero is someone who does something noble, requiring great courage, and risking life and limb. These guys qualify.

The word has become completely degraded and meaningless in today's world. Everybody who joins the police or the military is automatically a "hero" if you listen to political speeches or the lapdog media. Actually, these people are just subservient, yet dangerous, government employees—until they prove themselves less than subservient.

I wasn't optimistic that Snowden would manage to get asylum in any country in the world. They are all basically similar criminal organizations, run by the same sorts of sociopaths who see the little people as beasts of burden or cannon fodder. They all have secrets they don't want exposed, so they hate people like Snowden. None is keen to encourage whistle-blowers like him. Even Putin, who is generally happy to poke the United States in the eye, said that Snowden could only remain in Russia if he promised not to reveal any more secrets. Snowden has said he can't agree to those conditions. But Venezuela and Nicaragua have offered him asylum, and I guess Cuba will as well. Not because they're beacons of freedom—they absolutely are not. They'll do it to taunt the beast in DC.

Actually, I've spent considerable time in all three places: Venezuela, Nicaragua, and Cuba. The fact is that, if you're a foreigner with money and you don't meddle with their internal politics, you can live quite freely and well in any of them. It's quite paradoxical actually; an American is far less likely to get into trouble with the police or the government in those places than he is at home. You have to recognize what's important to the local government. Is it ideology? Is it power? Is it simple theft? Then, especially if they can't consider you a possession because you're not one of their citizens, you can make an accommodation with them. Like you might with the local mafia: It's business.

It's truly unfortunate that there's no place in the world that's truly free. Or where you can even legally defend yourself against the state. I only hope that the United States doesn't kidnap Snowden from wherever he chooses to go—assuming he's able to get there in the first place. The diversion of Evo Morales's plane on suspicion Snowden was aboard proved just how risky it will be for Snowden to try to go anywhere.

My guess is that the Snowden case could be the biggest upset over a single individual since the Dreyfus matter in France over 100 years ago. It could be the start of something big.

L: Life becomes stranger than fiction every day. I wonder if Snowden will end up in, of all places, Belarus. The government there is one of the few in the world that might say "no" to the United States— maybe North Korea and Iran, too—but Snowden could slip from Russia to Belarus on a "domestic" flight, which the United States could not divert.

D: Yes, we do indeed live in interesting times. It actually is Orwellian, in the sense of things being the opposite of what they proclaim themselves to be. The United States, once the land of the free and the home of the brave, is rapidly becoming the biggest threat to individual liberty in the world. I believe that's already the case today. It seems an inevitability in the evolution of empires. It happened with the Athenians in the fifth century BCE after they formed the Delian League, which was kind of the NATO of its day. And it happened to the Roman Republic as it expanded.

L: The incident with Morales's plane sure shows how long the arm of Uncle Sam has grown.

D: Yes, it'd be shocking, if we hadn't been saying for some time that this sort of thing was coming. It's yet another sign that while things may seem calm and well here in the eye of the storm, the storm winds are gathering speed and will be that much more destructive when we exit the eye.

Other countries increasingly feel they're either satellites of Washington or potential enemies. Nobody likes to be treated like a menial or a lackey. Especially when all the U.S. government has going for it anymore is its bloated, overstretched military; its gigantic spy/security networks; and the U.S. dollar. The whole world recognizes the U.S. government is bankrupt.

At some point, someone is going to pursue Nietzsche's famous dictum: That which is about to fall deserves to be pushed. It's hard to say who that will be. Maybe the Chinese, simply by speeding up their dumping of dollars—although their economy is so close to a disaster, I'm not sure they want to upset any apple carts. More likely they'll continue getting out of dollars by using them to acquire companies in the United States and Europe, and farmland in Africa and South America.

Maybe the Saudis will stop taking dollars if the Arab revolutions spill over and their corrupt theocracy/kleptocracy is overthrown. Already they're dealing directly with the Chinese. In fact, a dozen countries have cut the dollar out of the equation on at least a bilateral basis. There will be many more.

Remember that appearances can look fine until the last moment. Almost nobody, certainly including the worthless CIA, knew the USSR was going to collapse—until it did.

L: That follows. But, with all due respect, you did say we were exiting the eye of the storm almost two years ago.

D: [Chuckles] Yes, and I pointed out that when Harry Browne made a similar prediction in the 1970s, he was right about everything except the timing. I also said then, as I always say, that I don't like to predict both what will happen and when it will happen; it's too easy to mistake what's inevitable for what's imminent.

I'm not a fortune teller. Nobody has that power. The best we can hope for is to be on the right side of the most important trends. Exact predictions are impossible in a world that increasingly resembles a lunatic asylum.

That said, while I don't know how long the inevitable can be put off, I do know that once it gets underway, things will fall apart quite quickly. Anything could happen, at any time. The gigantic amount of unemployment in Europe and the Middle East, especially youth unemployment, is an extremely volatile situation. Youth unemployment in the United States is high as well, for that matter, and the latest rosy employment numbers put out by the government ignore the fact that full-time employment plunged while seasonal and other part-time employment gained; according to Shadow Stats, the "real" rate for June [2013] was actually 23.4 percent.

Interest rates going up in the United States is another sign that things are getting out of control. The economic news from China is also rightly alarming investors. Japan is in big financial trouble. The IMF is more bankrupt than even the average American or European bank. There's much, much more. And it's all likely to break loose at once, as we exit the eye of the hurricane.

The fact that Bernanke caused markets all around the world to plunge last month, just by hinting that the Fed might cut back on its money printing, is another sign that things are not as rosy as politicians and Wall Street brokers would like you to believe. If Bernanke stops printing, we could have a deflationary collapse. If he keeps printing, it's likely to be catastrophic inflation, worldwide. That worthless little bureaucrat is incredibly lucky to be leaving office soon. Now he can just collect his $50 million in book contracts, speaker's fees, corporate directorates, sweetheart deals, and the like, while someone else takes the fall. It's absolutely disgusting.

I don't know how long we can stay balanced here, but I do think we're really on the edge.

L: Mr. Cheerful again?

D: Well, there is good news, and it is genuinely good news, even if it alarms some of our readers: Gold is on sale again, back to around

$1,200 an ounce as we speak. I didn't expect the retreat to become this overdone, but I'm very happy about it, because it's providing a great buying opportunity to everyone. It's not quite as good a deal as it was under $50 in the early 1970s, or under $400 at the turn of the century. But it's now again a great deal. So, of course, no one will buy it.

L: Only the contrarians. And it's worse for junior miners, many of which are back to 2001 levels—just before the things you said would happen started happening.

D: That's right. This may be the last chance for people with the courage to be contrarians to buy gold at reasonable prices and gold stocks while they are actually cheap. I'm confident that all the money printing will ignite a bubble in gold, and a super bubble in gold stocks, over the next few years.

L: So, you're backing up the truck?

D: Yes, I am. I'm buying more gold, and I'm buying gold stocks too. My only fear is that storing gold safely can be a real problem. But this, of course, is a perpetual problem of living on this planet. My fear isn't of garden-variety thieves; they're a nuisance at best. It's what will happen when the financial system collapses. Most of the real wealth will still be there, of course. But what governments will do, and the degree the rule of law holds up, present a different order of problems.

L: If you don't mind my asking, since you advocate buying gold and distributing it in different jurisdictions, how much gold do you feel safe carrying when you fly?

D: I try to keep all negotiable instruments I carry under the $10,000 limit that has become the norm for snoops to ask about the world over. There used to be some comfort in the fact that most people had forgotten that gold was money, and you could arguably carry a whole bunch of Eagles or Mapleleafs with you because their face value is only $50. But these days, many customs forms, including those of the United States, specifically ask if you are carrying gold, as well as dollar bills and other forms of cash. So it's best to opt on the side of safety.

L: Even though Bernanke says gold is not money and we only keep it for traditional reasons.

D: That's correct; just look at the way Iran has been using gold to get around international sanctions and how the United States has responded.

That cat is out of the bag, even if no one in government will admit it: Gold is money. More and more of the people who denied or forgot this are starting to be forced to face the fact.

Which makes it all the more imperative for those U.S. taxpayers who understand what's going on not just to buy gold, but to get much of it out of the United States. I'd say the same goes for Europeans, Canadians, and people everywhere; it's your own government that poses the greatest danger to you, and everything we've been talking about today says that the noose is tightening. It's becoming not only essential, but more and more urgent with each passing day that you internationalize your assets—and your lifestyle—to mitigate this threat.

Absolutely everybody should have a crib outside their home country. And significant financial assets as well. If you aren't in a position to do so, then cut back on your standard of living, work harder, and start selling stuff so that you can. Pretend you're living on the Franco-German border in 1913.

L: Okay, but let's back up a second to the story about rising interest rates. It's quite striking that the Fed doesn't seem as in control as it imagines, even if we're talking about the 10-year and not the overnight rate. But the conventional wisdom says gold is not an asset to own when interest rates are high, because "gold doesn't pay interest."

D: That's not conventional wisdom, but conventional stupidity. Dollars don't pay interest either, if you just stuff them in your mattress. You have to lend them to earn interest, and you can lend gold too—the so-called bullion banks do it all the time. So of course gold can pay interest. But you have to lend it, and that entails risk.

But what's much more important about the interest rate story is that it's probably the key economic indicator to watch in the United States, in terms of when we exit the eye of the storm and things really start unraveling.

Consider that the United States is paying roughly 2 percent interest on a $17 trillion debt—about $350 billion per year. If rates go up to just 8 percent, which is about average since the last peak at 15 to 16 percent, then we're looking at about $1.5 trillion annually in interest alone. Not counting another trillion in deficits due to welfare and military spending—none of which will be cut voluntarily. Even the Chinese couldn't lend the United States that much every year. They couldn't even if they wanted to, which they don't, and increasingly can't, since they have big trouble at home. The only option that leaves is more government money printing, at even higher rates than today. And that puts us on the path made so famous in recent years by Gideon Gono, the central banker who oversaw Zimbabwe's hyperinflation.

L: What do you say to those who point out that we still have record-low inflation rates?

D: First, I'd say that the statistics the U.S. government puts out are now only marginally more reliable than the ones put out by Argentina. These fools really believe that psychology controls the economy. So they put out soothing numbers, which most people reflexively believe.

Second, the fact that certain assets are dropping in price does not mean that life is getting any cheaper for the average citizen. Just go to the store. Everything, and I mean *everything* we buy and use in our day-to-day lives costs more every year—I'd say on the order of 10 percent, not 2 percent. In other words, the average guy's standard of living is dropping. At some point, you have to wonder when he won't take it anymore. What will it take to get him off the couch and into the streets? I don't know, but hunger would certainly be one thing.

Again, the noose is tightening, and there's only so far it can go without something giving way. We are building toward a once-in-a-lifetime crisis here.

L: So, where does that leave us?

D: Still at the very beginning of the Greater Depression, which is going to be unbelievably bad.

L: Even worse than you think it will be.

D: Exactly. One year from now, we could be living in a completely different world than the one we live in today—a world considerably more scary, volatile, and unpleasant. And two or three years from now, I'm sure we will be there. Batten down the hatches.

L: Okay, is there anything else an intelligent investor should do, besides buy gold for prudence and gold stocks for speculative upside?

D: Stocks in general are overpriced; as interest rates rise, they should come down. Bonds are in a bubble. Most real estate is floating on a sea of debt supported by artificially low interest rates; plus it has huge carrying costs, not least of which are taxes.

L: What about productive agricultural real estate?

D: That's different—but you have to work on that. It's more like getting a job than being an investor, as absentee ownership is basically neglect. Farmland is good. But it's not cheap anywhere anymore, and management is critical. And mass commodity grain crops—soybeans, corn, and wheat—have their own set of risks. For one thing, they're all grown as gigantic monocultures. That's a risk which isn't adequately recognized. But now's not the time to get into that …

L: Nothing else?

D: Not really. Buy gold and silver and put it in places where it can't easily be seized. Our Hard Assets Alliance is a great way to do that. And, as a shareholder in GoldMoney.com, I should point out that that's another vehicle people can use. But you should first have coins in your own possession.

L: Very well. Thanks for another whirlwind update on the state of the world for investors.

D: No sweat. Even though it's 110 here in Vegas, where I am for the Freedom Fest. And to watch the hoi polloi wander around in tank tops and shorts, stuffing themselves as if they expect a famine. And to play in the WSOP, where my all-in call with pocket aces was beaten by a 7-8 of clubs. A complete fluke. It just goes to show that it's not unreasonable to be a cynic sometimes. On the other hand, it also goes to show there are no certainties in life outside the realms of physics and mathematics. Talk to you soon.

L: Good. Be well.

Part Two

THE ART OF INVESTING

Chapter 6

Doug Casey on the Education of a Speculator (Part One)

May 26, 2010

Louis: Doug, a lot of our readers have asked for you to tell some war stories. What were some of your biggest wins and losses, and what were the lessons learned?

Doug: Well, it may not all fit neatly under the rubric of "lessons learned," but I can tell you about some of the specific experiences that have shaped my career. There have certainly been some great deals and terrible deals that I've been in—and just as many of both that I've failed to get in.

L: It's all part of what Victor Niederhoffer would call *The Education of a Speculator*.

D: Vic's an old friend of mine, and his book by that title has some important insights. Although he's mainly a short-term trader. I prefer to only buy things I can hold on to for a few months, if not a couple of years. It gives you enough time to be right. And doesn't clutter your mind up with random noise and fluctuations.

L: Indeed; let the trend be your friend. Okay then, where do we start?

D: We've already told the story about my Ferrari business, in our conversation on cars, but that was my first business deal, so I do recommend reading it to those who haven't yet.

L: So, when you got out of the hospital, did you dive right into another deal?

D: Actually, I decided to start really educating myself at that point. Among other things, I read Harry Browne's seminal book, *How You Can Profit from the Coming Devaluation*, and that led directly to my first big score in the market. I read that book in 1970, and I bought gold coins. More important, as it turned out, is that I bought gold stocks and had a wild ride from 1971 to 1974. I made a *lot* of money, in percentage terms at least, since I was just out of school and had almost no capital to start with.

I then launched my second business venture—

L: Wait, wait. There was a big slump in gold in the mid-1970s. Are you saying you bought early, before Nixon closed the gold window, and then sold at the top of that first surge, realizing gains before the slump?

D: Yes, I did. But it's not as heroic as it sounds; I had no crystal ball. I sold near that interim top to invest in my second business, which was a company to market precious metals to the public. I have to say that I learned more painful lessons on that deal than I did crashing the Ferrari. Not only did I lose all the money I had built up, but I lost a bunch of money I didn't have. It took me years to dig myself out of that hole. I never declared bankruptcy, but I had significant negative net worth for some time.

L: That brings up an interesting point. You're a libertarian, and libertarians believe in the sanctity of the contract. That being the case, are there any moral grounds under which a libertarian *can* declare bankruptcy? There were times in my past when I was pretty deep in the red as well, and I couldn't bring myself to file for bankruptcy, even though it would have taken a great pressure off me. I'd made promises, and I just couldn't break them.

D: I completely agree with that, and that's why I didn't declare bankruptcy. I've always considered bankruptcy to be the act of hiding behind the state for the purpose of defrauding your creditors. It may be legal, but it's unethical; there's increasingly only an accidental overlap between what's legal and what's ethical. But most debt today is owed to banks. I have to wonder, with the banks increasingly becoming creatures of the state, if the morals involved haven't become inverted in today's world.

L: It could be a moral positive to borrow money from the government and then declare bankruptcy to help hasten the state's own demise?

D: Could be. Inflation is well known to corrupt a society's morals in many ways. It's a dangerous thing, a slippery slope, to start rationalizing why one needn't make good on debts. But that's what's happening all over the United States, with people walking away from their mortgages and their credit card debt, and declaring bankruptcy in record numbers. It's a trend that's going to end very, very badly.

What the state has done by increasingly insinuating its tentacles into every aspect of life is to completely corrupt society. Both the intended and unintended consequences are going to be ugly, because it blurs the morality of daily life. It's entirely perverse that defaulting on debts can even be considered as a good thing, and inversions like this are proliferating.

L: We should do a conversation devoted to ethics—someone sure needs to. But let's go back to the 1970s. What happened next?

D: Well, I had to dig myself out of that hole, so I redoubled my efforts to earn money. One of the things I did to earn money at the time was to write my first book, *The International Man*.

L: And thus was born a guru.

D: Well, it was *Crisis Investing*, a couple years later, that really put me on the talk show circuit. The other thing I did back in the mid-1970s was to become a stock broker. Have I told you the story of how I managed to buy precisely at the very bottom of the mid-1970s market trough?

L: No, please do.

D: I became a stock broker in 1976, which was fortuitous timing for someone who liked gold stocks. So, I'm sitting there at my office in Washington, DC, and I got a call from a guy—his name was Elmer—who impressed me as being one of these rich good old boys. I talked to him about what I thought would be good investments for him, and he said, "I'll come into town and put a little bit of money with you." The way he talked, I thought "a little bit of money" was going to be several hundred thousand dollars, at least.

When he came in, it turned out that he was an average Joe who rode in on a bus and really didn't have any money to speak of. But I put a portfolio together for him, worth about $2,500, which included 1,000 shares of a stock called Grootvlei, a thousand shares of Bracken, and several hundred shares of Anglo American Corporation of South Africa. Because gold had fallen almost 50 percent, from $200 at the end of December 1974, Grootvlei and Bracken were penny stocks—substantial producers, but with high cost and short-life mines—that were each yielding indicated dividends of about 50 to 75 percent. Even Anglo was yielding something like 15 percent.

L: Those are pretty amazing dividends.

D: It's incredible what you can get in dividends alone when a market is at a bottom—something people seem to have totally forgotten about today.

At any rate, the day Elmer came in happened to be the day that gold hit its absolute bottom for that cycle—$103.50, if I recall correctly—and also happened to be the very same day there were big riots in Soweto that made headlines in the United States.

So, Elmer gets hit with these two things at the same time, calls me back up, and says he wants to cancel his order. I said, "Elmer, this isn't Woolworth's. You can't really take the merchandise back." But rather than paying me for what he ordered, he hung up the phone on me.

Having entered the orders for the stocks the previous day, I had to ask myself what I would do about it. It was something of a revelation to me—it was clear that I was dealing with a typical member of the public, a representative of their mindset. I figured he must be the perfect contrary indicator. In today's terms, I had to ask myself if I was just talking the talk, or if I was willing to walk the walk.

So, I journaled those stocks I bought for Elmer into my account and held them until I sold in 1980 or thereabouts. By then, I was getting several times, annually, what I paid for them in dividends alone. It was a fantastic hit, at least in percentage terms.

L: So it was an accident?

D: Yes, completely. I didn't know it was the bottom. I just knew the stocks were really cheap. I believed what I had told Elmer about those stocks, and I figured it was more intellectually honest to keep them.

It turns out that I was right. People didn't want stocks that were off 90 percent and yielding 60 percent; they figured there had to be something wrong. They'd rather buy something that's gone up 10 times, proving it has a good "track record." Track records are the best way to judge people, but the worst way to judge stocks.

L: I don't think I've ever heard of anyone picking the exact bottom of that cycle.

D: I got lucky, but it's a perfect example of why it's essential for a speculator to be a contrarian. You've got to believe in your thinking enough to buy when everyone else is selling, even with frightening images on TV, like the riots in Soweto. That's why it's critical to have an understanding of economics, politics, and the technical details of various businesses; only then can you hope to be immune from the blather you'll hear on TV and read in the popular press.

And when it came to gold, few people had a clue. I remember one politically connected investment guru of the day, Eliot Janeway, saying that if the U.S. government didn't support the price of gold at $35, it would fall to $8. He didn't have a clue. But he influenced scads of people.

L: That's a great story. What a pity for good old Elmer.

D: Yes. I have no idea what happened to him after he hung up on me, but I thank him for appearing at the right time. Elmer was completely ignorant of economics and the markets, but he nonetheless taught me a more valuable lesson than any teacher in four years of college.

L: So what happened next?

D: The late 1970s were very good to me, despite the fact it was the worst time for the economy since the Great Depression—high unemployment, high inflation, and skyrocketing interest rates. I was making great money in my regular business, royalties from *The International Man*, fees from speeches and occasional articles, and putting all my savings into mining stocks and gold, which was on its way to $800.

I wrote *Crisis Investing* in 1978. It was published in 1979 and hit number one for many weeks on the *New York Times* Best Seller list in 1980. Then, in 1982, I wrote *Strategic Investing*, which was more focused on the stock market, Dow Jones–type stuff. I got a very large advance, $800,000, from Simon & Schuster. That's a lot of money today, but was a lot more money back then, and it confronted me with the question of what I would do with the cash.

I can't say that I thought gold was done then, but the gold stocks didn't seem as cheap, so I bought things like Treasury bonds, which were yielding 12 to 13 percent, and electric utilities, which were also selling for 12 to 15 percent yields, and other things I recommended in the book. It's an excellent book, still worth reading today. I was dead right about the markets, even though I foolishly remained bear-ish on the economy—the markets and the economy are not at all the same thing.

L: That was at the beginning of the 20-year bull market for Wall Street.

D: Yes, it was my next big hit in the market. At the time, the DJIA was less than 1,000, and I said it was going to 3,000, which was an outlandish and outrageous prediction. Unfortunately, I didn't keep the things I bought long enough—I didn't think the bull market in stocks or bonds would go on anywhere near as long as it did.

I was gone by the time it hit 3,000. That was one of the biggest mistakes of my career. I didn't foresee interest rates dropping as long and as far as they did, eventually driving stocks, bonds, and real estate to manic heights. I could have held on and done almost nothing else for the next 20 years, but I didn't. Nonetheless, I bought pretty close to the bottom and held on for a good, long run.

L: So what did you do after cashing in, in the 1980s?

D: That's when I started getting into the mining stocks you now cover. I liked their incredible volatility. But it took me quite a while to really understand the way the game was played. Even though the third thing I wanted to be when I was a kid was a geologist, it took me years to get geologically active, so to speak. But no regrets. It was a great time to get into the field, because there were some fan-tastic gold stock runs in the 1980s, right up to the Bre-X scandal in 1996. . . .

Chapter 7

Doug Casey on the Education of a Speculator (Part Two)

June 2, 2010

Louis: So what did you do after cashing in, in the 1980s?

Doug: That's when I started getting into the mining stocks you now cover. I liked their incredible volatility. But it took me quite a while to really understand the way the game was played. Even though the third thing I wanted to be when I was a kid was a geologist, it took me years to get geologically active, so to speak. But no regrets. It was a great time to get into the field, because there were some fantastic gold stock runs in the 1980s, right up to the Bre-X scandal in 1996.

I went out into the field, as you do now, building first-hand understanding for the fundamentals of the business. That's as opposed to treating these things strictly like trading sardines—which, of course, most of them are. But even so, you can trade them much more effectively if you have a solid grasp of the technical areas of the business.

And there's no book for learning this; there's really no way to learn how to sort the wheat from the chaff, other than to get out there and apply boot leather, spend a lot of time talking to geos, learn the psychology of the players, and watch the economics of mining companies as they develop.

The 1980s were really a period of learning for me, playing around with wins and losses, all of which prepared me to profit from the bull market of the 1990s. It's been a wild ride, with resource stocks cyclically going up 1,000 percent, and then falling 95 percent—again and again.

L: Heh. You didn't have the advantage I had of a Doug Casey who'd done it before and could teach me the ropes, and whose experience I can now draw upon at any time.

D: Yes, it really would have been helpful if I'd had a mentor, but I can't think of anyone back then who could have taught me what I needed to know. If there had been, I sure as hell would have sat at his knee and saved myself a lot of money and aggravation. But all that effort at self-education did prepare me for the 1993 to 1996 bull market, which was a wonderful, fantastic time to be in the junior mining sector. That was the time when I had the three biggest wins of my career.

L: Ah yes, the famous "accident, scam, and psychotic break." We mentioned those before, in our conversation on winning speculations, but you didn't really tell the stories.

D: Well, the scam was Bre-X, of course. I was introduced to that by my friend Rick Rule, who also introduced me to Silver Standard Resources and several other huge wins I've had in my career. The company was coming out with fantastic results from its drilling in the orangutan pastures of Indonesia. At the time, the stock was trading for about a buck, and there weren't too many shares out. I started buying, and the story just kept getting better, so I started buying with both hands. Who could have guessed that someone was salting the drill core?

I ended up with a very large position, and as I said before, I finally came to the realization, when the stock was trading over $100, that this exploration play had a market capitalization greater than that of Freeport McMoRan, which had already put billions of dollars into its Ertsberg and Grasberg mines, and was paying dividends, to boot. I asked myself what the point of holding on was, couldn't think of one, and sold on that basis. As you know, the whole thing was exposed as a fraud, and $4 billion of value disappeared.

The accident was Diamond Fields, of which I was a founding shareholder, simply because I was a friend of Robert Friedland's. I did a second private placement in it later, based strictly on the diamond assets. That was an offshore Namibian diamond play that looked great, as so many of these things often do, but didn't work out.

The only reason that Diamond Fields went to over $100 instead of near zero is because a couple geologists on a helicopter ride in Labrador, where the company was closing up shop, saw something out the window that looked interesting. They landed on the discoloration, sampled it, and that led to the world-class Voisey's Bay nickel discovery. It was pure luck those two geos were flying over that place and happened to look down at that time.

The psychotic break was Nevsun, which is still around today and is still active in Africa, as it was back in those days. I did private placements in that stock at $1 and $2, with full warrants, and rode it all the way up to $20, when I sold. I call it a psychotic break because there was a broker in Chicago, now deceased, who, for some reason, went wild and decided to put 100% of his clients' money into that stock. He personally took it to $20, after which it slid all the way back to becoming a penny stock, before this cycle breathed some new life into it.

This all just goes to show that even armed with the best intentions and expert knowledge, sometimes extraneous events can make all the difference.

L: Which underscores the importance of sticking close to the action, so you're not "out of the room, out of the deal."

D: Just so. Ted Turner supposedly attributes a lot of his success to just going where the action is and letting the law of large numbers work for him. It's true. You've got to be out there. Just running on the 9-to-5 treadmill is unlikely to result in anything other than mediocrity. It also helps not to be too risk averse, not to be intimidated by volatility, to have a contrarian nature, and to be inclined to go places others aren't interested in.

L: So, since we've recorded your three biggest wins for history, it would only be fair to record some of your biggest losses. Care to let one of those out of the bag?

D: It's funny—I tend to forget about those, actually. It's painful reliving them. Let's say I try to forget the incidents, while remembering the lesson.

L: It's just human psychology. You might think we'd want to remember our most painful experiences so as to never make the same mistakes again, but there also seems to be a tendency to push painful things from our minds, to enable us to continue functioning at all. If so, the unfortunate consequence is that people often repeat their worst mistakes.

D: That might explain why I've lost so much money on private deals. When you put money into a company at its founding, while it's still private, and it never goes public, you never get an exit, not even at a loss; the money just dies and goes to money heaven. At least if it was good money.

There are companies I bought decades ago that are, to this day, still not public. For all I know, they never will go public. I won't name names, but for all practical purposes, this is dead money. So I'm extremely reluctant to buy into private deals, although I can't help but look at them and still take the plunge occasionally. Some of these things that were deposited with brokers still show up on my monthly statements. Seeing them there is like getting poked in the eye anew every time, so I recently told the brokers just to delete them—the ones I know are bankrupt, anyway.

There's a lot that can go wrong before a private company gains a listing on a stock market. As well as after.

L: But you still do it. I've seen you do it this year.

D: You're right, but the price was really, really cheap, and I knew the people involved. If I have high confidence that the people involved will do what they say they'll do, that helps, but it still needs to be at fire sale prices.

L: Words to the wise, duly noted.

D: I'll tell you my best "woulda, coulda, shoulda" story. The stupidest failure to act in my career. A sin of omission, not commission.

L: Okay, shoot.

D: One of the largest publishing companies in the United States was started by a friend of mine in 1979. At the time, I was just start-ing to publish my newsletter, the predecessor of the "International

Speculator" you now run. He said he'd like to publish it, and I said: "Great, because I'm not a publisher and I don't want to be one." He said he'd sell me 10 percent of his new company for $10,000, with the idea in mind that that would be the seed capital for publishing the newsletter. I passed on the deal, thinking I was being a shrewd businessman.

Today, I estimate that my 10 percent share of the dividends would have added up to $3 to $4 million over the years, plus my 10 percent stake would be worth $5 to $10 million.

L: Wow. But if you knew your $10,000 was going to be seed capital for the publication of your own newsletter, why on earth didn't you take the deal?

D: Well, I had other offers from other publishers, and they seemed more experienced and stable; they didn't need capital to get the job done. My friend's company was private, with no experience in the newsletter publishing business, and I just didn't think it would work. I was simply, totally, dead wrong about it.

It's still a private company, but it would be one of the most productive pieces of my portfolio today, had I not been so clever back then.

And I've got to tell you that another of my best deals was, and still is, a private company. Believe it or not, it was a placer deal in Alaska—

L: You're kidding!

D: No! Talk about all the things you shouldn't do in investing: It was private, a placer deal, and with people I didn't know well.

L: Why is it that when you hear of a mining scam, it's so often a placer deal?

[**Ed. Note:** Placer mining is the dredging of rivers, sifting of sandbars, and so forth for gold that has accumulated in dirt, gravel, sand, and other "alluvial" matter.]

D: The same reason that so few are in public companies—there are just too many X factors. The first thing that happens is that when you get going, your workers see nice nuggets of gold, and those nuggets somehow manage to disappear. More technically, it's really difficult to estimate mining reserves in a placer setting; the flakes and nuggets are inconsistently dispersed into pods. On the other hand, it tends not to be very capital intensive, and values are easy to recover by simple gravity separation. But that also means most of them have already been played out by prospectors. Placer is a fun thing to play with during your summer vacation, but typically is not commercially viable.

L: So, why'd you do it?

D: It seemed like a good idea at the time—famous last words. Actually, an old friend, who did know the people, urged me to. And—not that this is an excuse for doing something goofy—it wasn't much money. Sometimes it's better to be lucky than smart, although that's no way to invest.

Anyway, I got into this deal for $20,000, back in the early 1980s. That $20,000 got me 200 ounces of gold over the years, which is still on deposit with a major broker to whom they shipped it. They stopped producing in 2001 at the bottom of the market, when it was just uneconomic, but it's going back into production soon, so I may still get even more gold without putting another penny into the deal.

L: That's more than 10 to 1 on just the gold they've dividended to you so far.

D: Yes. The $20,000 was tax deductible, since it went directly into expenses. And the gold is tax free until I sell it, which I have no intention of doing until there's a better place for the capital. Perhaps U.S. stocks when dividends are in the 6 to 8 percent range.

But actually there's another one, an opportunity brought to me by Jim Gibbons, a longtime subscriber who started a company called Seattle Shellfish. In spite of the fact that I'd grown to hate private deals, Jim's project looked good, so I invested some money. It's still private, but it's paying me about 30 percent per year in dividends, and they've been increasing. Incidentally, he's just written a book with a lot of insights that are especially relevant now: *The Golden Rule: Safe Strategies of Sage Investors*.

L: Sounds like a love-hate relationship you have with private companies. How does one even start to make a rational decision in that environment?

D: Well, they could start with my friend Arthur Lipper's book, *The Guide for Venture Investing Angels: Financing and Investing in Private Companies.* I've had a lot more losers than winners investing in private companies, but almost everybody does. You just hope that the occasional winner is big enough to make up for the losses, plus give you a worthwhile risk-adjusted return. What that means is trying to go only for deals that, in your subjective opinion, have 10 to 1 potential. Better yet, try to negotiate for some type of security, to reduce your downside risk. A study of Arthur's books, and he's got several, is a cheap education.

L: Sounds like one I need to read, with so many students sending me business plans. Any other painful lessons learned to share?

D: Like I said, I seem to have pushed most from my mind. But maybe I should also say that some of my biggest winners have been outside of the world of gold stocks and mining, and in the world of real estate.

L: Ah, yes, real estate is the other great passion of yours we've talked about, aside from poker, which we've also talked about.

D: Spain was a good example. I bought real estate in southern Spain before Spain joined the EU, and I recommended doing so in the newsletter. That worked out very well indeed, not just because of the influx of tourists and money from Northern Europe, but because the dollar was much higher back then, making it cheaper to buy all kinds of things for giveaway prices. All of Europe was relatively cheap at the time. I also bought in Hong Kong during a China crisis. Same in Argentina, but crises there come quite often.

L: I'd guess any trend-watcher who was paying attention could have guessed that after Generalissimo Franco took his long-overdue exit from our weary world stage, things must have been at or near a bottom for Spain.

D: That's right. Another "woulda, shoulda, coulda" story in real estate is that I was in South Africa looking at beachfront property back in about 2000. It was very cheap at the time, because the rand was about 12 to 1 against the dollar (because the price of gold and other metals was down). Had I done that, I could have made 10 to 1 on some of those beachfront properties during the following boom.

L: So why didn't you?

D: I didn't want to live in South Africa. The problem with many foreign real estate deals is that if you're not going to be there and watch over things, you just don't know what is going to happen. You get squatters, you get rapacious town councils, and so forth. It's always messy, but it gets out of hand if you're not there, or frequently there.

Anyway, gold and gold stocks were so cheap, I thought that was a better place to be. So, there are a lot of big ones like this that got away.

L: Like that castle you could have bought in Rhodesia during the war for $85,000—you told that story in our conversation on real estate.

D: Sure, but things can go wrong just as easily as they can go well, if not easier. Twenty years ago, I was talking with John Templeton, at his office in Lyford Cay, about real estate, and he told me about how he bought some land in Costa Rica back in the early 1970s. That was a smart move on his part, because Costa Rica was very cheap back in those days. But his lawyer, who was an ex–vice president of the country, managed to defraud Templeton. The master at this game lost $200,000, which was a lot of money back in those days; incidentally, I'd even met the guy who took the money. So you just have to be very careful about making long-distance investments in real estate, especially if you're not going to use them personally or stay close to them yourself.

L: Hm. Speaking of real estate, I heard a story about you that perhaps you can verify for me. I heard that when you started speculating in mining stocks, you'd actually been wiped out, or had very little cash at any rate. So you took out a second mortgage or something on a house you had in Vancouver, and that became the seed capital for your current fortune.

D: I forgot about that—it's true. I bought that house in West Van, which had 900 feet of really beautiful waterfront, for just under a million Canadian, when the Canadian dollar was about 65 cents U.S. I sold it at the beginning of the 1993 bull market, because I was really tight after the late 1980s bear market, and I just really needed the cash more than I needed a big fourth house. So I sold it for $2.3 million [Canadian], when the Canadian dollar was at about 83 cents. Today, the house would go for about $15 million [Canadian], with the Canadian dollar at near parity. At this point I definitely would urge its owner to hit the bid, whether he needs the money or not. Vancouver property is riding for a fall.

L: That explains a lot. I always wondered about that story, because you always say that people should never risk money they can't afford to lose on mining stocks—"the most volatile stocks on earth." So it seemed strange that you would have gone deep into hock to gamble in the market. But you didn't; you liquidated a noncore asset and remobilized your gains. You missed out on more gains on the house, but that move provided the capital for the three biggest wins in your career, which you just told us about. Sounds like a great move to me.

D: Another lesson learned that this brings to mind is that whenever I've made big gains in the market, I've made it a habit to invest the profits I've scraped back off the table into something that can't dry up and blow away.

L: Hence the emphasis on real estate.

D: Yes, though real property has carrying costs, and it's illiquid. That's the bad news. The good news is that it—usually—stays where you leave it. That's another advantage of salting away gold coins; you don't tend to liquidate them.

L: So noted. Any more lessons learned?

D: Well, I don't regret much in life, but the things I really regret the most, even more than the big losses I've taken, are the opportunities I've let slip through my fingers. It happens to everyone, and you shouldn't regret it too much, but they sure do smart. In most areas of life, not just investments, it's not the things you did that you regret, but the things you failed to do.

But investment-wise, for example, some friends of mine were founders of Digital Switch some 30 years ago. I didn't really understand the implications of the switch, no pun intended, from electro-mechanical to purely digital switching, so I passed on what could have been a *huge* amount of money.

The founder of AOL was also a friend of mine; I actually used to work for him at one point, when I was in the brokerage business. He made a billion dollars on AOL, another boat I missed. Coming close but no cigar hurts sometimes.

L: So what's the lesson to be learned from that? I bet there are even more deals you were quite right to pass up.

D: Lots and lots of bad deals I didn't get in on, for sure. Which reemphasizes the necessity of looking at hundreds of deals, just so you can afford to walk away from 99 percent of them. I've got to plug Marin Katusa here at our energy division. He is an exceptional judge of private companies, and he does look at hundreds of deals of all kinds. And he actually does walk away from 99 percent of them.

One more thing, I don't think it's possible to overemphasize the importance of having a voracious mind, of letting your curiosity run wild, into every subject and to every part of the world. To be a good speculator, you should have the broadest and deepest range of knowledge possible. If I had known more, I wouldn't have missed Digital Switch or AOL; it was my own ignorance that cost me those opportunities.

I said before that it's good to be lucky, but luck favors the well-prepared. For speculators, that means having the widest range of experience and knowledge possible, so you can see an opportunity for what it is when it comes knocking.

L: Hence our company motto: "Intensely Curious, Focused on Facts." Great stories, Doug, thanks for sharing them.

D: My pleasure. My guess is that this decade is going to feature some of the most volatile markets in history. That's a very good thing for those who are prepared and know what to look for.

Chapter 8

Doug Casey on Winning Speculations

December 16, 2009

Louis: Doug, these conversations are going out to a wider and wider audience—almost 100,000 now. A lot of these readers are new to our style of investing. They've heard of your 30-year track record of picking winning investments, and many are wondering how you do it. Can we tell them the secret?

Doug: Well, it's not really a secret. I have a method for picking resource stocks and other speculations; all our analysts at Casey Research use it. We even have a free report on our website describing this method, called *The Eight Ps of Resource Stock Evaluation*. We try hard to educate our subscribers in using this method themselves, and encourage them not to follow our recommendations blindly. Our goal is to educate subscribers in all the important aspects of our business: geology, engineering—all aspects of the markets. We make a lot of investment recommendations, but we don't just tout stocks—it's not like being a railbird at a racetrack. Each speculator has different amounts of capital available, different tolerance for risk, different areas of interest, and so on. But it's not just about knowledge; it's critical to have a method of some description. And to exercise discipline.

But before we get into that, let's talk about speculation itself.

L: As distinct from investing.

D: Yes. Properly speaking, investing is the act of putting capital into a business in anticipation of making a profit. Sounds easy and simple, but it's not. The best description of good investment methodology is *The Intelligent Investor*, Graham and Dodd's seminal work on securities analysis, first published in 1949. The book is still a financial best seller today, because it's clearly written, very well thought out, and covers all the bases. I don't just recommend it. I'll go so far as to say it's totally indispensible. If you're not thoroughly familiar with the concepts in the book, you're going into "the battle for investment survival" (another good book, incidentally, by Gerald Loeb) unarmed.

But the truth is that I don't consider myself an investor. I'm a speculator. Which is to say, someone who allocates capital in order to profit from distortions in the market caused by government intervention. The definition I just gave is the proper one for *speculation*, but the word is also used to describe investing in high-risk things, which may be totally different. It's a source of great confusion, often leading to disaster, when people use words inaccurately, and often without actually even knowing what they mean. Anyway, the times ahead of us are going to be tough on prudent investors, but a boon for speculators.

I've long said that it makes no sense to risk 100 percent of your wealth on "conservative" investments that might give you a 10 percent return—if you're lucky. There are a lot more GMs and Fannie Maes out there, I promise you. To me it makes more sense to allocate 10 percent of your portfolio to speculations that can yield [gains greater than] 1,000 percent. My ideal is to divide a speculative portfolio into 10 unrelated areas, each of which (in your subjective opinion, because certainty only exists in the minds of fools, bureaucrats, and ideologues) has at least a 50-50 chance of winning, with the potential for a 10 to 1 win.

Especially in volatile times, with inflation written on the wall, you can't afford to sit on cash or supposedly "safe" investments; you need a portion of your portfolio invested in speculations that can double in a year, or pull much higher multiples if their ships come in.

L: We talked about this a bit in our conversation on gold stocks, but even then you said that diversifying speculation into other areas improved the odds of success. The same reasoning applies.

D: Right. I believe in diversification, but not into just everything in general—like a lot of mutual funds. The problem is that it's very hard to find many really appealing speculations, although I do like cattle and some other rather obscure things. It's a good reason to read about everything, everywhere, because it might better attune you to an opportunity very few others might see. That is where life-changing amounts of money can be made.

L: In these highly volatile times, in which many "safe" investments are proving to be not so safe, might you increase your normal 10 percent guidance?

D: Sure, 20 percent might make sense for the people who can tolerate the exposure to higher risk. But, as you say, the conventional "safe" stuff is at higher risk as well. It's a question of do as I say, not as I do, however, because I'm a lot higher than 20 percent, although most of my money is still in physical gold, silver, and unleveraged real estate in the right places. Here a distinction must be made between volatility and risk: Risk is something you should always minimize, especially right now, with the Greater Depression just getting started.

Unfortunately, most people don't understand systemic risk and believe the government can shield them from it. And they're afraid of volatility, although volatility can be your best friend. Now is a great time to put that friend to work for you, as we do in our energy, metals, and technology letters. If you can afford to sustain some hefty losses and rebuild your portfolio, should you be dealt a losing hand, you might go as high as putting [more than] 30 percent into volatile speculations—basically, the one-third of our general portfolio recommendation that we suggest for stocks (the other thirds being gold and cash). But be careful about making "all-in" bets. You can't be an effective capitalist without capital.

L: I know you play a lot of poker, so the gambling metaphor comes easily to mind, but I've also heard you say many times that speculation, done properly, is not gambling. Can you explain that?

D: Yes, there's a huge difference. Gambling relies strictly on dumb luck: Will red or black come up next on the roulette wheel? Of course there's an element of luck in both investing and speculation, just as in life itself. But it's mitigated and controlled. You can apply your intelligence and effort researching a speculation, greatly improving your odds over random chance. Throwing darts at a list of stocks, even gold stocks, would be gambling. Researching companies and applying the eight Ps changes it from a game of pure chance. Of course poker is neither investing nor speculation—it's gambling, but a very sophisticated form that relies heavily on math and psychology. It takes intelligence to play poker well.

Another thing is taking a step back, looking at the big picture, and correctly identifying trends that have clear implications for you as a speculator. For example, when everything you see, read, and hear convinces you that major inflation is on the way, which I believe is so, then there are clear implications for speculators, such as rising gold prices (and gold stocks, even more so) and rising interest rates. And while it won't do so equally, a rising tide does tend to raise all ships—at least the ones with no holes in their hulls.

That means you can stack the odds greatly in your favor, and I don't just mean reducing thousands-to-one against, as in a lottery, to a 100 to 1, or even 50 to 1 against. I mean, a one-in-five chance of winning, or 50-50 odds, and even, in some cases, better than a 50 percent chance of coming out ahead. And when you do win, you can win 100 to 1, which makes up for lots of little losses.

This is why we put so much effort into *The Casey Report*, our big-picture newsletter. It's essential for us to keep the big picture in mind when we review possible speculations, to keep the odds skewed in our favor.

L: Can a high-stakes speculation really have better-than-even odds of winning?

D: It'd be senseless to try to put specific odds on a stock pick, of course, but when you spot an undervalued story with real merit, there are times when something truly unexpected and disastrously bad would have to happen to the company, or the market itself would have to turn against your expectation, to keep the stock from rising.

And if you can buy into a private placement, you can usually get warrants that offer you an option to profit from success without having to pony up the cash until you *know* you'll make money exercising.

L: Ah, the power of private placements, but let's come back to that. First, let's have a quick look at the eight Ps, for those not familiar with them.

D: Okay, but I do recommend that report, even to those who have little appetite for speculation. It's not that long and has a lot of my 30-plus years of experience as a speculator boiled down into it. The Ps are usable for all stocks, but are especially valuable for companies that don't have significant assets and have no history of earnings— probably not even any sales. Graham and Dodd's analysis simply doesn't apply to such companies. But that doesn't mean they can't be excellent speculations.

So, the first P is *people*. No matter how great the rest of the Ps might be, if you don't have confidence in the people, you can't have confidence in the rest of the story. There's no shortage of crooks, incompetents, and just plain stupid people in the resource sector we concentrate on, but that's equally true of real estate, tech, and any other business. Actually, it's possible to make money on crooks, incompetents, and even stupid people, but you have to get the timing right (buy in early and sell before the deal goes sour), and that's exceptionally risky—and remember, I like volatility but not risk.

In general, I stick with people I know have the skills, determination, and track record of success it takes to beat the odds and deliver huge amounts of added value. If I don't know the people involved, I usually know someone who does, such as yourself or Marin Katusa [Senior Editor of the Casey energy letters]. I also like to see management sharing the same risk and therefore having incentives aligned with shareholders—and I don't mean freebie stock options. I mean they put their own money into the deal and have a substantial stake in adding shareholder value.

If I'm not satisfied with the first P, it's usually not worth looking at the rest. There aren't enough hours in the day.

L: I've heard you say in several speeches that your biggest wins were an accident (Diamond Fields), a scam (Bre-X), and a psychotic break (Nevsun). How does that square with the above?

D: Well, I said you could make money on crooks, and we made something over 5,000 percent gains on Bre-X—but I didn't know it was a scam at the time. Nobody did. We got in early on a great story and sold when we had a huge win and it started sounding too good to be true—about when its market cap exceeded that of Freeport McMoRan. That sell turned out to be slightly early, but that was much better than being late, because it went to zero.

Diamond Fields was a completely accidental discovery of the massive Voisey's Bay base metal deposit in Labrador, when they were about to bail and concentrate on offshore diamonds in Namibia. The psychotic break was on the part of a broker friend of mine in Chicago, now deceased, who personally drove the share price of Nevsun through the roof by sheer willpower.

These were all penny stocks that went well above $100 a share in the first two instances, and $20 in the third. Happy anomalies like these are part of why I have solipsistic tendencies.

But you can never know those things are coming; there's no speculation strategy for increasing your odds of having one of these in your portfolio, other than the general strategy of being in the resource sector, where it's actually possible to make 50 times your initial investment in a couple years. Resource stocks are, by far, the most volatile class of securities on the planet.

L: And backing the best in the business does improve your odds. Got it. What's next?

D: After people, the Ps don't really have a fixed order, but the next most crucial ones are *property*, *paper*, and *phinancing*.

Property is pretty obvious: Whether it's an oil field, a mineral exploration project, a tech deal, or a real estate development, the project should be of genuine merit. That's why I ask you to go all around the world to check up on these things. Even with the best of people involved, we want to make our own judgments on the merits of the properties in question.

Paper refers to a company's share structure; you want to watch out, for instance, for large numbers of restricted shares that might come free trading soon; they can put a lot of selling pressure on a company if they're in the money, especially if their owners have warrants. More on that in a minute. A relatively large number of shares selling at low prices is also usually a sign of a checkered past. But on the other hand, too tight a share structure can be problematical as well, because there's not enough trading volume to make it possible to buy or sell at good prices.

Phinancing (apologies to any language purists out there—the rest all start with P) refers to the cash on hand, compared to the cash needed to achieve the next milestones. When credit is tight and financing hard to come by, there's just no sense in buying shares in a company that's low on cash. Even if they have great property being advanced by the best people, you know they are going to have to finance soon, which usually means you can get in at a cheaper price if you exercise a little patience (either because you can buy into the private placement or because the placement causes the share price to drop, as often happens). And if they don't finance, they won't have the wherewithal to add value, so either way, I rarely buy companies that are low on cash, unless it's on the back of an attractive financing.

L: Roger that. And the rest of the Ps?

D: They are *politics*, *promotion*, *push*, and *price*.

Politics refers to the risk of political intervention (or "social" problems, which amount to the same thing) that can ruin a perfectly good project. Anything from trouble with indigenous populations, to local bans on your company's proposed activity, to raised taxes and royalties, to new regulations that ruin a project's economics—there's so much economically suicidal politics that can kill a deal, it could take years to list all the specific risks. But these things really have killed, are killing, and will kill projects, so you have to research local, regional, and national politics carefully and avoid speculations with clear political red flags. Or use them to your advantage when you think others are reading things wrong.

Promotion refers to a company's ability to get its story out to the market. I've lost money on good people working on great projects because they simply could not promote their work to a market that would have cared had it known about it. "Promotional" has negative connotations, but that's only justified when a company has nothing but promotion going for it. All sizzle and no bacon. If your pick really does have the bacon, it's essential that it be effective at getting the market to hear the sizzle.

Push is related to promotion, but is not the same thing. It's the specific set of milestones that you can reasonably expect to push share prices higher. This could be a value-accretive acquisition, important drill results from a mineral or oil/gas play, a feasibility study—basically any good news you have reason to believe lies ahead and should be good for the share price. A catalyzing event that makes the deal a "buy" right now, as opposed to at some unknown time in the future.

Price is not simply the share price, nor just a company's market capitalization (share price times number of shares issued and outstanding), but those things in relation to the price of the underlying commodity or asset a company was working on. In other words: Is the price of gold, oil, uranium, copper, nickel, lithium, or whatever—a hundred other commodities—going up or down? You've got to have a grip on the big picture of the world economy, as well as the technologies that are using, will be using, or may stop using these things.

L: These eight Ps have become my Eight Commandments, and they sure have worked for me. So, I think our astute readers can see how private placements fit into this, but can you spell that out for us in brief as well?

D: Sure. When a company needs cash, it usually either borrows it (bonds, debentures, and lines of credit) or issues more stock. There are other options, like selling royalties or doing JVs, of course. For going concerns, it's usually debt, but if a bank won't lend the company money, it's usually forced to dilute existing shareholders by issuing new paper. That's generally a bad sign in a company that has cash flow. But in the junior exploration companies, both in oil and gas where Marin concentrates and in metals where you concentrate, there is almost never any significant revenue, so they are constantly back at the trough, raising more money—and that's a good thing, if they add value burning that cash.

L: As when a company spends $50 million exploring and developing a gold project that ends up with a $500 million NPV.

D: Speak to me. If it's a good company, meaning, solid on the eight Ps except for needing more cash, a financing via a private placement of new shares to existing and new shareholders can be a great opportunity.

L: A lot of people seem reluctant to go there. There are trading holds placed on the new shares, hassles getting brokers to cooperate, and qualification requirements. Can you tell us why all of this is worth the effort?

D: Leverage. Think about it, why would anyone buy new shares in a public company when they can just buy shares on the open market? Because the company offers them incentives, usually in the form of selling the new shares at a significant discount to market, and/or offering a warrant—a kind of free option to buy more shares in the future at a set price.

The warrants, in particular, are very powerful. Listen, if you like a company enough to buy the shares anyway and you can do so at or under market and get a free warrant as well, it's a no-brainer. When the shares come free trading, which is only after four months in Canada, where most of our stocks trade, you can sell them and retain upside free of risk through the warrants, or you can hold them, in which case the warrants multiply your potential upside.

If a warrant is good, say, for two years, that gives the company a long time to add value, and you only exercise the warrant if you can sell the shares you'd get for more than what you'd pay for them. You either know you're going to win, or you don't spend another dime.

L: Okay, but what about the hassles?

D: They exist, and they can be quite onerous. Many private placements offered by Canadian companies are not available to U.S. persons, and even when they are, you generally need to be a qualified investor, which, among other things, usually means having a net worth in excess of a million dollars.

But if you qualify, you're walking away from free money if you don't participate in private placements, and a good broker can help you handle the hassles.

L: And if any readers don't qualify, I'd be happy to help them build their portfolio values to the point at which they do qualify, as would Marin.

D: And you both do a fine job at it.

L: Aww, come on, you're making me blush.

D: Well then, we'll try to talk about something that has nothing to do with you next week.

L: I look forward to it.

Chapter 9

Doug Casey on the Biggest Danger to Your Wealth

June 17, 2009

Louis: Good morning, Doug. This week, I'd like to ask you about diversifying your assets outside of your home country. What is the danger for investors who keep all their assets at home, and what are the alternatives? It looks like there's a real risk of exchange controls blocking capital from leaving the United States. The Obama tough talk on tax havens is one sign. What should people do, while there's still time, to avoid getting trapped?

Doug: Well, investment risks are huge in today's world. But political risks are even greater, and most Americans are completely unprepared. The biggest danger to your wealth isn't the markets, as ugly as they are. The biggest risk today is your own government. The only way you can protect yourself is by internationalizing your assets.

So, while it is still possible—and I don't think it's going to be possible for very much longer—you should get as much money out of the United States as you can and put it into something that will be hard for them to force you to repatriate. If you open a foreign bank account or brokerage account, that's a step in the right direction, and you may be grandfathered somehow, but those things are liquid, so you could be forced to bring the assets back before you want to. I think the best thing that you can do is to either buy foreign real estate or to buy gold coins and put them in a foreign safe deposit box.

L: You mentioned something that Americans aren't familiar with: political risk. You've traveled and done business in a lot of countries. What kinds of negative policies are common in other parts of the world that you think are coming here?

D: Well, governments are capable of absolutely anything because they consider their citizens a national resource available for exploitation, almost like cattle. There are numerous things that the U.S. government might do, now that it has become so much like all the other governments. They could put a tax on foreign investments, to discourage you from buying them. You'd still be able to send money out of the country, but you'd be charged an exit tax of 10 or 15 percent, or whatever the government wants. There might be a tax on foreign travel to cut down on Americans sending money abroad. There might be a prohibition on opening up new bank or brokerage accounts outside the United States. There are all kinds of possibilities. It would probably be politically popular; the average guy thinks that foreign investment is somehow unpatriotic, and foreign travel is frivolous, something for only "the wealthy."

L: If you have assets outside the United States but you're a U.S. citizen, aren't you at risk anyway?

D: Yes, you absolutely are. It's unfortunate that the tax laws have turned U.S. citizenship into an albatross. The United States is the only major country that demands taxes from citizens living outside the country. And even if you renounce your citizenship, they still want taxes from you. First of all, they tax you at the time you expatriate, as though you had sold everything you own. Second, they still tax you on any income you earn in the United States for the next 10 years. And they levy a special tax on anyone in the United States who receives a gift or inheritance from you. So, over the years, America has become a roach motel for capital.

L: Planning can help, but it is getting more complex?

D: Yes. It is becoming very complex, and setting up a foreign company is subject to all kinds of reporting requirements. It's quite problematic. Really, the simplest and best way to gain some measure of political insulation is to buy gold and put it in a safe deposit box and/or buy foreign real estate. Neither move triggers any special reporting requirements.

L: Let's talk about your first recommendation, buying gold and storing it abroad. How do I go about it?

D: We had an article recently in "Big Gold," one of our letters that covers that question pretty thoroughly. In essence, you need a safe deposit box or a secure safe in your offshore property.

L: Over the years, you've bought real estate in many places—Spain, New Zealand, Canada, Hong Kong, Africa, South America, and elsewhere. I understand that you've recently invested in Argentina and Uruguay. Aren't you also at the mercy of the governments there?

D: The Argentine government has been amazingly stupid over the last 60 years, destroying the currency repeatedly, among other things. Now the U.S. government seems to be taking lessons from them. But on the plus side, the average Argentine has little love or respect for the government; most of them are transplanted Italians who seem to have a natural aversion to taxes. It's demographically about the most European country in the world, has by far the largest community and tradition of classical liberalism in Latin America, and is socially very stable. It's quite different from places like El Salvador or Bolivia, where there are masses of disenfranchised and landless peasants. Further, Argentines long ago learned how to deal with the nonsense the government specializes in; Americans have just enrolled for what's going to be an unpleasant learning experience. One of many things I like about Argentina—and I've been to 175 countries and lived in 12—is its extremely low cost of living, combined with a very high and sophisticated standard of living. That's why we chose Argentina to build what I intend to be the finest residential resort in the world. Check it out at La Estancia de Cafayate.

Chapter 10

Doug Casey on Protecting Your Assets

August 19, 2009

Louis: Doug, we're getting a lot of questions from readers on how to follow your advice to diversify assets, politically. I know it's a prickly subject, but what can you tell us about getting our money out from behind the new iron curtain that seems to be descending?

Doug: First—and I can't stress this enough—you've got to accept the grim reality of impending currency controls. The modern era of foreign exchange controls really started with the perversely Orwellian-named Bank Secrecy Act of 1970. For the first time, that made it obligatory for U.S. citizens to report any foreign bank or brokerage accounts they had to the government.

But the threat is older than that, of course, going back to 1933, when Roosevelt confiscated Americans' gold. Interestingly enough, only gold bullion held by Americans within the United States was confiscated. If you had gold outside the United States, you were insulated.

L: I didn't know that. If history repeats itself, that could be a key tactical factor for our readers to consider.

D: Yes. There are no guarantees, of course. Those in government today think they can do absolutely anything they deem necessary and expedient. But at least if it's out of their physical bailiwick, it improves your odds.

L: Why do you think they allowed that exemption last time? I doubt it was because they had any shred of respect for private property; maybe they just recognized that trying to seize gold overseas would be impractical.

D: Good question. Well, the 1930s were a different era. Communication, for one thing, was vastly slower and more expensive than it is now. And you have to remember that though we had an income tax in the 1930s—since 1913, actually—very few people were paying it, even among those allegedly legally obligated to pay it. It was hard for the government to find out who they were, and how much they were earning, and so on. Even though there were only 140 million people in the country then, the absence of computers, and much less centralization, made it very hard for Washington to keep tabs on them.

L: The income tax really was a voluntary tax back then!

D: [Laughs] Much more so than now; it really was a different era. At any rate, based on this history, and that the juggernaut is building momentum towards the bottom of the ditch, I have to reiterate my advice on the most important investment decision you can make. And it isn't one among the different classes of investment; it's political and geographical diversification. Simply put, that's because no matter where you live, your government is the greatest threat to your wealth today.

If you're a high-income earner, the state basically takes 50 percent of what you earn, and then from what's left, you have to pay your real estate taxes, sales taxes, and many, many other kinds of taxes. Government is without question the biggest danger to your financial health. You've got to diversify your assets so they are not all under any one government's control.

L: You say that in almost every speech you give these days, and you said it in one of our interviews a couple weeks ago.

D: Yes, and it bears repeating, constantly. It's the elephant in the room that very, very few people pay any attention to, and it's going to stomp most people to death, for just that reason.

L: Okay, so give us a primer. For those who want to avoid getting crushed by the elephant, where do they begin?

D: To start with, it makes all the sense in the world to have a foreign bank account. Not a hidden one—I'm not advising anyone to break any laws. You report it on your annual tax filings. So, the government will know about it, but if it's a foreign bank account, they can't just step in and lock down your assets in an instant.

L: Does Canada count as a foreign country for Americans?

D: I'll probably get hate mail for saying so, but it's important for investors to recognize that Canada is a sort of "USA-light." When Washington says, "Jump!" Ottawa generally says, "How high?" Nonetheless, if only for the sake of formalities and legal pleasantries, U.S. citizens would have some degree of insulation with a Canadian bank account. And, as a general rule, Canadian banks are more solvent than U.S. banks, so setting up a Canadian bank account is an easy first step for many U.S. investors.

The second thing to do would be to set up a Canadian brokerage account. Unfortunately, the SEC has made it so that no Canadian broker will open an account with an American unless they have a U.S. subsidiary. That, in effect, makes your Canadian brokerage account like a U.S. brokerage account. That doesn't help you much from an asset protection point of view, but it does let you trade directly in many of the stocks we recommend in the *International Speculator* and *Casey's Energy Report* (not through a U.S. market-maker via the pink sheets).

Third, I think that having a safe deposit box in Canada is vastly preferable to having one in the United States. You probably do remember that when Roosevelt confiscated gold in 1933, he also sealed safe deposit boxes in all U.S. banks. No American could visit a safe deposit box for some time without a government agent accompanying him. That could certainly happen again.

And all of this is true in other countries around the world.

But yes, as an easy place to start, Canada is a sort of plain-vanilla jurisdiction that's worth giving a try.

L: So, what would be the French vanilla, or even the Bailey's Irish Cream jurisdiction? Is there such a thing as a tax haven anywhere in the world anymore? Even the Swiss have caved; I just heard that they just started handing over new account info to U.S. authorities.

D: Yes, apparently there were some 50,000 accounts UBS had, owned by U.S. citizens. UBS, a multinational bank with a very substantial presence in the United States—and therefore exposure to extortion by U.S. authorities—was going to hand them all over. The Swiss government stepped in, saying they would prosecute UBS officials if they violated Swiss law by doing that. But the Swiss worked out some sort of compromise with the U.S. authorities, so only about 5,000 accounts are being handed over. On what basis they picked these 5,000 is uncertain.

So, the first tax haven rule is to never go to a place that's obviously a tax haven. If I were interested in bank privacy, I'd forget about places like the Bahamas or the Caymans. It makes no sense at all today. All those little island republics are totally under the thumb of the United States at this point. And they've always been infiltrated with stooges. They may have bank secrecy laws, but they don't have a tradition of privacy like Switzerland has—although that's no longer what it was.

You'll recall how the German government bribed a Liechtenstein banker to steal account names and information. The Germans then turned over relevant data to the UK, United States, and other governments, who were quite happy to receive stolen goods. And there was about zero protest over the appalling theft. It's a testimony to how thoughtless and ethically complacent most people are; when a state commits a crime, they just overlook it.

L: Are you saying that all of the little havens are unreliable?

D: Well, I don't know of any that are reliable.

Instead, I would recommend places that are geographically distant from the United States, and culturally distant as well. To me, the best places to be are in the Orient. That's partially because the Chinese, and other oriental civilizations, are much less prone to roll over and do what they are told. National pride assures that, if nothing else.

But if you go this route, with, say, an account in Hong Kong, you certainly would not want to use a bank like HSBC. It's got branches all over the world, prominently in the United States—so, like UBS, they'll do what they are told.

Actually, there are still Swiss banks that will open an account for a "U.S. person," if you can convince them to do it. But you definitely do not want a Swiss or Liechtenstein bank that has any presence in the United States. The same would be true in the Orient, so forget about HSBC. You want a real Chinese bank. That way, when the U.S. government calls, the phone will be answered in Chinese and no one will speak English with them.

The best places are the least obvious places. Malaysia is interesting. Thailand. These are completely non–tax haven types of places, and that might make them suitable.

L: What about step two, getting a brokerage account?

D: Well, it's tough these days. If you want to trade in U.S. and Canadian stocks, you pretty much have to have an American or Canadian broker. But one thing that can be done that is completely legal (and reportable) is to open up a foreign company. Then the company can open up a brokerage account. That way, you do have a level of insulation I think is very valuable, both from a practical and a legal point of view.

L: I gather you're not talking about the Banana Republic IBCs I see peddled on the Internet?

D: Right. Most of what you see on the Internet offering to open up an IBC, which is just an offshore company, are just scams, if not stings. The fees are too high. The people are usually sleazy. They often come up with all sorts of cockamamie tax-avoidance schemes. You may be encouraged to do things that are illegal. They are just disasters waiting for you to walk into. I strongly encourage people not to even consider such offerings.

If you want an offshore company for the purpose of convenience or a measure of privacy, completely reportable and within the law, the best thing to do is to go to the jurisdiction you've picked and see a lawyer who deals in that sort of business. Cut out the middleman. Ideally, the jurisdiction would be one that meets the criteria I outlined above, but is also a place you'd actually enjoy spending time in.

L: So, you hop on a plane to, say, Panama, and how do you go about finding a reliable attorney to set up your corporation?

D: That's the intelligent way to do it. There's nothing illegal, nor particularly tricky about it; you just find a lawyer who specializes in it,
pay the fees, and off you go.

How do you find a good lawyer? Same way you do at home; you
go and start interviewing lawyers until you find one that impresses
you as being sound.

Panama, by the way, is probably the best place to do this at this
moment. The British Virgin Islands may be another. And, of course,
if you're an Australian or a New Zealander, you should think about
Vanuatu; it's only a two-hour plane ride from Sydney or Auckland.

Back in the Western Hemisphere, the only other reasonable alternative I see is Uruguay. It's always been promoted as the "Switzerland
of South America" and there's still a lot of truth to that, although less
and less. Uruguay is a small country, about the same size and with
the same-size population as Switzerland, and a very big part of their
national income is foreign banking. They have no tax on foreign-
earned income—though, unfortunately, they recently instituted a tax
on domestic-earned income. Too bad.

Another unfortunate thing about Uruguay is that when you
import gold there, such as by carrying Krugerrands in your briefcase,
their customs form asks you to report it. It's not against the law, but
they want to know, and a small import tax is payable.

L: That's really all it takes? Find a lawyer and pay the fees?

D: Yes, though there can be nuances worth paying attention to. For
example, there are various jurisdictions with different tax treaties that
can be used to your advantage—the Dutch Antilles being a famous
example, as far as dividends treatment goes. This is a specialist area
that, well, you should discuss with a specialist. But you should definitely give it some thought.

Oddly enough, you can import gold into Argentina with no
problems nor reporting requirements, and you can buy and sell gold
in Argentina just as legally. It's much easier than in Uruguay, but I
wouldn't dream of doing any significant banking in Argentina, and
neither do Argentines. The government is just completely untrustworthy when it comes to things like bank accounts.

So, it's rather perverse; you can deal easily in gold in Argentina, but
not bank accounts, and you can't deal in gold easily in Uruguay,
but bank accounts are easy.

Frankly, the best place to look for one-stop financial services shopping is Panama. Banking is easy, and there's no gold reporting. And I think Panama City will one day replace Miami as the financial nexus of Latin America.

And yes, you can still take gold in and out of the United States without reporting it. It's like stamps or rare coins. The exception would be, if you had enough of them, to remember that Double Eagles have a face value of $20, and the new Eagles have a face value of $50. But you can never be sure how any particular minion of U.S. Customs will interpret the law.

L: What about your cash, once you have your offshore bank account set up? You have to declare it if you take more than $10,000 on your person, but can you wire whatever you want?

D: Yes, you can send any amount of money you want, currently. It gets reported, but it's legal. And by the way, the $10,000 limit doesn't appear to cover gold, but it does cover stock certificates and other financial instruments—but you can still send those by Federal Express.

L: I wonder how long that will last.

D: I'm sure they'll get around to closing all the loopholes. So, the time to act is now. We'll keep monitoring the situation in *The Casey Report*, but when this happens, the Powers That Be won't want anyone to see it coming, so it will zing in from left field. Your only chance to protect your wealth is to start diversifying its exposure to any one particular predatory state as soon as possible.

We'll talk more about foreign currency controls again, but I have to stress again the urgency of diversifying the political risk your assets are exposed to: Do it *now*.

L: Okay, Doug. Thanks!

D: You're welcome.

Chapter 11

Doug Casey on Gold

September 23, 2009

Louis: Doug, we've talked about cars, cows, and cash, but the investment world thinks of you as a gold bug, so let's give that a go. Why gold?

Doug: Sure. First of all, it's because gold is actually money. It's an unfortunate historical anomaly that people think about the paper in their wallets as money. The dollar is, technically, a currency. A currency is a government substitute for money. Gold is *money*.

Now, why do I say that?

Historically, many things have been used as money. Cattle have been used as money in many societies, including Roman society. That's where we get the word *pecuniary*: The Latin word for a cow is *pecus*. Salt has been used as money, also including in ancient Rome, and that's where the word *salary* comes from: The Latin for salt was *sal* (or *salis*). The North American Indians used seashells. Cigarettes were used during World War II. So, money is simply a medium of exchange and a store of value.

By that definition, almost anything could be used as money, but obviously, some things work better than others; it's hard to exchange things people don't want, and some things don't store value well. Over thousands of years, the precious metals have emerged as the best form of money. Gold and silver both, though primarily gold.

There are very good reasons for this, and they are not new reasons. Aristotle defined five reasons why gold is money in the fourth century BC (which may only have been the first time it was put down on paper). Those five reasons are as valid today as they were then. A good form of money must be durable, divisible, consistent, convenient, and have value in and of itself.

L: Can you elaborate on that?

D: Yes, and from them, we can draw inferences that will help us anticipate the fate of the dollar.

First, let's take durable. That's pretty obvious—you can't have your money disintegrating in your pockets or bank vaults. That's why we don't use wheat for money; it can rot, be eaten by insects, and so on. It doesn't last.

Divisible. Again, obvious. It's why we don't use diamonds for money, nor artwork. You can't split them into pieces without destroying the value of the whole.

L: If I paid for a new Ford GT with the Mona Lisa, what would be my change—a small canvas by Picasso?

D: That's right. Maybe you'd get millions of those paintings of Elvis or Jesus on velvet.

Consistent. The lack of consistency is why we don't use real estate as money. One piece is always different from another piece.

Convenient. That's why we don't use, for instance, other metals like lead, or even copper. The coins would have to be too huge to handle easily to be of sufficient value.

Value of itself. The lack here is why you shouldn't use paper as money.

Actually, there's a sixth reason Aristotle should have mentioned, but it wasn't relevant in his age, because nobody would have thought of it.

L: It can't be created out of thin air.

D: Right. Not even the kings and emperors who clipped and diluted coins would have dared imagine that they could get away with trying to use something as essentially worthless as money.

L: I think we can forgive Aristotle for the oversight.

D: I think so. At any rate, these are the reasons why gold is the best money. It's not a gold bug religion, nor a barbaric superstition. It's simply common sense. Gold is particularly good for use as money, just as aluminum is particularly good for making aircraft, steel is good for the structures of buildings, uranium is good for fueling nuclear power plants, and paper is good for making books. Not money. If you try to make airplanes out of lead, or money out of paper, you're in for a crash.

That gold is money is simply the result of the market process, seeking optimum means of storing value and making exchanges.

But it's not something that suits governments, because paper money is an excellent means for governments to tax people indirectly, surreptitiously, through inflation. That's one reason central bankers love paper money, but also, phony economic theories, like those of John Maynard Keynes, hold that the government not only can but should meddle with the economy, and the ability to print paper money gives them a means to do that.

In today's world, not only do people around the world take it for granted that paper is money, but that it should be so.

But it's all nonsense. It's one reason for taking a gloomy view of humanity—people will believe almost any kind of claptrap, if the story is retailed by those in authority.

After the current system collapses, as every paper money system in the past has collapsed, some form of money will have to replace it, and it's almost certainly going to be gold.

L: There are already experiments with digital gold currencies. E-gold got taken out behind the woodshed by the Feds, but GoldMoney. com seems to be doing well. Do you believe those could see widespread adoption, as paper currencies lose their credibility?

D: Sure. You know, in the nineteeth century, the "paper money" you carried in your wallet was called bank notes. Why? Because they actually were notes from your bank representing a specified amount of real money on deposit. People carried these things because they were much more convenient for large amounts of money than chests of gold. Dollars today say "Federal Reserve Note," not "XYZ Bank Note" on the back, because they aren't redeemable for anything besides more Federal Reserve notes. That's why today's paper money substitutes are called fiat currencies; they have zero intrinsic value and are not redeemable for anything, but are accepted because the government will put you in jail if you don't. It's a fiat accomplished by force, not real value recognized by those who accept the notes.

Things like GoldMoney.com are simply modernized, updated versions of bank notes. They are basically transferrable warehouse receipts that represent amounts of gold you have on deposit someplace. I do recommend GoldMoney.com, incidentally, because it allows you to hold your gold in digital form, outside the United States. And to my understanding, these accounts are not reportable under current U.S. rules. It's an excellent alternative to storing large amounts of gold in a safe deposit box.

L: But will people believe in them? Will the public accept them so they can be used in everyday transactions, as paper money is used now? Hundreds of years ago, people accepted bank notes because they knew the reputations of the banks issuing them (when you traveled, you went to a reputable local bank, which knew the reputation of the bank that issued your notes, and the local bank could issue you new notes in local currency, et cetera). There was no central authority to certify these notes. But today, people don't think that way. They think it takes a government to assure the value of money.

D: You're quite correct on that; a sea change in thinking will have to take place. Of course, anyone in Zimbabwe can tell you a government's guarantee is not necessarily worth anything. A collapse of the dollar—the world's de facto reserve currency—could spark such a change in that way of thinking. With GoldMoney.com or the Perth Mint—another worthy alternative—it's a question of predicting the solvency of an actual company, and we have tools for that. I believe this is exactly what is going to happen in the future. As far as I'm concerned, either of these outfits is more reliable than, say, Citibank. And gold is far more desirable than the dollar. So I'd rather have a thousand ounces of gold stored with GoldMoney.com than a million dollars deposited at Citibank.

The dollar will be phased out of the world economy, because everyone can see that it's a hot potato. The Chinese have 2 trillion of them. They want to get rid of them because they aren't stupid, and they can see what the ultimate fate of the dollar is. This is true of every country around the world at this point; their central banks know they are sitting on hot potatoes, and they are going to want to unload them.

What's going to happen is that one or more countries are going to institute a sound, stable, gold-backed currency. Ten years ago, Mahathir Mohamad of Malaysia tried to get Islamic countries to return to hard money, adopting the gold dinar and the silver dirham, which are defined in the Koran as specific weights of gold and silver. It didn't work because of mistrust between the players; the governments of Muslim countries are almost universally corrupt. But I think it's entirely possible, nonetheless, that something like that might arise in the Islamic world. After all, they believe that the Koran is the actual word of Allah, and there is a resurgence of Islamic fundamentalism everywhere.

According to press reports, the Chinese government is actually encouraging Chinese people to accumulate gold at this point. They might go for a gold-backed yuan—it would put them on the map as an international monetary leader. The press also reports that the Russian government has been consistently buying large amounts of gold. We might even end up with a gold-backed ruble.

Meanwhile, the U.S government is creating trillions more dollars per year. This could result in the entire world monetary system being overturned. But there's no reason for anyone to trust any of these other governments more than they trust the U.S. government. And rightly so; they shouldn't trust any currency that doesn't come with a guarantee of redemption for something specific. And as Aristotle and history have shown us, gold is the best choice.

L: So the question now boils down to, what is gold really worth in terms of today's dollar? How do we compute that?

D: Well, aside from a few Spanish galleons at the bottom of the sea and dentures returned to the earth after a lifetime of use, pretty much all of the gold ever mined and refined is still sitting on the surface of the earth somewhere. Nobody really knows how much that is, but the most reasonable estimates I've seen are something like 6 to 8 billion ounces. That happens to work out to about one ounce of gold for every human being on the planet at this time.

Out of this, the U.S. government reports that it has 265 million ounces of gold in its treasury. If we divide the money supply by the number of ounces the U.S. could back its paper with—and here we'd have to decide what measure of money supply we want to use. Nobody, including the Federal Reserve, actually knows how much money they have floating around out there. It would seem that there are about 6 trillion dollars outside the U.S. alone. Let's estimate that in the United States, M0, the narrowest measure of money supply that consists of just notes and coins, amounts to 1 trillion. So, 265 million into 7 trillion gives you about $26,420 dollars per ounce of gold.

Now, if we add in the total obligations of the U.S. government, which it will either need to print more money to meet, or it will have to default on, that's about 100 trillion. If those dollars are printed, that would give us $377,430 per ounce.

All of these numbers are far, far above the current level of roughly $1,000 per ounce. And that's the answer to the question you started this interview with. Why gold? Because it's got only one way to go: up. It seems to me that everyone should have a very significant portion of their wealth in gold.

That's not just for safety, security, and prudence, though those are reasons enough, but because gold is cash in its most basic form. Better yet, even though it's quadrupled since its bottom in 2001, it's also still an excellent speculation. I can see somewhere between 3 and 10 times your investment in current capital. And there's no limit to the upside in dollars, depending on how rapidly the government destroys the currency.

To my view, that offers an exceptional combined opportunity; by buying gold, you protect your wealth but also have enormous speculative upside.

L: Plus, as you like to say, gold is the only asset class that is not also simultaneously someone else's liability.

D: Absolutely right. And in a world as financially unstable as today's, you just don't want to hold on to someone else's liabilities any more than you have to. Especially if that's a liability of an entity like the U.S. government.

L: Got it. You should own gold because it's money, because of its security, and because it's an excellent speculation. In our publications, we've been telling readers that they should have as much as one-third of their portfolio in gold, one-third in cash, and one-third in investments that could do well in times of crisis, including gold stocks, commodities, certain kinds of real estate, etcetera. Do you think those are still the right proportions? That worked out very well for our readers last year. Those who actually followed our advice would have had one-third in gold and one-third in cash, so even if they lost 50 percent of their remaining third, they would still have only been down 16.67 percent by the end of the year. But that was then, and there were signs of short-term price deflation, and now things are different. How should we be deployed today?

D: That's still a good balance, but if you start really thinking of gold as cash, and the dollar as a merely temporarily fashionable means of exchange, you'll find yourself loading your portfolio with much more gold and gold proxies. That will protect you against the very rapid loss of value the dollar faces in years to come. Inflation is going to truly get out of control.

The only reason to hold any dollars at all right now, other than what you need for a few months' living expenses if you live in the United States, is that there is still a possibility of a very short-lived but catastrophic deflation. That could make the silly things worth more in the short term and give you liquid capital to deploy quickly into other asset classes. But certainly within one year, I would start moving more money out of dollars and into gold and other investments, possibly including well-positioned real estate and stocks that could benefit from the destruction of the dollar.

And once again, I want to emphasize, especially for Americans, that it's not just a question of what you have and what you're doing in the market, but where you're keeping these things. Everyone, not just Americans, should try to have half of their gold, cash, and investments outside of their countries of citizenship and/or residence. You don't want all of your assets within easy reach of whatever government considers you its milk cow.

L: Good reminder. Well, we've talked a long time again, but briefly, what are the best ways to own gold?

D: I prefer gold coins to bars. They are more recognizable and convenient. You can walk into a coin shop in many places around the world, and they will recognize your Gold Eagles, Krugerrands, Philharmonics, etcetera. Dealers, or the public, may not recognize the hallmark of some bars.

For larger amounts, I like GoldMoney.com, as I mentioned above, and I believe Kitco offers secure and convenient accounts accessible online. I also think highly of the Perth Mint Certificate program, especially for those who feel more secure with some sort of government backing (though government involvement is a reason to run in the opposite direction, in most cases). And, of course, there are various banks that will store gold for you in vaults in London or Zurich, that sort of thing. We cover these sorts of things in "Casey's Gold and Resource Report."

L: Okay, then, one last question: How about the gold stocks—where do they fit into this picture?

D: That's a whole new conversation, and we should cover it soon. For now, I'll sum it up with three words: leverage to gold.

L: Very well then—I look forward to our next conversation. Thank you for your time.

D: A pleasure, as always.

Chapter 12

Doug Casey on Nuts and Bolts: Handling Bullion

July 15, 2009

Louis: Doug, we get a lot of questions about how to handle significant amounts of bullion. So let's talk about physical gold, and what to do with the stuff. First off, do you really think that people should put as much as one-third of their asset portfolios into physical gold?

Doug: Yes, I do, and at considerable risk of repeating myself, I'll tell you why:

First and foremost, precious metals bullion is the only financial asset class you can own that is not simultaneously someone else's liability. When you own an ounce of gold, you own an ounce of gold. It's not just a piece of paper that conveys a right to it from parties that may or may not even exist if and when you want to turn their liability into an actual, unencumbered asset in your pocket.

With today's markets suffering from volatility and disruptions of truly historic proportions, that sort of solidity is worth a lot, as you can see from gold's continuing strength. The dollar is in huge trouble and is on its way to reaching its intrinsic value, which is very bullish for gold.

Second, gold is natural money. It's uniquely well suited for use as money. Aristotle explained why, over 2,000 years ago, but in brief, it's because it's convenient, consistent, durable, divisible, and has intrinsic value (or, in Austrian economic terms, it has high intersubjective value).

So, if things get *really* bad and push comes to shove, you'll always find someone willing to take your gold in exchange for things you need. Come hell or high water—actually, especially in cases of unleashed hell and high water—your bullion will still be an acceptable form of payment, long after people stop bothering to pick up paper money blowing along the cracked streets of dying cities.

Third, gold offers excellent speculative upside at this time, precisely because the markets are so turbulent, with relatively little downside risk—again for the same reason: The fear factor will keep gold prices strong for the foreseeable future and could drive them to the moon with little notice. That's not a ride you want to miss.

L: What about people for whom one-third of their portfolio constitutes a substantial sum—much more than you can stuff under a mattress? Do you use Perth Mint Certificates?

D: You're right. Carrying a significant amount of value in gold coins is bulky, and forget about silver, which gets extremely bulky for larger dollar amounts. That's an important consideration given how critical it is to diversify your assets internationally, so you're not totally controlled by your own government.

It's still legal to carry gold coins across borders. Gold isn't currently considered a "monetary instrument," so you can still arguably carry, say, 100 Krugerrands (worth about $100,000) across a border legally, even though you're supposed to declare "monetary instruments" in excess of $10,000 in most places these days. But a large amount of gold could get you referred to a TSA supervisor, and I'd rather see a dentist who doesn't believe in anesthesia than that. The rules and their interpretation are quite Kafkaesque. Although I promise that almost none of the TSA's 50,000 employees will have ever heard of Kafka.

Vehicles like the Perth Mint Certificate are excellent choices for securing larger amounts of gold. They basically boil down to outsourcing your storage and security needs to a highly respected and secure vault, and in the case of PMCs, they are backed by the government of Western Australia. You own the gold, not just a paper or electronic promise representing gold, and can take delivery via FedEx any time you want. And the certificates are transferable, so there's some liquidity to owning gold in this way, without having to take delivery.

But that's for after you've set yourself up with all the physical gold you want in your possession. Because as good as PMCs are, it's still only a piece of paper you have in your actual physical possession. It's only one step removed from physical gold, but a step removed, just the same.

If you are worth many millions, it's obviously problematic to go around with several million in gold bullion on you, but you should have at least a few hundred thousand dollars of gold in your personal possession. The rest can be held in things like PMCs or GoldMoney.com, another good alternative. GoldMoney.com stores your gold in London and Zurich and allows you to transfer it electronically, which is quite convenient. I've known Jim Turk, who runs it, for many years and have a great deal of confidence in him. The last alternative is a safe deposit box in a foreign country.

Be careful with that, however. I was just in Switzerland last week, and they have gone from simply discouraging Americans to unilaterally closing accounts held by Americans (unless you also live in Switzerland and are a resident of the country). They're sending checks to last known addresses, so you can't have a dormant account anymore, like in the old days. And it's even worse: If you're an American with a safe deposit box in Switzerland, watch out, because they are closing those as well. If they can't find you, some of the banks are opening the boxes and removing the contents. They set the stuff aside somewhere, not in a safe deposit box anymore.

L: What? They just dump the stuff in a cardboard box and shove it into a corner of the basement until you come and get it?

D: Well, not cardboard, but it's serious. You can't have a safe deposit box in Switzerland anymore, certainly not with a major bank (though there are private companies in Switzerland that still offer the service). And it'll happen in other countries too.

L: Switzerland isn't even Switzerland anymore.

D: I know. Switzerland was an idea, and like America, it doesn't exist anymore.

L: So, are safe deposit boxes anywhere safe any longer? The long arm of the law is long indeed when it comes to the U.S. IRS.

D: That's right. These agencies can do pretty much anything they want, and it's become very problematical. You could establish a safe deposit box in Russia, and they wouldn't be likely to cooperate with the U.S. tax authorities, but you'd be at risk from their own bureaucrats with guns. I'd forget about Europe—wouldn't trust any of those governments.

Of the remaining possibilities, I favor Uruguay. Hong Kong might not be bad, since the Chinese aren't going to roll over for U.S. officials, and Thailand has always been very neutral. Panama is a reasonable possibility. Canada is a possibility. With the exception of Canada, these places have the advantage of not getting a lot of American traffic, so it's less likely that U.S. authorities will bother with the time and expense it takes to bully a foreign power into submission. Switzerland was well known and frequently used as a financial shelter, and that's why it became the focus of so much arm-twisting by various tax authorities.

L: What about skipping the safe deposit boxes then, and going private? Would it make sense to leave smaller caches in various countries with people you trust?

D: Yes, it would, but you have to watch out for the mistake W.C. Fields made, of opening a new bank account in every new town he went to. After a while, he had hundreds of bank accounts and forgot where they all were. You don't want all your eggs in one basket, but you also don't want so many baskets you can't watch them all.

You've got to be thoughtful and innovative. The governments are changing the rules, and you have to think of ways to keep ahead in the game. Think for yourself and be independent.

And this doesn't just apply to Americans. The U.S. government is the big problem in the world today, but there are certainly other problems. The French and the Germans, for example, are pressuring the Swiss in the same way that Americans are.

L: Anything people should think of stashing, besides gold?

D: Well, they keep raising the taxes on cigarettes—a pack now costs $10 in some places in the U.S, that's 50 cents per individual cigarette. If you're American and are going to be storing things, you probably can't go wrong building a stash of cigarettes. Even if you don't smoke—or perhaps especially if you don't smoke—every time you return to the U.S., you should buy the maximum amount of duty-free cigarettes allowed and store them.

The other thing Americans should do is buy a lot of shotgun shells, 9mm, .45, .223, and .308 ammo. Even if you don't shoot, you can set those aside and store them too, because they're going to be taxed and regulated to the nth degree. And properly stored, they keep for a very long time.

In fact, anything regulated by the Bureau of Alcohol, Tobacco, and Firearms—one of the most corrupt, dangerous, and useless of all federal bureaucracies—is likely to go up considerably in both price and value. It's perverse that the U.S. has a bureaucracy to regulate the three things you need for a hunting trip or a good party. Maybe their next trick will be to convert the DEA into the Bureau of Sex, Drugs, and Rock 'n' Roll.

L: I used to write about the wisdom of stashing the three Gs: gold, guns, and generators. All three are useful in and of themselves and have high resale values.

D: Yes, exactly. I hate to sound like an alarmist, but I really do think things are going to get scary—and if they don't, you can still sell these commodities in the future.

L: What about diamonds?

D: I wouldn't do diamonds. That's a really specialist market, and diamonds have long seemed to me to be subject to artificial pricing. There are at least two separate technologies now that create totally flawless, real diamonds. They are indistinguishable from natural diamonds, except that they don't have any flaws. But people will figure out how to introduce some flaws into those too, so I think the diamond market is in for a collapse at some time in the future. I could go on—let's just say that for many reasons, diamonds are the one gemstone I wouldn't touch.

L: Besides, they are less liquid. Relatively few individuals are trained to evaluate the color, clarity, cut, et cetera of diamonds, whereas it's easy to identify a gold Eagle and know how much it's worth.

D: That's right. And they are not divisible—I just wouldn't touch them at all.

L: Okay. Is there anything else you would put in your safe deposit box today? Cash? Stamps?

D: I wouldn't put any significant amount of currency in one; that's a guaranteed depreciating asset. I used to collect stamps, but no longer. I have no opinion on them as investment vehicles, but I came to realize that they are all relics of government monopolies, and I just didn't want them anymore. In fact, it makes no sense to collect anything for mainly financial reasons; doing so is to get sucked in by the greater fool theory.

Rare coins are tricky too, though I've always enjoyed collecting ancient Greek and Roman coins, which are actually a form of artwork; they all have very individual personalities. But I've never seen the fascination with collecting slugs turned out by the U.S. Mint, that essentially differ from each other only in the date stamped on them.

In general, I focus on gold bullion coins. And own them simply because they're the most convenient and fungible form of gold.

L: Okay, Doug, thanks for another interesting conversation.

Chapter 13

Doug Casey on Buying Physical Gold and Silver

September 28, 2011

Louis: So Doug, gold has dropped from its $1,917.90 high last month down to $1,540 yesterday and is currently hovering around $1,650. I know you don't believe $1,900 was the top, but is this correction good enough? Are you buying again?

Doug: Well, I hate to recommend buying anything that's gone up six or seven times in the last decade, but for all the reasons we've discussed in our recent conversations, as we exit the eye of the storm—first and foremost of which being the creation of trillions of new currency units—I am convinced gold is going much higher. So, yes, I do see the current correction as a buying opportunity.

L: In addition to the United States roughly tripling its money supply in the last couple of years, the EU just announced taking its bailout fund to $2 trillion, so saying trillions is no exaggeration. But gold dropped about 20 percent in a month—that's a pretty impressive correction.

D: It's par for the course. Gold is a volatile commodity for the time being, although that will change when it's reinstituted as money. If you think about what the word *correction* means, it suggests a price either dropping back when it gets too far ahead of itself or catching up when it gets unreasonably low. If you look at longer-term—multiyear—gold charts, the surge this summer looked like gold was going vertical. Hyperbolic curves are always danger signs. Gold has now reverted to the mean it's established over the last decade.

That doesn't mean it can't go lower before heading higher, of course, but it does make this a much more reasonable time to buy than a month ago. The point to remember is that you don't want to try to trade gold. You simply want to accumulate it, as an asset. Consistently, and in quantity.

L: But a line on a price chart doesn't explain anything; it just shows us a result over time. Why do you think gold dropped in the face of exactly the sort of economic fear that should send it higher?

D: We saw this in 2008 as well. When the global markets get whacked—and they just got whacked hard—everything tends to dip, as various individuals and institutions are forced to sell whatever they can get a bid on to cover margin calls, redemptions, and such. As gold became more volatile, exchanges naturally raised margin requirements, which forced a lot of weak longs out of the market. Some people say it's because some "bullion banks" are in a conspiracy to suppress the price of gold, but I find that reasoning ridiculous. No bank—no government even—can fight a decade-long secular bull market, entirely apart from the fact that most U.S. and European banks are dead men walking. They're bankrupt, and only seem alive because of massive government bailouts with newly printed paper money. Survival is the main thing on their minds now, not trying to suppress the price of some commodity they still believe is nothing more than a barbarous relic. And even if some group of fools was trying to drive down the price of gold, they'd only be giving the Chinese and the Indians a bargain as they buy more.

L: I've heard that hedge funds are the big sellers, looking to lock in gains on gold, which is still up for the year.

D: Very likely, in that the end of the quarter is coming up. It's possible some of these types were trying to book some wins, while building cash ahead of a possible wave of redemptions sparked by the now rampant fear in the global marketplace.

L: If that's right, the weakness in gold should dry up by the end of this week. Also, it seems to me that investors will remember that gold was the first thing to bounce back in 2008; I suspect we'll see less correction and a quicker turnaround this time.

D: I agree. Plus, you have all these developing economies, many of which are, ironically, in better shape than the so-called developed nations. The central banks of countries like China, India, Russia, and Taiwan have relatively little gold, and don't want to be caught holding the USD "Old Maid card." I think we'll see a lot of buying from them, taking advantage of relatively low gold prices, and that will backstop the potential downside on gold in the near term. These countries will be buying gold in ever-larger amounts, even at these prices, just to get rid of their excess hot-potato dollars. They are, in effect, offering gold buyers a free "put" on the price of the metal.

L: Okay, so when you go shopping for gold, what do you buy? Bars? Bullion jewelry? Coins?

D: I buy bullion coins, almost exclusively. American Eagles are now probably the most widely recognized and readily accepted bullion coin in the world; they're becoming mainstay of my stash. But I also have a lot of Canadian Maple Leafs, Austrian Philharmonics, South African Krugerrands, Mexican 50-peso coins, and the like.

The Mexican coins usually have the lowest premiums, by the way, and they're also the largest common coin, in that they contain 37.5 grams of gold, which is, not just coincidentally, equal to a Chinese tael (which is in turn equal to 1.2 troy ounces). In the Orient, people think of gold as much in taels as they do in grams or ounces. The Mexican 50-peso is perhaps the most popular coin in Latin America, especially in Argentina, where I spend a lot of time, because it's minted in grams. Krugerrands used to be the bullion standard, but they've fallen from favor.

The British sovereign is perhaps the most common gold coin, and there are several hundred million out there. It's also got a low premium, and is worth owning, since it's only 0.2354 ounces of gold;

it's convenient having something about the size of a nickel that's worth around $450.

Right now there's a good opportunity in semi-numismatic gold coins too—not rare collectibles, but pre-1933 U.S. bullion coins, like the Saint-Gaudens and other double eagles.

L: Why? I thought you didn't like rare coins for investment purposes.

D: I don't. Coin dealers will often try to steer buyers toward rare coins because the premiums are higher; if they sense the buyer is an easy mark, they can and will mark the coins up as much as 100 percent. Rare coins should only be bought by knowledgeable collectors who enjoy collecting rare coins. They shouldn't be purchased by amateurs— but the same is true of stocks.

Just to be clear, I have bought certain rare coins, particularly ancient Roman and Greek coins. I used to collect them actively. But I buy them as works of art that I find beautiful and interesting. Each one is unique and full of history. The reason we have so many is that people used to bury them, to keep them safe from government tax collectors, common thieves, and invading barbarians—but fate prevented their retrieval. Even today there are lots of hoards from ancient times discovered every year in Europe. But paying huge sums to buy coins that were mass produced 100 or 200 years ago makes no sense to me; they have no history, and they're not usually art.

But that's not what I'm talking about. The Saint-Gaudens is a collectible—and that can be very important, if and when the government starts confiscating bullion. That's because such historic artifacts are not considered the same way modern bullion coins are. At least last time around, they were not confiscated. Plus, because of their semi-numismatic value, they do attract a premium over the price of the gold they contain. Historically that's been between 50 percent and 100 percent. I was talking with my friend Van Simmons at David Hall Rare Coins, and as it happens, those premiums are currently down to about 12 percent—historic lows. Now, normally I'd rather pay a 4 to 5 percent premium—which is the current level for popular modern bullion coins—than a 12 percent premium. But in this case, you get both a measure of protection from confiscation, and the additional speculative upside from the potential for higher premiums in the future.

L: So, once you buy your coins, what do you do with them? You can't stuff them all in your mattress.

D: I usually try to dodge that question, in part because I don't want to publish the details of my own arrangements, and in part because the answer is different for different people in different circumstances. But first and foremost, I have to warn people not to use bank safe-deposit boxes. They are typically not insured, and they put your valuables on record. The last time the U.S. government stole private citizens' gold, the first thing they did was seal all the bank vaults.

L: I somehow doubt that other governments would be any better.

D: Certainly not in places like Argentina; Argentina is great for land and living, but it's a very bad choice for anything to do with banks. Uruguay is much better in that regard, but idiotically, you have to declare your gold when you take it into the country, which you don't have to do in Argentina. In the UK, they impounded thousands of vault boxes a couple years ago, so I wouldn't go there. The UK is on the slippery slope in many ways; it was prescient to have used it as the locale for *V for Vendetta*. Switzerland is still good, but it's tough for Americans to get in the door there. Austria is okay. But for larger amounts, the respected, private, insured bullion storage companies are the way to go.

It's a sign of the bad times we're going into that almost nothing is safe—anywhere—from governments. Your ownership is increasingly uncertain whether you have someone store things for you, or you store things yourself. It gives you an understanding of how the Romans might have felt from the third century on.

L: And for smaller amounts? The average safe in the closet is an obvious target and won't stand up long to a determined thief with power tools and sledgehammers.

D: That's right. And in the future, home invasions are likely to become more common in the United States as well. In addition, houses can burn down—gold and silver have relatively low melting points. As paranoid as it may sound, I'd generally say that "midnight gardening" may be the best way for the average individual to store highly portable wealth securely on his or her own property. Gold is nonreactive, but remember that silver tarnishes and corrodes easily, so you want good, durable, watertight containers to plant in your garden.

L: And what constitutes a "smaller" amount?

D: I might stash a handful of coins in really good hiding places around the house for quick access in case of need; a handful of gold coins can take you almost anywhere in the world these days and pay for months of frugal living, if necessary. At present prices, gold is actually easier to transport than its value in $100 bills. As for midnight gardening, your mileage will vary, but I'd say anything on the order of $100,000, perhaps 50 to 75 ounces, is a reasonable amount to keep under your own physical control. It's enough to do almost anything you might need to do in various scenarios, but not so much that your exposure to local risk is too high.

L: Speaking of confiscation risk, did you hear that Odyssey lost its appeal on the "Black Swan" case?

D: Yes, it's shameful. It's beyond me why the Spanish government should have any right to a treasure trove of coins lost hundreds of years ago and found by private entrepreneurs who put all the time, effort, and money into finding it. I'm especially sympathetic in that I spent about three months in the early 1970s on a treasure hunt for sunken treasure—blockade runners off Charleston, and then in the Caribbean. I did a lot of wonderful diving, but it was a financial disaster. On the bright side, even though I didn't get the gold, I did get some great experiences.

Also on the bright side, I read that Odyssey found another sunken treasure ship off the coast of Ireland, sunk by a German U-boat in 1941. In that case, they've apparently arrived at a deal to keep 80 percent of the proceeds.

L: Talk about international speculators—I've got to admire Odyssey. So, back to buying physical precious metals, I think we've covered the basics. Any additional thoughts?

D: Just remember that you buy physical gold and silver for prudence. For speculative upside, you buy gold and silver stocks. And while the precious metals have corrected, the stocks have overcorrected. There are some bargains out there, and that's excellent news given the still-high prices of the underlying commodities. Gold and silver could correct another 20 percent, and the kind of profitable producers Jeff Clark tracks in "Big Gold" would still make a lot of money.

But let me emphasize this as strongly as possible: We're headed into perhaps the most tumultuous time in modern history. It's critical to own a good amount of physical gold. If you, out there reading this, don't have a sufficient stash, your very next action should be to get on the phone and order some.

L: Roger that. Thanks for your thoughts.

Chapter 14

Doug Casey on Gold Stocks

September 30, 2009

Louis: Doug, we were talking about gold last week, so we should follow up with a look at gold stocks. If one of the reasons to own gold is that it's real—it's not paper, it's not simultaneously someone else's liability—why own gold stocks?

Doug: Leverage. Gold stocks are problematical as investments. That's true of all resource stocks, especially stocks in exploration companies, as opposed to producers. If you want to make a proper investment, the way to do that is to follow the dictates of Graham and Dodd, using the method Warren Buffett has proven to be so successful over many years. Unfortunately, resource stocks in general and metals exploration stocks in particular just don't lend themselves to such methodologies. They are another class of security entirely.

L: "Security" may not be the right word. As I was reading the latest edition of Graham and Dodd's classic book on securities analysis, I realized that their minimum criteria for investment wouldn't even

111

apply to the gold majors. The business is just too volatile. You can't apply standard metrics.

D: It's just impossible. For one thing, they cannot grow consistently, because their assets are always depleting. Nor can they predict what their rate of exploration success is going to be.

L: Right. As an asset, a mine is something that gets used up, as you dig it up and sell it off.

D: Exactly. And the underlying commodity prices can fluctuate wildly for all sorts of reasons. Mining stocks, and resource stocks in general, have to be viewed as speculations, as opposed to investments.

But that can be a good thing. For example, many of the best speculations have a political element to them. Governments are constantly creating distortions in the market, causing misallocations of capital. Whenever possible, the speculator tries to find out what these distortions are, because their consequences are predictable. They result in trends you can bet on. It's like the government is guaranteeing your success, because you can almost always count on the government to do the wrong thing.

The classic example, not just coincidentally, concerns gold. The U.S. government suppressed its price for decades while creating huge numbers of dollars before it exploded upward in 1971. Speculators that understood some basic economics positioned themselves accordingly. As applied to metals stocks, governments are constantly distorting the monetary situation, and gold in particular, being the market's alternative to government money, is always affected by that. So gold stocks are really a way to short government—or go long on government stupidity, as it were.

The bad news is that governments act chaotically, spastically. The beast jerks to the tugs on its strings held by its various puppeteers. So it's hard to predict price movements in the short term. You can only bet on the end results of chronic government monetary stupidity.

The good news is that, for that very same reason, these stocks are extremely volatile. That makes it possible, from time to time, to get not just doubles or triples but 10-baggers, 20-baggers, and even 100-to-1 shots in these mining stocks.

That kind of upside makes up for the fact that these stocks are lousy investments and that you will lose money on most of them, if you hold them long enough. Most are best described as burning matches.

L: One of our mantras: Volatility can be your best friend.

D: Yes, volatility can be your best friend, as long as your timing is reasonable. I don't mean timing tops and bottoms—no one can do that. I mean spotting the trend and betting on it when others are not, so you can buy low to later sell high. If you chase momentum and excitement, if you run with the crowd, buying when others are buying, you're guaranteed to lose. You *have* to be a contrarian. In this business, you're either a contrarian or road kill. When everyone is talking about these stocks on TV, you know the masses are interested, and that means they've gone to a level at which you should be a seller and not a buyer.

That makes it more a game of playing the psychology of the market, rather than doing securities analysis.

I'm not sure how many thousands of gold mining stocks there are in the world today—I'll guess about 3,000—but most of them are junk. If they have any gold, it's mainly in the words written on the stock certificates. So, in addition to knowing when to buy and when to sell, your choice of individual stocks has to be intelligent too. Remember, most mining companies are burning matches.

L: All they do is spend money.

D: Exactly. That's because most mining companies are really exploration companies. They are looking for viable deposits, which is quite literally like looking for a needle in a haystack. Finding gold is one thing. Finding an economical deposit of gold is something else entirely. And even if you do find an economical deposit of gold, it's exceptionally difficult to make money mining it. Most of your capital costs are up front. The regulatory environment today is onerous in the extreme. Labor costs are far above what they used to be. It's a really tough business.

L: If someone describes a new business venture to you, saying, "Oh, it'll be a gold mine!" Do you run away?

D: Almost. And it's odd because, historically, gold mining used to be an excellent business. For example, take the Homestake Mine in Deadwood, South Dakota, which was discovered in 1876, at just about the time of Custer's last stand, actually. When they first raised capital for that, their dividend structure was something like 100 percent of the initial share price, paid per *month*. That was driven by the extraordinary discovery. Even though the technology was very primitive and inefficient in those days, labor costs were low, you didn't have to worry about environmental problems, there were *no* taxes on whatever you earned, you didn't have to pay mountains of money to lawyers. Today, you probably pay your lawyers more than you pay your geologists and engineers.

So, the business has changed immensely over time. It's perverse because with the improvements in technology, gold mining should have become more economical, not less. The farther back you go in history, the higher the grade you'd have to mine in order to make it worthwhile. If we go back to ancient history, a mineable deposit probably had to be at least an ounce of gold per ton to be viable. Today, you can mine deposits that run as low as a hundredth of an ounce (0.3 g/t). It's possible to go even lower, but you need very cooperative ore. And that trend toward lower grades becoming economical is going to continue.

For thousands of years, people have been looking for gold in the most obscure and bizarre places all over the world. That's because of the 92 naturally occurring elements in the periodic table, gold was probably the first metal that man discovered and made use of. The reason for that is simple: Gold is the most inert of the metals.

L: Because it doesn't react easily and form compounds, you can find the pure metal in nature.

D: Right. You can find it in its pure form, and it doesn't degrade and it doesn't rust. In fact, of all the elements, gold is not only the most inert, it's also the most ductile and the most malleable. And, after silver, it's the best conductor of both heat and electricity, and the most reflective. In today's world, that makes it a high-tech metal. New uses are found for it weekly. It has many uses besides its primary one as money and its secondary use as jewelry. But it was probably also man's first metal.

But for that same reason, all the high-grade, easy-to-find gold deposits have already been found. There's got to be a few left to be discovered, but by and large, we're going to larger-volume, lower-grade, "no-see-um"-type deposits at this point. Gold mining is no longer a business in which, like in the movie *The Treasure of the Sierra Madre*, you can get a couple of guys, some picks and mules, and go out and find the mother lode. Unfortunately. Now, it's usually a large-scale, industrial earth-moving operation next to a chemical plant.

L: They operate on very slender margins, and they can be rendered unprofitable by a slight shift in government regulations or taxes. So, we want to own these companies. Why?

D: You want them strictly as speculative vehicles that offer the potential for 10, 100, or even 1,000 times returns on your money. Getting 1,000 times on your money is extraordinary, of course—you have to buy at the bottom and sell at the top—but people have done it. It's happened not just once or twice, but quite a number of times that individual stocks have moved by that much.

That's the good news. The bad news is that these things fluctuate down even more dramatically than they fluctuate up. They are burning matches that can actually go to zero. And when they go down, they usually drop at least twice as fast as they went up.

L: That's true, but as bad as a total loss is, you can only lose 100 percent—but there's no such limit to the upside. A 100 percent gain is only a double, and we do much better than that for subscribers numerous times per year.

D: And as shareholders in everything from Enron to AIG, to Lehman Brothers, and many more have found out, even the biggest, most solid companies can go to zero.

L: So, what you're telling me is that the answer to "Why gold?" is really quite different to the answer to "Why gold stocks?" These are in completely different classes, bought for completely different reasons.

D: Yes. You buy gold, the metal, because you're prudent. It's for safety, liquidity, insurance. The gold stocks, even though they explore for or mine gold, are at the polar opposite of the investment spectrum; you buy those for extreme volatility and the chance it creates for spectacular gains. It's rather paradoxical, actually.

L: You buy gold for safety and gold stocks specifically to profit from their "un-safety."

D: Exactly. They really are total opposites, even though it's the same commodity in question. It's odd, but then, life is often stranger than fiction.

L: And it's being a contrarian—"timing" in the sense of making a rational decision about a trend in evident motion—that helps stack the odds in your favor. It allows you to guess when market volatility will, on average, head upward, making it possible for you to buy low and sell high.

D: You know, I first started looking at gold stocks back in the early 1970s. In those days, South African stocks were the "blue chips" of the mining industry. As a country, South Africa mined about 60 percent of all the gold mined in the world, and costs were very low. Gold was controlled at $35 per ounce until Nixon closed the gold window in 1971, but some of the South Africans were able to mine it for $20 an ounce or less. They were paying huge dividends.

Gold had run up from $35 to $200 in early 1974, then corrected down to $100 by 1976. It had come off 50 percent, but at the same time that gold was bottoming around $100, they had some serious riots in Soweto. So the gold stocks got a double hit: falling gold prices and fear of revolution in South Africa. That made it possible, in those days, to buy into short-lived, high-cost mining companies very cheaply; the stocks of the marginal companies were yielding current dividends of 50 to 75 percent. They were penny stocks in those days. They no longer exist; they've all been merged into mining finance houses long since then. Three names that I remember from those days were Leslie, Bracken, Grootvlei; I owned a lot of shares in them. If you bought Leslie for 80 cents a share, you'd expect, based on previous dividends, to get about 60 cents a share in that year.

But then gold started flying upward, the psychology regarding South Africa changed, and by 1980, the next real peak, you were getting several times what you paid for the stock, in dividends alone, per year.

L: Wow. I can think of some leveraged companies that might be able to deliver that sort of performance, if gold goes where we think it will. So, where do you think we are in the current trend or metals cycle? You've spoken of the Stealth, Wall of Worry, and Mania Phases of a bull market for metals—do you still think of our market in those terms?

D: That's the big question, isn't it? Well, the last major bottom in this sector was from 1998 to 2002. Many of these junior mining stocks—mostly traded in Canada, where about 75 percent of all the gold stocks in the world trade—were trading for less than cash in the bank. Literally. You'd get all their properties, their technology, the expertise of their management, totally for free. Or less.

L: I remember seeing past issues in which you said, "If I could call your broker and order these stocks for you, I would."

D: Yes. But nobody wanted to hear about it at that time. Gold was low, and there was a bubble in Internet stocks. Why would anyone want to get involved in a dead-duck, nineteenth century, "choo-choo train" industry like gold mining? It had been completely discredited by the long bear market, but that made it the ideal time to buy them, of course. That was deep in the Stealth Phase.

Over the next six to eight years, these stocks took off, moving us into the Wall of Worry Phase. But the stocks didn't fly the way they did in past bull markets. I think that's mostly because they were so depleted of capital, they were selling lots of shares. So their market capitalizations—the aggregate value given them by the market—were increasing, but their share prices weren't. Not as much. Remember, these companies very rarely have any earnings, but they always need capital, and the only way they can get it is by selling new shares, which dilutes the value of the individual shares, including those held by existing shareholders.

Then last fall hit, and nobody, but nobody, wanted anything speculative. These most volatile of stocks showed their nature and plunged through the floor in the general flight to safety. That made last fall the second best time to buy mining shares this cycle, and I know you recommended some pretty aggressive buying last fall, near the bottom.

Now, many of these shares—the better ones at least—have recovered substantially, and some have even surpassed pre-crash highs. Again, the Wall of Worry Phase is characterized by large fluctuations that separate the wolves from the sheep (and the sheep from their cash).

Where does that leave us? Well, as you know, I think gold is going to go much, much higher. And that is going to direct a lot of attention toward these gold stocks. When people get gold fever, they are not just driven by greed, they're usually driven by fear as well, so you get both of the most powerful market motivators working for you at once. It's a rare class of securities that can benefit from fear and greed at once.

Remember that the Fed's pumping up of the money supply ignited a huge bubble in tech stocks, and then an even more massive global bubble in real estate—which is over for a *long* time, incidentally—but they're still creating tons of dollars. That will inevitably ignite other asset bubbles. Where? I can't say for certain, but I say the odds are extremely high that as gold goes up, for all the reasons we spoke about last week and more, that a lot of this funny money is going to be directed into these gold stocks, which are not just a microcap area of the market but a *nanocap* area of the market.

I've said it before, and I'll say it again: When the public gets the bit in its teeth and wants to buy gold stocks, it's going to be like trying to siphon the contents of the Hoover Dam through a garden hose.

Gold stocks, as a class, are going to be explosive. Now, you've got to remember that most of them are junk. Most will never, ever find an economical deposit. But it's hopes and dreams that drive them, not reality, and even without merit, they can still go 10, 20, or 30 times your entry price. And the companies that actually have the goods can go *much* higher than that.

At the moment, gold stock prices are not as cheap, in either relative or absolute terms, as they were at the turn of the century, nor last fall. But given that the Mania Phase is still ahead, they are good speculations right now—especially the ones that have actually discovered gold deposits that look economical.

L: So, if you buy good companies now, with good projects, good management, working in stable jurisdictions, with a couple years of operating cash to see them through the Wall of Worry fluctuations—if you buy these and hold for the Mania Phase, you should come out very well. But you can't blink and get stampeded out of your positions when the market fluctuates sharply.

D: That's exactly right. At the particular stage where we are right now in this market for these extraordinarily volatile securities, if you buy a quality exploration company, or a quality development company (which is to say, a company that has found something and is advancing it toward production), those shares could still go down 10, 20, 30, or even 50 percent, but ultimately there's an excellent chance that

that same stock will go up by 10, 50, or even 100 times. I hate to use such hard-to-believe numbers, but that is the way this market works. When the coming resource bubble is ignited, there are excellent odds you'll be laughing all the way to the bank in a few years.

I should stress that I'm not saying that this is the perfect time to buy. We're not at a market bottom as we were in 2001, nor an interim bottom like last November, and I can't say I know the Mania Phase is just around the corner. But I think this is a very reasonable time to be buying these stocks. And it's absolutely a good time to start educating yourself about them. There's just such a good chance a massive bubble is going to be ignited in this area.

L: These are obviously the kinds of things we research, make recommendations on, and educate about in our metals newsletters, but one thing we should stress for nonsubscribers reading this interview is that this strategy applies *only* to the speculative portion of your portfolio. No one should gamble with their rent money nor the money they've saved for college tuition, etcetera.

D: Right. The ideal speculator's portfolio would be divided into 10 areas, each totally different and not correlated with each other. Each of these areas should have, in your subjective opinion, the ability to move 1,000 percent in price.

Why is that? Because most of the time, we're wrong when we pick areas to speculate in, certainly in areas where you can't apply Graham-Dodd-type logic. But if you're wrong on 9 out of 10 of them, and it would be hard to do that badly, then you at least break even on the one 10-bagger (1,000 percent winner). What's more likely is that a couple will blow up and go to zero, a couple will go down 30, 40, 50 percent, but you'll also have a couple doubles or triples, and maybe, on one or two of them, you'll get a 10-to-1 or better win.

So, it looks very risky (and falling in love with any single stock *is* very risky), but it's actually an intelligent way to diversify your risk and stack the odds of profiting on volatility in your favor.

Note that I don't mean that these "areas" should be 10 different stocks in the junior mining sector—that wouldn't be diversification. As I say, ideally, I'd have 10 such areas with potential for 1,000 percent gains, but it's usually impossible to find that many at once. If you can find only two or three, what do you do with the rest of your money? Well, at this point, I would put a lot of it into gold, in one form or another, while keeping your powder dry as you look for the next idea opportunity.

And ideally, I'd look at every market in every country in the world. People who look only in the United States, or only in stocks, or only in real estate—they just don't get to see enough balls to swing at.

L: Okay, got it. Thank you very much.

D: A pleasure, as always.

Chapter 15

Doug Casey on Protecting Your Cash

August 26, 2009

Louis: Doug, we talked last week about getting assets out of your home country, especially the United States, where to take them and what to do with them. In so doing, you touched on the inevitability of currency controls just ahead, especially for Americans. Can you tell us more about that?

Doug: Yes, I'm quite serious about what I said about "the grim reality of impending currency controls." As the global economy continues to deteriorate, governments will have to appear to be "doing something." It's going to become very fashionable to institute some sort of foreign exchange control.

Why might that be? Because obviously, people who are taking their money out of the country are unpatriotic.

L: Those bastards.

D: That's right. Jingoistic Americans naturally, but stupidly, see taking money out of the country as being unpatriotic. They don't understand

121

that it's mainly those prudent people who will be able to supply the capital to rebuild a devastated economy later. Besides, getting money abroad is obviously something that only rich people would do, and of course, it's time to eat the rich, as well. For those two reasons, there won't be much resistance to controls. And the state gets to appear to be "doing something."

And when they do, more people—at least those with any sense—will get scared and *really* try to get their money out, which will exacerbate the run to the exits. The bottom line is that if you want to get your money out, the time to do it is now. Beat the last-minute rush.

I don't know what form the exchange controls are going to take, but there are two general possibilities: regulation and taxation.

The regulations might take the form of a rule prohibiting you from taking more than X-thousands of dollars abroad per year without special permission. No expensive vacations, no foreign asset purchases without state approval.

As for the taxation, if you want to, say, buy foreign stocks or real estate, you might have to pay an "interest equalization tax" or some such. So, you could do it, but it'd cost you a lot of money to do it.

Something like either of these, or both, is definitely in the cards.

L: But aren't FX controls something from the past? I mean, where do they exist today?

D: Well, FX controls have been used since the days of the Roman Empire. A country debases its currency, raises taxes beyond a certain level, and makes regulations too onerous—and productive people naturally react by getting their capital, and then themselves, out of Dodge. But the government can't have that, so it puts on FX controls. They're almost inevitable at this point.

Almost every country—except for the United States, Canada, Switzerland, and a few others—had them until at least the 1970s. I remember leaving Britain once in the 1960s, and a border guy searched me to see if I had more than 50 pounds on me. In those days, currency violations in the Soviet Bloc countries could get you the death penalty. Things liberalized around the world with Reagan and Thatcher, and then the collapse of the USSR. But you have to remember that that was in the context of the Long Boom. Now, during the Greater Depression, things will become much stricter again.

Right now, the United States just has reporting requirements. But some places, like South Africa, make it very expensive and inconvenient to get money out. South Africa, perversely, may serve as a model for the United States.

L: Okay, so, we talked last week about Americans at least setting up a Canadian bank account and safe deposit box, and better yet going in person to Panama, Uruguay, Malaysia, or a similar place to do the same. And once there, you advised getting with a lawyer, either referred by someone you trust or found through an interview process, to set up a corporation that can handle your assets and investments for you. This all needs to be reported, but it's wise to do it in advance of the higher costs or other limitations to come.

D: Yes. While U.S. persons must report foreign bank and brokerage accounts, safe deposit boxes are not—at least not yet—reportable. This leads me to the biggest and best "loophole" when it comes to potential foreign exchange controls, and that's foreign real estate.

I'm of the opinion that, broadly speaking, real estate as an asset class is going to be a poor performer for a long time to come, but that won't be equally true across all countries. Real estate in countries that rely on mortgage debt to buy and sell will continue to be the worst hit.

People don't understand that buying property with a mortgage is just the same as buying stocks on margin. It's caused speculative bubbles and malinvestment. Until the malinvestment in those countries is entirely liquidated, you don't want to invest in real estate in them. But a lot of countries, especially in the third world, have no mortgage debt whatsoever. Zero mortgage debt. You want a piece of property, you pay for it in cash. That keeps prices down and the market much more stable. And it makes for more interesting speculations, because if a mortgage market develops in the future, it could light a fire under prices.

But, from the viewpoint of FX controls, the nice thing about real estate is that there is *no* way they can make you repatriate it. Other than owning a business abroad, real estate is the only sure way to legally keep your capital offshore.

L: I suppose it would be difficult for even Uncle Sam to seize your estancia in Argentina, without starting a war.

D: Yes. Although I don't doubt he'll be starting more wars as well.

L: So, part of your thinking here isn't just speculative. You're talking about strategies for wealth preservation, not just in the face of foreign exchange controls, but more aggressive, predatory taxation and confiscation by the state; they can seize your assets, even real estate, in the United States, but not abroad.

D: Exactly. Argentina is excellent from that point of view; rights to real property are, if anything, better than those in the United States. In many ways, Argentina is culturally and demographically more like Europe than Europe. Uruguay is also excellent, although culturally it's like a backward province of Argentina. Paraguay is quite secure, but a bit weird as a place to live.

I'm not currently up-to-date on the Chilean real estate market, but Chile is definitely now the richest and most advanced South American country, and an excellent choice. Brazil is fine. Colombia is improving greatly. Ecuador has a goofy president, but parts of it are very nice, and it's about as cheap as Argentina. Eastern Bolivia is interesting, actually, despite Morales; it's actually two totally different countries—the highlands controlled by the native Indians, and the lowlands centering on Santa Cruz controlled by those of European extraction. Only Venezuela is out of the question in South America—but Chavez won't last forever. It's just a pity they have all that oil, which is always a corrupting influence. At least when it's a state asset.

L: Well, then, what about Central America? I know you prefer South America for speculative purposes, but what if someone wants to park a lot of wealth by buying a couple miles of beautiful beachfront property in Costa Rica, or someplace like that?

D: I was a big fan of Costa Rica for many years. The first time I went down there was 35 years ago, but it's a different place now. Then, it was very cheap, and now it's very expensive. And it's totally overrun with gringos. So, Costa Rica is not of that much interest to me at this point; it's pleasant, but there's limited upside.

I think an excellent place to be in Central America is Belize. Although culturally and ethnically, it's not really part of Central America; it's part of the Caribbean.

L: And they speak English there.

D: They do indeed, though things are changing. The Guatemalan government has always regarded British Honduras, which is what Belize used to be called, as part of Guatemala. There have actually been confrontations between Britain and Guatemala over this. But that's in the past; now there's a different problem. Guatemalans are rolling over the border in much the same way that Mexicans are in Texas, New Mexico, Arizona, and California.

So, the character of Belize is changing, but for the foreseeable future, it's still going to be Bélize, and I rather like it. Aside from Panama, Belize would be my first choice in Central America.

The problem with Central America, however, is that it's a bunch of small countries that have historically been very unstable. And culturally backward. Most are under the thumb of the United States; there's a long history of U.S. invasions, most recently in Panama with Noriega. There are Frito Banditos running around these places.

The most culturally advanced country in Central America, not counting Mexico, of course, since it's in North America, is Guatemala. But Guatemala has had huge troubles with violence, which has only recently come to an end. I hate going through checkpoints at night, manned by jumpy, uneducated, heavily armed teenagers.

Nicaragua is the low-cost alternative, but it's relatively backward. Panama is probably the best choice. It's very international, very urban (in Panama City), and it's very sophisticated, infrastructure-wise. In fact, I believe Panama City will replace Miami as the financial and shopping center of Latin America. It's a great place, and almost certain to get better with the improvements being made on the Canal.

If I didn't like Argentina and Uruguay so much, I would put Panama at the top of my shopping list.

L: Got it. Back to the exchange controls themselves. Do you think people will have any warning at all? It seems to me that this is the sort of thing the Powers That Be would want to spring on people.

D: I think it's going to come out of left field. It always does, with at most an official denial just before it happens. In August 1971, Nixon devalued the dollar, which immediately dropped against gold and all foreign currencies. I think there's a reasonable probability that the government will do that again. Gold may not be part of the equation, but they may decide to put in some sort of fixed exchange rate between the dollar and various foreign currencies.

The reason for thinking this is simple: With all the dollars outside the United States devalued by that much, that much of a liability just vanishes into thin air. And in the short term—it's never a long-term fix—U.S. exports would go up. This would "stimulate" the domestic economy. Imports to the United States would go down, which would make for fewer dollars leaving the United States and adding to the $7 trillion overhang the United States already has.

L: I know you hate making predictions, but can you tell us if your "guru sense" is tingling on this so strongly that you think it could happen this year? Or is this more of a 2010 possibility? 2011?

D: The timing on this is really unpredictable. These people don't have a plan. They're acting "ad hoc" to whatever seems most urgent. All the so-called economists around government today are really just political hacks. Their worldviews are totally unsound.

If you don't believe me, check out the YouTube video of the clueless chief inspector of the Fed that's circulating on the Internet. (See www.youtube.com/watch?v=PXlxBeAvsB8.)

L: With all the problems the United States has, do you think this could happen *now*? Could we be reading about new exchange controls on CNN.com this afternoon?

D: Sure. Although they typically pull these stunts over a weekend. I expect something of this nature to happen any time between tomorrow morning and two years from now. If some form of currency controls are not instituted within two years, I'm going to be genuinely surprised. Although, in point of fact, very few foreign banks or brokers want American clients—or will even accept them—since there's so much liability and potential pressure from the U.S. government. Rather clever, actually. De facto controls through making foreigners reluctant to accept American business.

So, if you're going to take action, you should start heading for the exits *now*. Not next month, and certainly not next year.

L: For those who don't take action until it's too late, under the scenarios you mentioned, they'll still be able to get money out. It's just that it might be more difficult, time consuming, humiliating, and certainly more expensive to do. For every $100,000 they move, only $90,000, or $70,000, or whatever will get to where it's supposed to go. Can you foresee a more Stalinesque alternative, where they simply can't get anything out at all?

D: Hopefully not. Anything is possible, and things can change so rapidly, but I'd hate to think of what conditions would be like if they ever became that draconian. It'd be so bad on other fronts that there would be all sorts of even more urgent things on your mind; Americans would get a very quick and unpleasant education in the real meaning of Maslow's hierarchy.

L: Like the Mad Max–style neobarbarians at the door with a battering ram.

D: That's when you'll definitely want to be in more pleasant climes. I'd want to be watching it on my widescreen, in comfort, not out my front window.

L: We're talking about extremes here.

D: You know, back in the 1970s, there was a spate of books published on financial privacy. In those days, financial privacy was still possible. Now, it's not only no longer truly possible, short of embracing a completely outlaw lifestyle, it's very dangerous to write about it or even talk about it. I kid you not. These days, people who ask too many questions about privacy techniques may well be government stooges.

There's lots of handwriting on the wall. All those books on financial privacy were published in the 1970s; if you look on Amazon, you can still find them. But there's nothing really worth reading that's been written on the subject in 20 years. It's actively discouraged by the government. I could name—but I won't—at least two authors that got themselves into a real jackpot this way. Forget about the First Amendment.

In fact, I even feel uncomfortable talking about it in this interview.

So let me once again emphasize that I advise everyone to stay fully within the bounds of the law.

That's not for moral reasons, of course; there is no morality to the law. It's strictly for reasons of practicality. Risk-reward ratio.

L: Understood. Loud and clear. Any more investment implications, besides foreign real estate, that you want to draw attention to here?

D: Yes—and it's another reason for those so very clever boys in Washington to embrace currency controls. They will be disastrous for the U.S. economy, but there's a very good chance that, in the short run, they'll be very good for the stock market. That's partly for the reasons I already mentioned about it temporarily boosting U.S. exports, and hence earnings of U.S. exporters, but also because all that money that can't leave the United States will have to go into something.

Investors will probably want to put it into equity, rather than debt, while the dollar is depreciating. Again, it's disastrous over the long term, but as a short-term play, buying the blue chips the day the exchange controls are instituted could be a good move.

L: You'd buy the Dow?

D: I might, if I couldn't think of anything more intelligent or original to do. We'll just have to see what the situation is like.

L: This will be a development we'll have to keep an eye out for in *The Casey Report*, then.

D: Yes, we will. The more politically controlled an environment, the more distortions are created. And the better it is for a speculator.

L: Thanks again, Doug—you've given us a lot to think about.

D: My pleasure.

Chapter 16

Doug Casey on Cattle

September 9, 2009

Louis: Doug, we talk a lot about metals and energy, but you've also made money in agriculture, as have our subscribers who got in early on corn and potash. In the February 2008 issue of the *International Speculator*, you made the case for speculating on rising cattle prices. Would you explain your rationale for that and give us an update?

Doug: Sure. There is such a thing as a cattle cycle, and right now, all over the world, cattle are in liquidation. Farmers and ranchers just can't make any money on cattle. Nobody has made any money on cattle in North America or Europe for years, and it's especially serious now. So worldwide, cattle herds are being slaughtered, and that's depressing the prices.

The interesting thing is that even as prices are being depressed by all the selling, counterintuitively, cattle herds are collapsing. That means the number of cattle and the price of cattle are going down at the same time. That obviously can't go on forever; at some point, the relative number of cattle is going to be quite small, and prices are going to explode upward. Why? Because people in China, the rest of the Orient, and across the developing world are going to want more beef—in addition to the traditional consumers. And the numbers of cattle are going to be very low.

I think that cows are an excellent place to be.

L: If it's not a traditional part of their diet, why would such people want more beef?

D: As you become wealthier, you want better-quality food. Beef is generally at the top of the food chain.

Why is that? It takes about two pounds of grain to produce a pound of chicken meat; four pounds of grain to get a pound of pork; seven pounds for a pound of beef. So from a production point of view, beef has always been, and I suspect always will be, the most expensive type of meat.

L: Of common meat animals. Some unusual meats are a little more expensive.

D: Yes, of common meats. Bald eagle drumsticks are much more expensive. But beef is traditionally the rich man's food. Crisis notwithstanding, a lot of people around the world are getting wealthier, particularly in China. India is not far behind, but there is a cultural issue with beef and Hindus, of course. I think we have a rare opportunity right now to buy low, while beef herds are collapsing.

That's exactly what I've done with a number of friends; we've bought a lot of land in Argentina and are raising cattle.

L: It's basically a bet on rising global affluence as the underlying trend.

D: To a degree. But it's more a bet on significantly lower supply combined with steady demand. In real terms, cattle prices are at about 40-year lows. As bad as the global economy has been, one might think they could have gone even lower—the economy does affect them—but they're very low. In fact, the worst day I ever had trading commodities personally was back in 1987, when I thought that cattle were quite cheap. And you remember that day in 1987 when the stock market fell out of bed like 500 points or something like that.

L: Black Friday.

D: Black Friday. And I was personally one of the largest players in the cattle market at that point. I was short puts and long contracts, of both feeder cattle and live cattle. It was a horrible day, because the day after the market collapsed, the cattle market collapsed. Everybody figured: "Oh my god, it's a depression, nobody is going to be able to afford beef, so we better sell." It was a nightmare for me. So, you're quite right; cattle are a play on prosperity.

So why, if I believe we're sliding into the Greater Depression, am I long cattle? Because you've got to be a buyer when everybody else is a seller, and everyone else is a seller right now, because no one can make any money on cattle. That's number one. Number two is that, despite the fact the world is going into a depression, the world population will continue growing, and the countries in the Orient are going to do relatively much better than countries in the West, so I'm willing to bet on rising beef consumption. Number three, real cattle prices are at generational lows.

But I'm not speculating in cattle; I'm investing in cattle. I'm not doing anything with them in the futures market.

L: There's no leverage on what you're doing; you are actually buying cattle.

D: Yes. I've bought land in northwest Argentina, which to me is the most attractive part of that country—and the country itself is very attractive indeed. We've bought a number of large, dormant farms where we clear the land, fence it, put in wells, and plant grasses the cows like. We bought Braford females—heifers—and they calf every year. We now have about 1,500 cows. Every year we get about 1,200 new babies, and then the babies have babies in two years. We sell the male calves for current income, to finance the clearing and fencing of more land and putting in more wells. And we let the heifers grow and reproduce. It's a form of compound interest. Plus, the land is worth considerably more after we improve it—a big bonus.

And since our cattle are all grass-fed, and we own the land for cash, and the Gauchos earn roughly $250 a month, we don't have much in the way of costs.

I'm a big fan of grass-fed beef. Most cattle spend the best part of their adult lives in feed lots. They're packed chock-a-block next to each other (moving burns calories and takes off weight). They're fed things cows don't naturally eat. And they're pumped full of growth hormones and antibiotics. The end product is okay for a mass market that wants cheap beef, but it isn't what I want.

L: Is your reason for doing this in Argentina because the market is there (Argentines love to eat beef)? Or is it because land and labor are cheap, and it's such a good place to be in the business? Why Argentina?

D: I picked Argentina because out of the 175 countries I've been to, the fact of the matter is, I just like Argentina more than any other place I can think of. Despite the fact that it's been in economic decline for many decades, and the government is . . . let me be diplomatic, and say highly dysfunctional.

L: Even Thailand?

D: Well, it's perverse. Thailand is exactly the antipodes of the globe; it's as far from Argentina as you can get geographically, and it's about as far as you can get from Argentina culturally as well. They are just opposite and antithetical in so many ways. But the fact of the matter is, those are my two favorite places on the planet.

L: But Argentina edges Thailand out.

D: It does. That's because I like the wide-open spaces. I like the *estancias* [ranches]. I like the barbeques—the *asados*. And in Thailand, as much as I like it, the fact is that as a Westerner, you are never going to be a part of Thai society. Forget about it. No matter how many Thai friends you have and so forth, even if you have a Thai spouse, you're always going to be an outsider. But that's not true in Argentina, because it's culturally about the most European country in the world. It's more European than Europe at this point, quite frankly. And, completely unlike Thailand, it's a country of immigrants. So, especially as my Spanish improves, I can actually become part of the society. Entirely apart from the fact that the upper classes and the kids all speak excellent English. In addition, Argentina is by far the most outward-looking of any country in Latin American, and by a huge margin, has the biggest libertarian/classical liberal tradition.

On the other hand, in Thailand maybe there's an advantage to not being part of the society, because you really don't exist. You are like what Chinese would call a *Quai Loh*—a foreign ghost or foreign devil. You are not an element to officialdom; you're a permanent tourist. It's a double-edged sword; it depends on what you like.

L: If you're an anarchist, why would you *want* to be part of society?

D: Well, I'm a fairly social anarchist. We like society as well as anyone—we just don't like the state. I just want to be left alone by the authorities. An anarchist can feel pretty mellow in Thailand because of the foreign-ghost effect. And pretty good in Argentina for different reasons; it's full of Spanish-speaking Italians who don't like to do what they're told.

We got into the cattle business as a consequence of wanting to buy estancias, because the land prices were so low. They were just begging. The country is so pretty, and the society is just so nice, I wanted to become a part of it. When you have this land, you have to do something with it.

In addition to buying a beef cattle herd with some friends, I personally bought a dairy farm—but, again, with no cattle. I bought the dairy herd from another farmer—a wealthy guy—who wanted to get rid of it. This was during the soybean and corn boom of 18 months ago. He had 130 Holstein dairy cows, and he told his farm manager: "Get rid of these things. They are a rounding error on my balance sheet, and the ground they are taking we can use to plant soybeans and corn." So I bought them at an excellent price.

In fact, the deal I cut with the guy, because dairy herds were also already in liquidation then, was this: He said, "Alright, you take the cows in exchange for one year's milk production from them."

So, the cows graze on land—that doesn't cost me anything. And my Gauchos, they were just sitting around, and I had to find something for them to do. So now they can milk the cows, and I just gave him a year's milk production.

L: So, in addition to the beef play, is there a dairy play? I've heard that not only beef cows are in liquidation, but milk cows are being turned into hamburgers. That should create a supply crunch, and there should be money to be made in the dairy business. Is that right?

D: That's totally true. Dairy prices have fallen about 50 percent in the last couple of years.

L: But are dairy prices really falling? It doesn't seem that milk is any cheaper in the supermarket.

D: They must be, because the milk prices the farmers receive most places in the world are down 50 percent. The ideal solution might be for dairy farmers to sell raw milk directly to consumers—they'd make much more, and consumers would pay much less. But that's against the law most everywhere today.

Going back to what you said earlier, one of the reasons I thought that Argentina would be the best place to do this, is because of the stupid fascist government down there. They try to control everything, including the price of beef. All your input costs are very low, partially because it's a depressed economy, and partially because of price controls. Land and labor are extremely cheap. But when you sell beef, you don't sell it at the world market price in Argentina. And when you sell milk, you don't sell it at the world market price in Argentina either. So, I'm looking for significant profit from the fact they are now controlling the prices. But that will come to an end. At some point, Argentina will be forced to bow to the market, and I hope to make a killing as a result.

Want to hear something unbelievable? It's possible Argentina will soon become a net beef importer. One reason is the drought in Buenos Aires province, which is exacerbating the already extraordinary liquidation of herds. But more important by far are the price controls. Between the drought, the boom in grain prices, and the controls—meant to artificially depress beef prices to bribe poor voters—Argentina is creating a beef shortage for itself. It's like creating a sand shortage in the Sahara. Reality alone will bring the controls to an end.

Also, I have a feeling that we may see a shift to the right when the next elections come up in 2011. Two of the leading candidates to replace Christina [Argentine President Christina Kirchner] are both free-market-oriented guys. I don't mean radically free market, but pretty free market. Either could turn the place around, however, much the way Roger Douglas turned New Zealand around in the mid-1980s. And if that happens, Argentina could boom and blossom, and the value of my land and cattle would jump just from the releasing of controls. Joining the real world market could result in a double overnight.

L: So, there's a political speculation as well.

D: Yes. The best speculations always capitalize on politically caused distortions. My dairy herd, within the next couple of years, will be up to 300 cows, which is the maximum capacity of my milkery or *tambo* [the word *tambo* comes from the Inca language, and in Argentina it's a synonym for dairy farming]. And eventually, we should get our beef herd up to 10,000 or 12,000 head.

And of course, when we are up to 12,000 head, we'll have 10,000 head that we can sell into the market every year. This would be a significant income stream.

I think it's a good time to get into the business, and Argentina is the right country, because of the price controls.

L: For people who don't want to go to Argentina or fear that the price controls may never be lifted, what other countries would you recommend? Obviously you wouldn't want to do this in the United States. Where would you go, if not to Argentina?

D: The United States and Canada are huge beef producers, but they're not ideal environments. For one thing, they have long, cold winters, especially in the plains states and Alberta. Cold takes weight off animals, so you have to feed them more. And the winter pretty much precludes their eating grass, so you're feeding them hay or silage—very expensive.

Surprising to most people is that the largest beef-producing state in the United States is Florida. The winters are perfect, but the summers are way too hot, and heat is also the enemy of beef. Plus, the pasture is generally very poor. Beef cattle can live on Florida grass, but horses, for instance, absolutely cannot. And the insects are a problem in a lot of places. Where we are in Argentina, the climate is ideal year-round, the grass is good, and insects aren't a problem.

I'd be willing to look at Brazil or Bolivia. Paraguay is very interesting, actually, in a lot of ways. The problem with Paraguay is that there are no transportation facilities there, besides trucks. It's one of the best places in the world for growing everything from cattle to corn to soybeans, but the transportation for shipping the stuff out is very problematical.

And if you want to get even stranger than that, I would go to the eastern provinces of Bolivia, the so-called Media Luna. Bolivia is really at least two different countries that are sociologically, demographically, and geographically as different as night and day. I think there is an excellent chance that Bolivia is going to split up in the future into at least two countries. The Santa Cruz/Media Luna area, which is the agricultural lowland, is also an excellent, politics-based speculation. The land in the Media Luna is very cheap and it's really beautiful, albeit in the middle of nowhere. Let the Quechua and Aymara [the languages and the people who speak them in the Bolivian highlands], which Morales [Bolivian President Evo Morales] belongs to, in the dry highlands have that area.

I like Brazil, too, but it has done so well in recent years, it's not particularly cheap anymore. So I'd rather go for places that are cheap, where I can see a possible explosive upside as opposed to a place that's nice like Brazil, but where the market recognizes that it's nice, and that's already reflected in the prices.

L: Are there places you might go outside of Latin America? Europe is as controlled as the United States, but some governments might decide to support some agriculture. Say, Denmark suddenly decided it's going to subsidize the dairy business, would you consider going there?

D: Well, dairy is the biggest form of agriculture in Denmark; and since it's Europe, I presume it's already heavily subsidized. But I don't know of any such opportunities there right now. Western Europe is high cost, high regulation, high tax. And too far north to be very productive. I'd forget it. Eastern Europe is a possibility. Land is still relatively cheap in Serbia.

L: Yes, and they have a flat tax structure and free trade with Russia, so you'd have access to the whole Russian market.

D: Yes. Ukraine and Romania might also be interesting, since the Eastern European property market has collapsed. But the problem with farming operations is that you've got to supervise them. There is a saying in Spanish: *El ojo del amo engorda el ganado.*

L: "The eye of the master fattens the cattle."

D: Yes. The fact is, if you are not there, and you don't have people who are really reliable.

L: I get it—as you said, you *like* living in Argentina. So you'd have to like living in Serbia or the Ukraine for it to make sense to get into the cattle business there.

D: Right. That goes for Argentina, too. So that's the problem with investing in farming, on a first-hand basis: You've got to be on the spot several times a year, and you've got to have some degree of confidence in the guys on the ground running the operation.

But I think it's a good thing to do if you have an inclination, have the capital, and want to spend time there.

L: And for the people who don't want to buy a ranch, is there an ETF in cows? Or is there an easier, less laborious way to invest that you can recommend?

D: Yes, there are a couple of relevant ETFs—at least one for cows. There are futures in all the agricultural products. But that's a day-to-day kind of thing that requires its own due diligence and effort.

L: If you grow your own herd, you don't have to be right on the timing, you just have to be long when the time is right?

D: That's right. When you are actually growing the cattle, you just have to be right on the trend, as opposed to picking the right day when you are speculating. All things considered, I think the countries in South America are the most interesting, for all kinds of reasons. But part of that is my taste.

   The key is this: If you're going to buy real estate abroad anyway, for the kinds of reasons we discussed in our conversation on currency controls, or others, you should pick land in a place you enjoy being. And if you're going to do that, you might as well put the land to work, with cattle and dairy herds being an obvious way to do that. For me, this adds up to a working estancia in Argentina.

   For others, it'll be wherever the stars align for them.

L: Got it. You know, I do like Serbia, and Belarus. I wonder . . .

D: Have fun.

Chapter 17

Doug Casey on Real Estate

November 18, 2009

Louis: So, Doug, it's well known that in addition to investing in resource stocks, especially gold juniors, you also have a passion for playing the real estate market. What can you tell us about real estate in today's world?

Doug: Real estate has been very, very good to me. The reason that's true is that I buy only things that I like myself. I don't try to second-guess what other people may want. If you do that, you're guaranteed to wind up with mediocre stuff that nobody really wants. I have an inclination to buy unique properties, as opposed to commodity-type stuff. That approach is not for everyone, but it's worked for me.

But let's start with the big picture. I've bought real estate in many countries, all around the world, and I find that it helps to have an international view.

L: We'd expect no less from the original International Man.

D: You wouldn't, I know. But most people still think like medieval serfs, tied to the land of their birth. People say that real estate is a local

market, and of course that's true. Location, location, location—you
have to know enough to pick good locations, so you should deal in
an area you know well. But at the same time, if you take a global
view, with over 200 countries in the world to look at, you have 200
times the chances of finding an anomaly, either on the buy or the
sell side. Those anomalies make for exceptional deals—exactly what
you want to capitalize on. It also gives you a better idea of what the
market likes, what works, what doesn't, and so forth. If you're isolated
and insulated in just your little community, you'll never get one up
on the rest of the crowd.

L: That makes sense, but let's start with the U.S. real estate market,
because that's where most of our readers are.

D: It's also the epicenter of the financial quakes spreading around the
world today.

L: A lot of people have to be looking at what seems like a degree of
economic recovery, and wondering if real estate has bottomed in the
United States.

D: Real estate has definitely not bottomed in the United States, and
probably not anywhere else either. You have to take a long-term view
of this. Remember that through most of U.S. history, residential real
estate was not viewed as an investment. You didn't buy a house to
make yourself wealthy selling it to someone else. It was viewed as an
expensive consumer good that depreciated—you bought or built a
house to live in it, just as you bought clothes to wear or a horse to ride.
It was just a part of life—a necessity, a convenience, but an expense.

But then, especially just after World War II, the government
started to institutionalize mortgages, which is to say, add huge leverage to the housing market. That's what has transformed houses into
speculative vehicles. That trend has been building momentum over
the decades, as more and more debt was centered on real estate.
Mortgages turned into commodities futures contracts. It was a huge
change from the days where you knew your banker, he knew you,
and he was lending his own money.

The result has been a *huge* amount of overbuilding, in residential,
office, and retail commercial real estate. It's going to take years and
years to work this off. In addition, the entire psychology of the market has changed.

I don't believe this recession is going to end the way all the other post–World War II recessions have, with a new and bigger boom. This is a major, secular turning point. It's not just another cyclical low to use to load up for the next run up.

L: Okay, so, U.S. real estate is still headed down, and maybe headed much farther down if this recession turns into the Greater Depression you've been calling for. But at some point, it will have to hit bottom. How will anyone who wants to own real estate in the United States know when it's time to buy?

D: I think the economic depression we're embarking on now—a depression being a period of time in which the average person's standard of living drops significantly—will be much worse than the one in the 1930s. So we can look at how bad things got then as a minimum guideline for when to start looking for a bottom. For example, Greenwich, Connecticut, was one of the hottest, glitziest real estate markets back in the late 1920s. A look at comparable prices in the newspaper ads from the period indicates that residential property fell 90 percent over a period of about 5 to 10 years. There's no reason that couldn't happen today, especially in overbuilt markets like Florida, California, et cetera, but it could easily be much worse.

L: Why do you say that?

D: Because in those days, most people paid cash, to start with. If you had a mortgage, you usually put at least 20 percent down, and the length of the mortgage was generally five years. Today, with even prime mortgages having much less money down, lasting 30 years, and floating rates, there's *much* more leverage.

But there's another reason. The bottom back in the 1930s was famous for people being able to buy properties for just back taxes. Today, you can buy square miles of some cities, like Detroit, for back taxes alone—but nobody's doing it. No one sees the $500 minimum bid as worth it, partly because the properties are likely to simply remain tax liabilities well into the future.

I've got to say that this is the big elephant in the room that no one is talking about. To me, more important than the overbuilding, more important than the amount of mortgage debt, is that real estate taxes are completely out of control in the United States. Nobody talks about this, for some reason, but the fact is that in many parts of the United States, you'll pay 2 percent of the assessed value of your house to the government, just to live in it. There are people across the United States paying $10,000, $20,000, and even $50,000 a year in taxes on what are actually quite normal houses.

L: You think you own your house, but you have to pay rent to the government, or else.

D: Exactly; if you don't pay rent to the government, you'll find out who really does own your house very shortly.

This is cash money that has to be coughed up, whether you have a job or not. And a lot of people are still going to be losing their jobs in the years ahead. We aren't anywhere near the bottom of the employment situation. So, I think there are going to be large numbers of places—and I mean all over, not just places like Detroit and Flint, Michigan—where you're going to be able to buy whole tracts of McMansions for past taxes. But you'll think twice before doing it, because those taxes are going to continue.

L: They'll get worse, won't they? With government revenue from other sources falling through the floor, they'll squeeze wherever they can, and your house is an easy target.

D: That's precisely right. It will get uglier for that reason, and I'll give you another reason why it will get even uglier: Interest rates are being suppressed to insanely low levels. This is an artificial rate set by the government in a truly stupid and doomed effort to stimulate the economy into renewing unsustainable patterns of production and consumption. Eventually, interest rates are going much higher—because they must, for reasons we've discussed in past conversations. *Real* interest rates are going to 10 or 15 percent, or more, as they did in the early 1980s. That's going to put the final nail in the coffin of U.S. real estate.

But there's more.

L: Wait! Don't order now! We'll throw in a free garage!

D: That's right, except that people are more likely to throw in the towel when they see what happens to their utility bills in the coming years. Water, garbage, but especially electricity, gas, heating oil—energy prices, for reasons we've also discussed, are going way up. That means more cash money that needs to be paid whether you have a job or not, if you want the air conditioner to run in the summer and the heat to work in the winter.

And it gets even worse; most of the overbuilding is way out in the suburbs. Bedroom communities. People moved out of downtown areas because they became expensive, and transportation was cheap. Many people are not going to be able to afford to drive their gas guzzlers 100 miles per day, round trip, to a job that won't have any prospects for a pay raise, since most people will be thankful just to have a job at all.

I think we'll find significant tracts of suburbs that will be literally abandoned in the not-too-distant future. Just as mansions were abandoned in the 1930s or sometimes turned into flop houses—nothing wrong with the houses, except people just couldn't afford to live in them. All that construction was a misallocation of capital, making the country poorer, even while—paradoxically—people thought it was a sign of wealth.

So, no, U.S. real estate hasn't bottomed yet at all. And it's not just going to be in residential real estate, which is where the little guy is going to get killed. It's going to happen in office space and other commercial real estate as well. This is *very* ugly, and it's just gotten started.

L: So, even when it does bottom, not everything selling cheap will be worth buying? I can imagine that an office building picked up for pennies on the dollar should work out okay at some point, unless the entire city it's in is abandoned. But huge swaths of bedroom community houses far from shrinking cities might have to wait generations before there's demand for them again—and you'd need to spend money maintaining them the whole time.

D: Agreed. U.S. housing stock will suffer from years of deferred maintenance by the time the final bottom comes. Although, right now, you can already buy a 30-story office building in downtown Detroit for a few million bucks. As I mentioned above, one of the reasons I've done well in real estate is that I tend to buy things that I like personally and can see using myself. Why? Because I understand these things, and you shouldn't invest in things you don't understand.

L: And if you ended up having to keep these properties, you wouldn't shed a tear, because you like them anyway.

D: Yes. I think these bedroom communities of ticky-tacky houses way out in the desert, or in places that should still be cornfields, are dead ducks. They'll end up being torn down or becoming new ghost towns. People forget that there are lots of ghost towns and always have been—and not just in the United States; it's happened in Europe too, where the land has been highly populated for over 2,000 years.

And as far as commercial real estate, fuhgeddaboudit. As we keep pointing out, a big part of the problem in the West is that we've been consuming more than we've been producing. That means that all these stores catering to unsustainable patterns of consumption and production are not going to have customers. They're going to go out of business. Their buildings will be empty.

Now, at some point, there will be a bottom, when buying such commercial property will make sense, but I can't tell you when that will be. We'll have to keep tabs on the situation and look for a confluence of a number of factors, including interest rates, taxes, demographics, energy prices, and politics.

It will happen, but I don't know when, so at this point, I'm completely uninterested in speculating in U.S. real estate—and I don't foresee being interested for at least five years. I reserve the right to change my mind, but I think it'll be at least five years.

Now, that doesn't mean that if I wanted a house, I wouldn't buy it now. You can get a fixed-rate mortgage now with an artificially low interest rate on houses below the jumbo level (I think it's about $550,000). Given where interest rates and the value of the dollars you borrow are going, that's going to be a gift in the future.

L: But that's not a speculation. You're saying that if I wanted to buy a house I like, to live in, the near term might be a good time to buy.

D: Yes, that would make sense, if only because that fixed-rate mortgage could be practically wiped out by the inflation to come. You're looking at what could be a very large gift. Too bad for the entity that lends you the money, but that's what they get for playing this government-rigged game.

There's a true story I tell to remind people of how cheap real estate can get under crazy circumstances. I was in Rhodesia at the tail-end of the war, in 1979; I must have been the only foreign tourist in the whole damned country. I took a bus from Salisbury to Umtali [they've renamed both of them: Salisbury is now Harare, and Umtali is now Mutare]. There were no other cars on the road at all; I guess it was actually rather risky.

Anyway, I got to Umtali and found that it had become an armed military camp. I looked around and asked people what I should go see, and was told to check out the Leopard Rock Hotel. It was a fantastic place on 200 acres, with a nine-hole golf course and 50 acres in coffee. Very beautiful. The hotel had about 15 suites and was built like a castle. It was huge.

I could have bought that place—silverware, linen, food in the fridge, everything, the whole shooting match—for $85,000, cash. When I went back to Rhodesia (now Zimbabwe) after the war, in 1985 or 1986, the same place had just changed hands for $13 million— about 150 times the price I was offered. Of course, if I'd done it, I would have had to live there and run the place, or it would have turned into a looted derelict within a week. My whole life would have changed course. But that can be true every day, depending on whether you turn right or left at any street corner.

Opportunities like this really do pop up from time to time around the world, if you're willing to go look for them.

L: That leads naturally to the question of where you do like real estate now, if not the United States? Where in the world are you buying today?

D: Let's look at the various regions of the world. For people in the United States, Canada is the easiest place to move to, and I do think Canada will fare much better than the United States in the Greater Depression. But that doesn't mean I want anything to do with Canadian real estate now. It's far from cheap; in fact, Vancouver real estate has become some of the most expensive in the world today. If I owned anything in Vancouver right now, I'd be hitting the bid.

I do have property in Hong Kong, which may be the most volatile major real estate market in the world. Right now, it appears to be at a manic top. I'm looking to sell my apartment there. This may be hard to believe, but I think I'll get something on the order of about 25 times what I paid for it. Of course, I bought it very cheap, during a China crisis.

L: Could today's high prices be the result of a bubble caused by the Chinese stimulus spending?

D: I suspect that's a major element, but frankly, I don't know. I have to visit and find out why these prices have risen to such crazy levels. But it doesn't matter; I'm hitting the bid.

L: Any time you see something go way above what the market fundamentals justify, it's time to take profits. We do that all the time with stocks.

D: That's right. I'm going to shoot first and ask questions later, in this case.

The question now is: Where are the nice places in the world today that are still cheap?

It's most unfortunate that governments all around the globe are increasingly rapacious and virulent. The institution of the nation-state as we know it is actually the biggest problem—other than the cosmic one of life and death itself—to living on this planet. Governments all over the planet are getting truly out of control, and that makes it less pleasant to live under their jurisdictions.

L: The number of nice places is shrinking.

D: It is. So, back to the regions to look for speculative opportunities. Forget Canada. Forget Hong Kong. And definitely forget about all of Africa. The continent is a basket case that's not going to change for a long, long time.

L: Why?

D: It's primarily because of the arbitrary lines the Europeans drew on the map when they divided it up into all these stupid nation-states. That divided tribes and turned each country into a vehicle for theft for whichever group got control.

You can also forget about Central Asia and the Middle East, partly for the same reason, but also because it's the epicenter of the war against Islam. You can forget about most of Europe for the same reason: The demographics in Europe are going totally the wrong way, and those governments are among the most voracious. I wouldn't even think about Europe now.

L: Does that include Eastern Europe, where there's been a trend toward liberalization since the collapse of the Soviet Union?

D: Good point. Actually, with the corrections those markets have seen, especially in the Baltics, they could be interesting. Some highly profitable anomalies could be shaping up. I was talking about Western Europe when I said it was going the wrong way. Eastern Europe deserves a closer look.

L: I've seen charts showing large drops in some of those markets.

D: I would expect so. Back in the Far East, places like Thailand, Laos, Cambodia, and Malaysia are very interesting. Especially Burma. I like them a lot, but as much as I do, assuming you're a person of European descent, they are not places where you will ever be accepted as a member of society.

That brings me back to South America—I think it's going to have its day in the sun. I think Argentina, Chile, and Uruguay are the places to be in South America. Brazil has gotten too expensive. Bolivia and Paraguay are too screwed up. I like the "southern cone" countries, and among them, for reasons we've discussed at length in the *International Speculator*, I think Argentina offers the best speculative opportunities. And I think it's the nicest place to be as well, even though Chile has become the most advanced and forward-looking of these countries.

Among the reasons I think Argentina is the best place to own real estate is that real estate taxes are basically nonexistent. And there's no credit. It's a completely cash market, which means that the prices are real. I don't think the political situation is likely to get any worse, and it's quite possible it could get better.

L: In the last Argentine crisis, a huge economic and fiscal crisis in which the Argentine peso lost three-quarters of its value overnight, as crazy as things got, the government never touched land titles.

D: No, they didn't. And, in fact, while land prices in Argentina are up since the bottom of the last crisis, they haven't exploded upward. I see a lot of European immigration headed to Argentina. Europeans that come to Argentina, or Uruguay, for that matter, are going to realize that real estate costs a tenth of what it does in Europe, the cost of living is a quarter of what it is in Europe, and they'd have much more freedom, because the governments are much smaller and much less effective—it's like they're still back in the 1950s. They'll realize that this is the place to be for real estate, and lifestyle in general.

If we were having this conversation 60 years ago, if I'd looked over the world then, I believe I would have said that the United States was absolutely the place to be. But it's not anymore. Everything changes. And it's way too early, as a speculation, to even *think* about buying U.S. real estate.

I can't stress this too much. You know, back in the 1930s, co-op apartments in Manhattan that today sell for millions of dollars—you literally couldn't give them away. The co-op fees were more than anyone wanted to pay. Residential units worth millions of dollars today were literally free. Could it happen again? I'm not going to say that it will, but prices of residential or commercial real estate in the United States should not be of any interest to a speculator today.

L: What about Spain? It's basically Europe, but cheaper.

D: Yes, well, I put my finger on Spain's Costa del Sol in my *Crisis Investing for the Rest of the '90s*, and I was absolutely right.

L: It was a 10-bagger for you, wasn't it?

D: Yes, it absolutely boomed. And now it's going into reverse, it's in freefall. That's because every European who wanted a place in the sun went to the Costa del Sol. It got hugely overbuilt with a tremendous amount of debt used to finance it. Now it's time to pay the piper. I don't know when the bottom will be in Spain, but I'm in no hurry to go back there. All the overbuilding has actually made it less desirable, from my personal aesthetic point of view.

I'd rather look at Portugal, which is still the backwater of Western Europe. If I had to live in Western Europe for some reason, Portugal would be my first choice. I have to say that I haven't been there for several years, so I can't say much about it from a price point of view, but from an ambiance point of view, it'd definitely be my first choice.

L: What about Down Under?

D: Australia and New Zealand are going to do relatively well in the Greater Depression. Prices, certainly in New Zealand, where I have property, are down considerably from their peak. The trouble with New Zealand, as much as I like it, is that it's . . . at the end of the road.

L: It's a long way from anywhere.

D: It is. It's a nice place to hang out, but while prices have come down a lot, the currency has come up a lot. The kiwi dollar has doubled since I was recommending that people buy real estate in New Zealand 10 years ago. So it's not a bargain anymore.

If you want a bargain, I've got to tell you, Argentina is it. Lifestyle, costs, benefits, freedom—even with all of the problems every country has, including Argentina, the place is without a doubt my best pick at the moment.

L: I know you're sincere in that, so I'll go ahead and play along with a "shameless plug" question, as David Galland might say: Are you still selling lots at your Cafayate project in Salta province?

D: Yep. I suggest that people go to www.CafayateLiving.com and check it out. It really is becoming a bit of a Galt's Gulch because of the kind of people who are showing up there. It's an oasis in the desert, next to a fantastic little town where you can get whatever you want and have every amenity known to man, at very reasonable prices. That's where I'm going to be spending a great deal of my time, and I suggest that others who see the world the way we do at least take a look at it.

L: As far as amenities on the project site, what's completed? Is the golf course done? The clubhouse? What can people actually do there, besides sit and watch the grapes grow?

D: Well, the 1,500 acres the project occupies are right adjacent to the town, so you can ride your horse into town, if you're of a mind to do so. We do have 200 acres of vineyards, and you can watch the grapes grow if you like, while drinking some of last year's harvest. The first clubhouse, the golf clubhouse, is built. The 18-hole golf course is built and the first nine holes are playable. The second nine will be playable by March. The first polo field is under construction. Forty kilometers of horse riding, biking, and jogging trails are being completed. Two lakes are built and being stocked with fish, so you can catch fish for dinner if you want a break from great beef. We're planting just about every kind of fruit tree, berry bush, nut tree, and vegetable variety you can imagine, and raising organically nurtured animals so the food we eat will be of the highest quality possible.

Within a year, about 30 houses will be completed, and the spa, the gym, and the social club will be done. You'll be able to play golf, chess, bocce ball, or read in the library. You could play billiards with your neighbors, or maybe just sit and smoke a cigar. I can't think of a more civilized place to hang out.

L: Very good—that was indeed pretty shameless. Thanks for your time, Doug.

D: I enjoy these chats. Whether you agree with me about Argentina or not, just remember: It's too early to buy a place in the United States, unless you want it for personal use and get it with a big mortgage you can afford.

Chapter 18

Doug Casey on Africa
February 22, 2012

Doug: Lobo, you were in Africa—the Congo—last time we talked. How did that go?

Louis: I saw a lot of changes from my previous visit to the DRC [Democratic Republic of the Congo, not the Republic of the Congo] in 2006. That brings up an interesting question, as we do invest in companies working in several African countries, and you've described the continent as "a perpetual basket case." What's your take on Africa today? Is it doomed to remain the heart of darkness, or could things be looking up at a last?

D: I think it's very much an open question at this point, as to whether Africa has a dim or bright future. It's all about management, not resources. Africa has always had plenty of resources, but the worst management possible. Resources are actually a liability for most places. The classic examples of places not needing natural resources for success are Japan and Hong Kong. They have essentially zero natural resources, but became immensely prosperous because they had good property rights and predictable laws. On the other hand, you've got countries like Venezuela and Nigeria that have been blessed—or cursed, as the case may be—with great mineral wealth, but are absolute basket cases. And they'll stay that way until the governing philosophy changes.

Success of a society is totally a "people" thing—management. Without social systems that encourage prosperity—which is to say, encourage personal freedom—natural resources are counterproductive. They just become something for the strongest thugs to steal. Since the mineral rights in Africa all belong to the state, the best way to steal the diamonds, gold, oil, or whatever, is to get control of the government. Governments are obstacles to prosperity almost everywhere, but in Africa they are totally counterproductive. They're exclusively vehicles for theft and repression.

All across the continent, every regime—and I can't think of a single exception—became a hellhole after the colonial powers left. They exported nothing but minerals—the farms and plantations all went back to the bush—and imported nothing but crazy ideas and luxury goods for the rulers, mostly from Europe. Then, to compensate, Western governments have shoveled a trillion dollars of "aid" into the continent over the past 50 years. That was all money stolen from poor people in rich countries that ended up lining the pockets of rich people in poor countries. It cemented the poor Africans to the bottom of the barrel. Crucifixion is too good for people who promote foreign aid.

I attribute almost all of Africa's disastrous problems to colonialism. If Europeans came there as traders, it would have been beneficial to everyone. But they came as conquerors, destroyed the existing native cultures, engaged in horrendous wholesale slaughters—the Congo being perhaps the worst example—and imposed alien religions and political systems on the natives. My friend George Ayittey details this in his books.

L: My 11-year-old daughter is somehow aware of this. When I came back this time, she told me she was deeply offended by the rulers and other rich thieves in African countries who redirect foreign aid to their bank accounts in Switzerland, while the people it's intended to help starve. But it occurs to me that what you said about the mineral rights is true of Latin America and other places as well; if you want to mine, you don't go to the people living on the land, you go to the government to buy or rent the right to do so.

D: Yes. The only exception I know of is the United States, where if you own the surface rights to a piece of land, you own the subsurface rights as well, including mineral rights. It's only if someone wants to mine on government land that they need to file claims and deal with the government. This is one reason why the United States was the world's most prosperous and least corrupt country in the past. Private property rights like this served as one limit to the size and importance of the state.

L: Right. And as a "people system," the ability of individuals to own mineral rights had a lot to do with America's westward migration in the nineteeth century—the great gold rushes and such. Mining was also one of the main things that paid for that expansion. But we're straying from the subject. It's new to hear you say Africa's fate hangs in the balance; I'm used to hearing you say the place is hopeless. What would be a possible pathway to improvement?

D: Well, unbeknownst to most people, it seems that GDPs on the continent have been expanding very rapidly over the last decade. Now, of course those figures—issued by inept, despotic, and kleptocratic governments—are highly questionable, but most of the countries in Africa are actually starting to turn around, and strongly. Part of it is because they're starting from such a low base. But most of it is because things have improved so much from the way things were in the 1960s and 1970s. In those days most of Africa was run like Haiti was under Papa Doc—or worse.

L: That may be so, but a major source of that growth is the Chinese money pouring into the continent to lock up natural resources—and escape the dollar trap, to boot. Is that really a reason for optimism, or does it just mean the new thieves in presidential ribbons will continue gorging at the trough, with no lasting benefit to the people?

D: I remember when I first went to Zambia, in 1985. I don't believe there was a bookstore in Lusaka, although they sold a few dog-eared Marxist tracts at what laughably passed for the best office supply store. The same thing in Tanzania, where I stayed in the best hotel, but had one light bulb to move between my bedroom and bathroom. That kind of thing was typical. Now the whole continent is changing. Everybody has a cell phone—except me, I hate the damn things—and access to the Internet. People are moving into the cities and joining the middle class.

Africans aren't stupid; they've just been sold on every stupid collectivist idea that's come down the pike from Europe. A bloated state controlled by a kleptocracy has been the pattern so far, but there's change in the air. The disastrous colonial period and the catastrophic post-colonial period are receding into history. As I recall, the first African country to free itself from its colonial overlord was Ghana in 1957, followed by a whole spate of independence movements in the 1960s. Ghana was a nightmare under Nkrumah, but by the time I went there in 1994, it was to play polo with our excellent partner at Casey Research, David Galland—talk about a small world—and the place was already on its way up.

L: That would be true for sub-Saharan Africa. I think the very first was Libya.

D: That's right; Libya in 1951, and then Egypt in 1952. At any rate, I suspect they had to go through a stage during which the people thought that independence alone would make their countries as rich as those of their former colonial masters. That was the stage where an African thought he was successful if he could wear a tie, have a pocketful of pens, and carry a clipboard, even if he didn't know how to write. When the Congo went independent, there were only something like a couple dozen natives who even had a high school education. They were ripe prey for Uhuru jumpers and neocolonialists from the IMF and World Bank. That's changed. Those worthless institutions are now on the ragged edge of bankruptcy, and Africans have become much more sophisticated. There's an understanding that it's not a matter of race; your enemy, or friend, can be white or black. And soon a lot of them are going to be yellow.

L: You really believe that?

D: I didn't say they've all become free-marketeers. But I do think they are starting to realize it doesn't matter if the thief is a white guy on a throne in Europe or a fellow black who's made himself president for life. People don't have to be deep political thinkers to simply want governments that work—meaning they allow prosperity to flourish. Of course, no government produces any prosperity. But even kleptocrats are starting to realize it's much better to steal 10 percent of a huge pie than to try to steal 90 percent of a tiny pie.

L: Okay.

D: On the other hand, there's a huge problem in Africa, stemming from the fact that none of these countries truly represents the historic homelands of a specific people. The lines on the maps were all pretty much drawn up in boardrooms in Europe during the nineteeth century without regard for tribal homelands, differences in language, or even to geographical barriers, in some cases. With the possible exception of Egypt—and to a much lesser extent, Ethiopia—each of these countries is an agglomeration of different tribes, ethnic groups, and religions that don't mix well together.

The result of this has been that the governments of these countries have become prizes sought after by each group, to be used for profit and to reward buddies by stealing from everyone else.

L: Could the countries be reorganized along tribal lines to result in something more peaceful and durable?

D: That would be a step in the right direction. But they'd just find other differences upon which to base plundering a new group of victims for the benefit of a new group of fat cats. The best hope would be the complete breakdown of the nation-state as a way to organize society, and for the various groups to self-organize into voluntary social systems, along the lines of the phyles we've discussed in the past. I'd say the same thing for Europe, Asia, and the Americas as well, where different sorts of tribalism are alive and well. The nation-state is definitely on its way out; it was a really suboptimal—I'm being kind—way for people to organize.

L: Perhaps so, but wouldn't you still have a threat of war between Hutus and Tutsis and other such feuding tribes?

D: Maybe. Maybe not, if they weren't forced to mix. South Africa has avoided a civil war in spite of having a dozen or more major black tribes, as well as two white ones.

L: That could be just around the corner there.

D: Yes, they've been very fortunate and dodged the bullet so far. We'll see. In Nigeria, where there were an estimated 300 different tribes at the time of gaining independence in 1960, they had a civil war that was knee-deep in gore during the late 1960s in Biafra. Now there's tension between the Muslims in the north and Christians in the south. Nigeria, like all these countries, is an artificial construct that should be disassembled. Sudan just broke in two for similar reasons, and the new trouble in northern Mali has similar roots. If these very different peoples weren't forced to live under the same political system, they wouldn't feel the need to fight for control of it. It's best to let others go to hell in their own way.

L: Okay, I can see that.

D: I think this is a global trend, by the way, as we discussed in our recent conversation on Europe. What about you—did you see much evidence of tribal conflict in the Congo?

L: I asked people about that, actually. I asked them if a country as big as the DRC—second largest in Africa, and eleventh largest in the world—could stay together with all its different tribes. I was reminded that the most recent war only ended in 2003, with residual problems lasting into 2004—they were still quite visible when I was there in 2006. It was all very fresh then, and the country still had the appearance of an armed camp, with many of the survivors dressed in rags, the ghosts of hundreds of thousands of dead still in their eyes.

This time, I saw signs of new prosperity; many of the family farms I flew over had new tin roofs on a building or two, and cheap Chinese motor-scooters swarmed the jungle pathways like insects. There's a highly visible UN military presence along the border between the DRC and Rwanda, but still, Sunday afternoon brought out a lot of smiling people in new, brightly colored clothes. It's just a beginning, but these people are busy rebuilding. The ones I spoke with think most Congolese don't want to hear about tribal divides and the like; they just want to get back to earning a living.

D: That makes sense. With hundreds of different ethnic groups and local languages, there's no reason for the place to pretend it's one country. I was a big fan of Katanga trying to secede back in the 1960s. At least they share a common language in the DRC—French. The tribes all have their own languages, but decades of Belgian colonial occupation at least left behind a *lingua franca* that helps them all to communicate. It was the first African country I took a real interest in. I still recommend a really good movie, *Dark of the Sun*, about the mercenaries in Kasai province in the 1960s. I passed through M'Buji-Mayi when I was there. One thing I remember clearly was an old 707, acting like a tramp steamer of the air. The plane was totally without ID, painted in primer. I walked up to the pilot, who was a really good-looking

Belgian girl in her 30s. One thing I asked her was how she navigated. She said, "I'm the queen of the GPS," and showed me her handheld device. I last saw that plane when I looked up as I was sitting in a café in Uganda several days later. It made me feel like that guy who saw the girl in the T-bird at the end of *American Graffiti*. Anyway, I love weird places, and Africa is still full of them.

L: I'm sorry to say that the people I met were more mundane. But again, the answer to the question is not that the people feel all united into one nation as a result of their history, but rather that no one had time for nonsense. The people are tired of fighting. Sort of like Colombia, at the end of the *violencia*.

That's very different from the answer I got in Ghana, where the largest tribal group—by a large majority—is the Ashanti, who are seen as warlike. Since they are fierce and a majority, none of the other tribes are willing to take them on, and there is a sort of *pax Ashanti*.

D: Which is different again from Zimbabwe, where the contest was largely between two tribes, one represented by Mugabe, who is a Shona, and the Ndebele tribe, led by Nkomo. The Shona won. Maybe that will mean the crates of Shona stone sculptures I bought there a few years ago will have political as well as artistic value someday. But back to the DRC—where did you go, just Kivu province?

L: Last time I flew into Lubumbashi in southern DRC, and this time I flew into Bukavu, on the southern shore of Lake Kivu, which straddles the border between the DRC and Rwanda. This is all to the west of Lake Victoria, in an area that's sort of Africa's equivalent of the Great Lakes. It's remote, mountainous, and covered with jungle known to harbor both guerillas and gorillas. Both seem to be dying out—unfortunately, in the case of the latter. I saw no sign of either, but I heard of a guerilla attack on a town near one place my chopper set down one day, six months prior.

D: I visited the same place in 1998, after the preceding war, the one that overthrew the dictator Mobutu, who was a U.S. stooge who looted the country for many years. That was just before the war you're talking about, in which Rwanda, Uganda, and several other countries got involved; something like 4 million people died. Nobody knows exactly how many. But I visited the city of Goma, on the north end of Lake Kivu. I stayed at a friend's house on the lake, and we'd go swimming in the lake each morning. The first morning, as we looked across the water at the Rwanda border, only a few hundred yards away, I asked my friend if he was able to take his daily swim during the big troubles in Rwanda, back in 1994. He said no, because there were bodies floating everywhere in the lake.

L: That's a big lake—it takes three hours to reach Goma from Bukavu by speedboat.

D: They say almost a million people died in that <u>particularly nasty epi</u>-sode. Mostly done in with machetes.

L: You'd never know it to look at the place today. There are colorful villages on the shores of the lake, bright tropical flowers in abundance, fishing boats on the water. Some very nice hotels and villas—I heard there are waterfront homes selling for a million dollars in Bukavu. The water was so clear, you could see the bottom of the lake in places, before the wash from the chopper ruffled the surface. I looked and didn't see any bones.

D: Maybe they're covered with sediment now, something for future archeologists to unearth and puzzle over the machete marks on the bones. A million bucks for a house? I'll wait until I can get something like that castle in Rhodesia on the Mozambique border I should have bought during the war there. That was a 100-bagger, as it turned out. Oh well, my whole life would have been totally different—an alternate reality.

L: So, again, why is it that you're more positive on Africa's prospects now than in the past?

D: Well, there are two ways you can look at the future of Africa. One is that when they have these wars that last decades, it changes the local culture and engrains bad habits in the people that can take a long time to get rid of. The other view is as you said: After a certain amount of such stupidity, people get tired of it and start acting more intelligently.

L: Is there a historical example of a country "cursed" with great mineral wealth and actually benefiting from it, in the sense of the whole society achieving a higher standard of living rather than just the thieves in control of the government?

D: The only ones—and this may sound biased, but it's just a historical fact that people would do well to think about—are societies that were offshoots of Anglo-Saxon culture. The America that was (before they turned it into the United States), Canada, New Zealand, Australia.

L: Why would that be? The Protestant work ethic?

D: That's part of it. I think the ideas of the Enlightenment era—specifically the classical liberal ideas that so influenced the likes of Jefferson and Franklin—combined with the "rugged individualism" imposed by frontier life had a lot to do with it. The concept of English common law was a big factor. Ideas matter. Actions flow from ideas.

Of course, Argentina didn't have the English tradition, but nonetheless was once dominated by ideas that enabled wealth creation, and it became one of the wealthiest countries on earth—though most of the silver that gives the place its name was actually in Peru and Bolivia. But that was over 100 years ago, and the steady replacement of liberal ideas with socialist ones has been accompanied by a matching fall in prosperity, in spite of great natural resources. It's no longer a place to start a business, but it's a spectacular place to live—unlike Africa, which I view as a great place for merchant-adventurer type business, but not so great as a place to live.

L: Well, Africa is no bastion of free-market thinking; this analysis doesn't seem very hopeful.

D: Perhaps not now, but when people are tired of old ways that not only don't work and periodically lead to genocide, they may open up to new ideas. Many good people there—like my friend Leon Louw, who runs the Free Market Foundation—are looking for what works, and the continent has improved immensely. Markets work. And there certainly are abundant opportunities for entrepreneurs there.

L: It is indeed a very good sign that such organizations are cropping up all over Africa. Thompson Ayodele has done a very good job with his Initiative for Public Policy Analysis in Nigeria, as has James Shikwati with the Inter Region Economic Network in Kenya, and my friend Kofi Akosah with his Africa Youth Peace Call in Ghana. But would you really encourage Westerners to try their luck in Africa?

D: As we discussed in our conversation on starting out or starting over, if I were a young adventurer, I'd go to Africa, even more so than to Latin America or the Orient. The skills and experiences and connections you have—ordinary and offering no particular advantage in the United States—would be extraordinary and of great advantage there. And the more obscure the country, the better. I wouldn't go to South Africa or Kenya, which are relatively developed. There are fortunes to be made in really backward and troubled places. Maybe Sao Tome, or Guinea Bissau, or Guinea Conakry. Maybe Cameroon, or Gambia, or Benin.

L: Maybe Burundi? I stopped there on my way to the DRC this time; I confess I'd never even heard of it before.

D: I first heard of it because I collected stamps when I was a kid. But yes, that's the sort of place I mean.

L: By the way, on my previous trip to Africa, I stopped in Togo, which you'd asked me to drop in on.

D: Really? How was it?

L: It was much nicer-looking than I expected, for a place so far off the beaten track that almost no one even knows it exists. But maybe I should have known that was a positive sign; if it was in the news, that would almost certainly mean there were bad things going on. Slowly winning the struggle for prosperity is not newsy. When I got there, I saw a typical West African country, but with a lot of visible wealth in the form of nice real estate around the capital city.

I also stopped in Rwanda on this last trip, and it too looked cleaner and more well-maintained than I expected. I found that very hopeful—a sign of a focus on economic progress, rather than picking fights with neighboring countries.

D: I'd like to go to Togo some day, it being one of the relatively few countries I haven't been to. I just want to check it out and see what makes the place tick. I remember its postage stamps too.

But, we should also mention that North Africa is something of a region apart, with its own political dynamics. It also has mineral wealth, particularly in hydrocarbons. Perhaps we should remind our readers of our conversation on the Arab Spring, which is the main trend to be watching in the area.

L: Sure. We should also say something about South Africa, which is still one of the wealthiest countries in Africa, and a destination for many investors' dollars, especially in the natural-resource sector that we focus on.

D: Yes. In spite of that wealth, both in terms of one of the single richest natural resource endowments in the world, and one of the highest per capita GDPs in Africa, I have to say I don't think the place is safe for investors—and it's getting worse by the day. We do not invest in any South Africa plays—not for ideological reasons, like those who opposed apartheid—but because of the country risk. The people running the show are not just thieves; they are so hostile to enterprise, they've taken the place from producing over 60 percent of the world's supply of gold a couple decades ago to less than 12 percent of world gold production today. There's a high risk of nationalization in the country, if not *force majeure* in the form of violent chaos. South Africa is a powder keg with a lit fuse of unknown length, but it's lit. I have lots of friends and relatives there and things seem mellow at the moment, especially in Capetown, which is one of the prettiest places on the planet. Then again, the whole world is at the edge of a financial precipice at the moment.

L: Okay, so if South Africa is on its way down, is there a place in Africa on its way up that you'd invest in?

D: Maybe Zimbabwe—I might have to go back there. Perhaps I could be persuaded that it has bottomed. It might have, now that it allows people to use whatever currency they want. Mugabe is on his way out, although African dictators seem to have preternaturally long lifespans. This could be the time to get in cheap, especially if I was interested in living there, which I'm not. The problem is keeping physical control of your property. It'd be highly speculative, but cheap is the key. I'll buy anything if it's cheap enough. At a low-enough price, the downside becomes negligible—the potential reward becomes vastly greater than the apparent risk.

L: "Cheap enough" trumps even country risk. That applies to some of our investments in Africa plays; they are discounted for being there, which creates acceptable risk/reward ratios.

D: Yes. You can lose everything, investing in Africa—but then, increasingly, you can lose everything investing in the United States, say, if someone finds a piece of wetlands on your farm or whatever nonsense they come up with next.

L: Okay, so for investors, the bottom line is that there are opportunities, but serious due diligence is required, preferably via boots on the ground, and by waiting for the perfect pitch in terms of a price low enough that the probability of a loss pales in comparison to the possibility of a win.

D: Exactly. And if you're of a certain age or mental inclination, then Africa is the closest thing to a wild frontier left on the planet, a place to go and seek your fortune. But enter at your own risk.

L: Very well, then. Thanks for your insights.

D: I just don't want to hear from anyone's lawyer if they wander into a war zone and don't resurface for a decade. Talk to you next week.

L: Until then, take care.

Part Three

A MORAL MINORITY

Chapter 19

Doug Casey on Ethics (Part One)

June 23, 2010

Louis: Doug, we touched on ethics in our last conversation on your education as a speculator, and we decided we should have a conversation on the subject. Now, most religious people base their personal ethics on the moral mandates of their religions, and I know socialists who base their ethics on the utilitarian principle (or at least say they do). Both types seem shocked when someone like you or I—atheists, anarchists, and capitalists to boot!—refuse to do something that may seem profitable, on ethical grounds. So let's talk about ethics: What are they, what are yours, and how do you apply them?

Doug: Well, as always, let's start with a definition. Although I fear we may end up with a lot fewer subscribers, because this is a subject like religion, politics, and the U.S. military, where people have all kinds of hot buttons. But they don't pay us the big bucks to talk about the weather and the state of the roads.

L: Sure. Webster's says:

1. The discipline dealing with what is good and bad and with moral duty and obligation.
2. (a) A set of moral principles: a theory or system of moral values; (b) The principles of conduct governing an individual or a group; (c) A guiding philosophy; (d) A consciousness of moral importance.
3. (*Plural*) A set of moral issues or aspects.

D: These are all workable definitions, depending on the context we're discussing. Now, there are clearly some people who have no ethics at all, which is to say no principles. They act on the spur of the moment, just doing whatever seems like a good idea at the time. Then there are other people who have flawed principles that will consistently set them in the wrong direction. My own set of principles can be summed up in two statements:

1. Do all that you say you're going to do.
2. Don't aggress against other people or their property.

    There are endless corollaries you can derive from this, but this is what it all boils down to.

L: The first one sets out the basis for contracts and fair conduct, the second one the basis for peaceful physical interaction. But the first is actually derived from the second, because breaking the first (committing fraud) is really just a deferred form of the second (initiation of force).

D: True enough, although I think it's helpful to make a distinction between force and fraud. I also think it's important to distinguish between ethics, an individual's own guiding principles, and morality, which is a set of community standards. Morals, being politically/culturally derived artifacts, really only have a coincidental, or even accidental, connection to ethics. Morality is something that's dictated by a group or even imposed on a group by some kind of higher power. Ethics deals with the essence of right and wrong. Morality is just a construct of rules. It winds up being a bunch of precepts. Some have a basis in ethics. Others are just dramatizations of people's fears, quirks, and aberrations.

The difference between ethics and morals is analogous to that between using a gyroscope or a radar to navigate. A gyroscope is an internal device that keeps you level and steady without reference to what's outside. Radar would use external cues, bounced off other people, to tell you which way to go. Morality tells you what to do; ethics acts as a guide to help you determine, yourself, what you should do.

Similarly, ethics is a branch of philosophy, not religion. Ancient Greeks studied, wrote about, and placed a great deal of importance on ethics, the guiding principles of good action, completely apart from whatever their frisky gods were up to. For them, religion had basically nothing to do with ethics, except for providing edifying stories from time to time.

L: Okay, but what's the basis for your principles, or the one fundamental libertarian commandment of nonaggression that they resemble? Why is this any better than, for example, the Ten Commandments in the Bible?

D: Which Ten Commandments? The part of Exodus 20 most people refer to when they say the "Ten Commandments" actually has more than 10 commands, and there's another version in Exodus 34, plus one in Deuteronomy 5. So the things are hardly written in stone, as it were. Some of the bible's commandments are basic common sense, of course, especially if you use the "Thou shall not murder" translation instead of the "Thou shall not kill" version Catholics favor.

But the first three or four, depending on how you count them, are totally useless admonitions regarding a supernatural being, the existence of which is not supported by any evidence whatsoever. As ethical guidance goes, the list is rather confusing, with the parts governing the way people treat each other looking almost like afterthoughts, thrown in after all the instructions on how to worship.

The Ten Commandments impress me as an arbitrary agglomeration of moral precepts and commands. They lead to thinking you'll be all right if you do as you're told, instead of figuring things out for yourself. They get people into the mindset of following orders, even if the orders are goofy or irrelevant or arbitrary. The Ten Commandments got Western civilization off to a bad start.

L: In the New Testament, Jesus boiled it down to two principles, as you do: first, to love God, and second, to love your neighbor as yourself.

D: The second one, interpreted liberally, looks good at first. But it's not. Love isn't something you should hand out for free; it's something that should be earned and deserved. If it's not, love is not virtuous, it's worthless and counterproductive. I believe in giving the other guy the benefit of the doubt and maintaining an attitude of good will toward others whenever possible. And I absolutely believe in cultivating a benevolent approach toward other people, creatures, and even inanimate objects. But to love one's neighbor as one's self is idiotic and degrading; it leads to self-abasement and destroys self-respect.

But the first one is nonsense to me. Which god? Allah? Zeus? Perhaps Yahweh, the one who calls himself "Jealous" in those commandments, periodically authorizes wholesale genocide, and says he will punish children for the sins of their fathers?

It appears most people in the United States worship Jesus. Why not Baal or Quetzalcoatl? If you must debase yourself before some construct, it makes more sense to me to have a household god, as did the Romans, that represents and personifies the virtues that are important to you as an individual. My personal preference in gods are those that show nobility, as do many of the Greek gods, but especially the Norse gods. But I don't see what gods have to do with ethics. At least any more than Batman, Wonder Woman, or other superheroes do.

L: Okay, okay, but let's not get distracted. Religion is not today's subject. What's the basis of your two ethical principles? Why are they better than others?

D: They demonstrably work. They allow you to live with other people, in any society, and in any time, whether those people are enlightened philosophers or bloodthirsty pirates. Understanding those two laws is all one needs to interact peacefully and productively with others. Even more important, they're what you need to live with yourself— and you are the final judge of what you do; the opinions and morality of others are just opinions.

You could say the two laws are right because they obviously benefit others, but they actually benefit you the most, and it would be stupid to adopt principles that benefit you less. You could say, as an economist might, that they maximize efficiency and hence well-being among members of a society. They're quite practical, and it doesn't take a legal scholar to understand them. In fact, a six-year-old can understand them, rather intuitively.

L: Sounds like the utilitarian principle of the greatest good for the greatest number.

D: They happen to be pragmatic and utilitarian, although I must say I don't like pragmatists or utilitarians, because their principles are situational, fluid, and unsound. Someone who holds to those things could wind up committing all manner of depredations. But it's *because* my ethical principles are sound that they tend to produce the greatest good for the greatest numbers, not the other way around.

The problem I have with utilitarianism is that anyone can argue that anything, even the great atrocities committed by the Soviets were right as rain, because they were intended for the greatest good. Pragmatism is anti-ethical because it holds something is right if it works; the Nazis fancied themselves to be pragmatists.

L: Anything sacrificed on the bloody altar of the greater good, even an innocent child, is made sacred and holy by that excuse. Utilitarianism devolves into expediency, the perfect excuse for any atrocity. The twentieth century sure showed how badly utilitarianism can be abused.

D: For sure. And all these cockamamie philosophies usually evidence themselves as some variety or another of economic collectivism and political statism. My view is that free-market capitalism is the only ethical economic system. It maximizes everyone's advantage and does so without coercion. That's no accident; that's the proof of the soundness of the principles.

And it's no coincidence that the two ethical principles I outlined are also the only laws you need. You certainly don't need some council or Congress or Parliament cranking out new ones by the score every week. Or, as you pointed out, one being derived from the other, they could be boiled down to one single law: "Do as thou wilt, but be prepared to accept the consequences."

L: We discussed that in our conversation on judging justices. And that makes sense; on the most fundamental level, the law is a substitute for personal ethics when those fail or appear to be lacking. So they should have the same basis. There is little in our world that is more perverse than unethical laws that require people to do what's wrong or punish people for doing what's right.

D: Sure, but it happens all the time. These laws are cranked out by governments like there's no tomorrow—they are basically visible dramatizations of the psychological aberrations of lawmakers and the people they pander to. In brief, I have no automatic respect for either law or morality, which I know sounds horrible. But that's only because they subvert people's judgment. They actually work to make a personal code of ethics unnecessary, by telling people all they have to do is obey the law and current morality. This tends to transform people into unthinking automatons who don't feel responsible for their own actions.

L: "I was just following orders!" Frightening indeed. But I want to stay on track here. Let's talk about how you apply your two ethical principles, and if such a simple system can really cover all situations.

D: Okay.

Chapter 20

Doug Casey on Ethics (Part Two)

June 30, 2010

Louis: So, Doug, you've told us your ethical principles can be summed up in two statements:

1. Do all that you say you're going to do.
2. Don't aggress against other people or their property.

I have seen you apply this in life. These are great rules that lead to peaceful interactions between people. The first covers how you interact with others and ultimately would govern everything from business to marriage. The second covers how you should not interact with others, and would ultimately govern—prevent—what we might regard as criminal behavior.

It's admirable to simplify—I know you like to make an analogy to the way physicists try to simplify all the forces in the universe down into one unified field theory—but do these two principles really cover everything?

Doug: Well, perhaps not entirely. But it is said ignorance of the law is no excuse for breaking it. In today's world, that's total nonsense, because there are literally hundreds of thousands of arbitrary laws, with new ones passed daily. So I like these two laws because they're simple, intuitive, and based on ethical principles. But as we discussed last time, I really think there's just one great law, and it's even more important: Do as thou wilt, but be prepared to accept the consequences. An observance of that principle would necessarily result in a much more thoughtful and ethical population.

In any event, I only said my principles work, not that they are perfect. For instance, it's possible to cause others pain without actually aggressing on them. If, for example, some twisted artist created an incredibly beautiful painting designed specifically to appeal to you, and then burned it right before your eyes simply to watch you suffer, he would not have aggressed against your person or property, but what he did would hurt you. It'd certainly not be a nice thing to do, but would it be unethical?

L: Hm. Well, that brings the question of harm into play, and harm is different from aggression. You can harm people quite by accident and perhaps be liable for damages to person or property, but it's not a breach of your ethics if you didn't do it on purpose—accidents and aggression are not the same.

D: Right. So, is hurting someone's feelings really harming them? I have nothing but contempt for the politically correct crowd and their attempts to sanitize—sterilize—all human interactions, lest someone's feelings be hurt. Hurt feelings are not something that can be documented with evidence, the way physical harm can be, and as such, are not a proper subject for the law. And yet, if someone does something for the specific purpose of causing pain, even though they don't aggress, that doesn't sit well with me. A person that does such a thing will have to accept its consequences, some of which will be the damage to his own spirit and psychology, some may be retribution from others who see what happened and don't like it.

L: Stalkers and paparazzi come to mind. If they do not physically aggress, is there nothing wrong with what they do? If I'm going nuts because some guy is sticking his camera in my face everywhere I go, am I within my rights to grab the camera, maybe smash it?

D: It likely would depend on the circumstances. I'm prone to think that a clear warning to them before taking action would be sufficient, and I suspect a jury would agree 99 percent of the time. One simply has to use his best judgment in assessing the consequences of actions—or nonactions. Certainly none of the religious books, like the Bible or the Koran, are of much help. They're full of contradictions, ambiguities, and absurdities, while generally lacking clear ethical principles.

L: Well, some people might say that that statement is insulting or hurts their feelings. However, if the statement is true—the Bible does tell us not to suffer a witch to live, and other things that make no rational sense—and you're not trying to offend Christians, but to have a rational discussion of ethics, you can't leave out relevant facts because they might upset some people's sensitivities.

But I will point out that Jesus did say to love others as you'd love yourself, which would cover at least trying not to hurt people's feelings—and being "brutally honest" as well.

Then again, I'm not asking you about what Jesus said, I'm asking you about your system. As a matter of law, many libertarians argue that you shouldn't try to pass laws to protect people's feelings because it's impossible. Not only are feelings unprovable—anyone can say their feelings were hurt, and there is no reliable, objective way to measure that or prove it—but they can be harmed without knowledge or intention all day long. Anything and everything can hurt the feelings of a sensitive person; trying to prevent that quickly becomes absurd. Is that what this comes down to? Causing psychological pain is not objective, so it's not subject to your ethical principles?

D: I try never to offend someone who I don't think deserves it. And I try not to offend unintentionally. But why do we have ethical principles? Because when people behave ethically, they have a positive, constructive system for interacting—a voluntary regulation of behavior that is much more convenient than breaking out into fist fights at every interaction.

Ethics are rules for good living in society; if you're Robinson Crusoe, alone on an island, ethics are largely irrelevant, because there is no one to do right or wrong to. Although I would also consider plants and animals, in that I believe all living things should be treated properly. In society, however, if you break the rules—that is, if you behave unethically—you definitely increase the chances of someone responding with force. Treating others ethically decreases the odds of violent conflict and increases the odds of pleasant and profitable interaction. Ethics are a survival mechanism. They help make life less solitary, poor, nasty, brutish, and short.

So, back to our stalkers and reporters: They may not be engaging in violent conflict, but they are engaging in conflict—a kind of nonphysical aggression. In so doing, they increase the chances that someone may respond forcefully because they degrade the peaceful quality of social interaction ethical behavior seeks to establish. That's one reason it's correctly said that an armed society is a polite society (as we noted in our conversation on firearms).

L: In other words, it's just not a very good idea.

D: And even if you might be wrong to grab the paparazzo's camera, he'd be an idiot not to realize that bad things might happen if he makes a practice of annoying people.

It's also a question of intention. If personal ethics don't cover psychological assault, then a healthy, human system of social mores might. I've never been a fan of "morality," as such, because it's a largely arbitrary social construct. It's a sort of psychological mob rule. And the mores of the mob usually amount to banning, or at least consigning to a dark closet, just about everything that's any fun: smoking, drinking, uncensored conversation, sex—

L: Everything you'd want for a first-class party.

D: It's so perverse, sometimes I think I must have been put on this planet full of violent chimpanzees and intrusive busybodies as a punishment for some horrendous crime I committed in some past life.

L: Working off bad karma.

D: There's something to be said for that concept. If you believe that everything you do has consequences—above all, to yourself—then it makes sense that you create your own reality. That's certainly true in the here and now. As to whether there's another kick at the cat, I'm open to evidence.

Interestingly, we got a little flurry of e-mails from religious folks—all Christians—who made all kinds of assumptions and jumped to a bunch of conclusions based upon last week's conversation. I believe most of them believe I'm damned to eternal perdition. But a couple were quite mellow and thoughtful, which was gratifying. You can't convince anyone on spiritual matters. The best you can do, as has been said, is let those who have eyes see. Trying to change people is foolish and counterproductive.

L: But if you're a solipsist, as you claim, then all of this is just happening in your mind, which makes you a sadomasochist.

D: Perhaps I am. If I could master the advanced techniques of Taoism, or Zen, or some martial arts, or some other disciplines, then perhaps I could be much more serene in dealing with both temporal and cosmic unpleasantness and inconvenience. But there are many paths up the mountain, and I'm working on it. As you know, I'm not saying I have all the answers. Thinking about this kind of thing is a rather cosmic undertaking, and trying to sort it all out, defining your own personal system of ethics and acting accordingly, is one of the most important things you can do.

    I'm reasonably confident that, at least in my universe, there is no Heaven, nor Hell, no seventy virgins, no world where you get to rule those you baptize here, or other things of that nature. What's it like after you die? Perhaps it's just like it was before you were born. But I certainly don't need some book to tell me what to believe.

L: It's interesting to me that ethics are not an obstacle to living a better life, as the greedy and shortsighted might think, but are actually the means for achieving the Good Life.

D: Just so. Ethics are, in fact, essential tools for survival for social beings like humans. That's the difference between a decent human being and a criminal; the criminal doesn't understand this.

L: The really interesting thing about this is that while your view is quintessentially selfish—Ayn Rand would approve—what economics has established, from Adam Smith to Hayek, to today's Austrian economists, is that such rational selfishness actually leads to the greatest good for the greatest number. That's especially so if you include your posterity (what's good for your children) in your view of your own rational self-interest. It's the very thing utilitarians have found so slippery. But it's not because it's utilitarian that it's good; rather, it's because it's good that it happens to be utilitarian.

D: I agree. No matter what people wind up believing, though, it should be the product of their own thinking and experience. Not something they believe because they were brought up that way or someone scared them into believing. But free thinkers are few and far between, I fear. It accounts for the degraded state of things on this planet.

L: Rand said that ethics is the one subject no one should delegate to experts. To what degree would you credit Ayn Rand with your own ethical development? We talk about her a lot, so she seems to have had a strong influence on you. Speaking for myself, though I've never agreed with her on everything, I will always owe her a great intellectual debt, most specifically for her eloquent defense of rational egoism.

D: Rand was the most important single intellectual influence I've had in my entire life. I didn't really learn ethics from her—I had always intuitively believed in an ethical system such as she articulated—but I had never put it together and structured it in so many words.

I remember very distinctly when I read *The Virtue of Selfishness*—after I read the first page of the book, I had to put it down, because I was so shocked that someone had actually crystallized, in words, exactly what I had been thinking, inchoately, for most of my life. So I picked it back up and quickly devoured the rest; it was an intellectual and psychological blockbuster for me.

It's a book I could not recommend more highly. It's only about 150 pages, a much easier way to get the idea than reading her 1,000-page-plus magnum opus, *Atlas Shrugged*.

I'm not, incidentally, particularly endorsing her whole philosophical system, Objectivism. It resembles a secular religion, and its followers tend to be strident and dogmatic acolytes. Once people develop a theology—it doesn't matter whether we're talking about Objectivists, Christians, Communists, Hindus, Muslims, or what-have-you—they tend to be dull company at best and very likely a danger to themselves and others.

L: I remember reading *The Virtue of Selfishness* as well, and the dirty looks it seemed to draw from my college professors. But let's get back to your personal ethics. They cover a lot of ground, with some questions around the edges on issues like psychological harm, but what about extreme cases? Take the purely hypothetical case in which you have a button you can push and kill anyone you want to, perhaps the politician you most despise, and—this is important—no one would *ever* know. If there could be no possible harm to you, ever, would you stick with your principle, or would you push the button?

D: Well, I can think of a lot of people this world would be better off without, but no, I wouldn't push the button. Even if I could get away with it completely, it would still seem . . . cowardly. There are people on this planet who need killing, but if I were going to do it, I'd do it face to face—and the other guy would have a sporting chance of shooting back. Although that's perhaps more a matter of aesthetics than ethics.

L: You'd bring back dueling?

D: Why not? If two people choose to fight, how is that the business of the state or anyone else? Can you imagine what the effect might be on the spineless, miserable excuses for human beings called politicians if people could call them out to duel, as a matter of honor? Apart from the fact that nobody gets out of here alive anyway, I find the people that are willing to preserve their lives at any cost tend to be those whose lives seem to be the least worth preserving.

L: Well, dueling did make a good riddance of Alexander Hamilton. But are matters of so-called honor really matters of aesthetics? And if you'd consider it unaesthetic to kill someone without confronting them, fine, but what's the ethic involved?

D: Well, as a matter of ethics, I would point out that politicians who steal from the people, start wars just to get reelected, and so forth, have in fact initiated the use of force, and so force used against them is not aggressive but defensive. And defensive force is ethical, according to my principles.

But your question was if I would push your hypothetical button, and my answer was no, based on my aesthetic values, not my ethical principles. Aesthetics help make life worth living, especially since I don't think life has meaning in itself. You have to endow it with meaning. The cosmos may have a life of its own, but you're totally in charge of your life, even if they're going to throw you in a dungeon or execute you tomorrow morning.

L: All we are is dust in the wind—but unlike a virus or a patch of interstellar gas, we can give meaning to our lives in our own eyes. In my mind, that's the true glory of being human. But let me refine my question: What if it's not a politician or anyone who has initiated the use of force against you? Suppose you fell in love with a married woman, and she loved you but for whatever reason could not divorce her husband. Here's the button again. He's a complete innocent, but no one would ever know. He's not a bad man you want to challenge to a duel, but simply an inconvenience whose death would benefit you. If your ethics are based on selfishness, why not push the button?

D: No. First, she may have an overweening duty to him. If not, then if she really cared that much for me, she'd leave the man. I'm certainly not going to commit a serious aggression because of an emotion.

But beyond that, the kind of person who tries to build a relationship on force or fraud is either a knave or a fool, and likely both. In the real world, all actions have consequences. Becoming a mass murderer is not a good survival strategy, and spending your days trying to hide deadly secrets from the whole world ensures you'll experience a spiritual hell in this lifetime, regardless of whether there's another after it.

L: Okay, one last try then. And this really does happen: Suppose you were on your deathbed, with weeks or even just days to live. And suppose you were a man of considerable means. Why would you let the ethics that guided you through life prevent you from joining Heinlein's Committee for Aesthetic Deletions—that is, taking a few of those who need killing with you when you are in no condition to duel and pretty much dead anyway?

D: It would make no difference to me. As I said earlier, we're all under a death sentence anyway; I can't see how the amount of time remaining to you can change the ethics of a given act. Nor do I think you can ever escape the consequences of your actions. And I'm not talking about those that may be imposed on you by a legal system. I'm talking about those within yourself. Plus, if you have loved ones, partners, children—or even ideas and beliefs that you care about— becoming a murderer on your deathbed could subject them to reprisals and social backlash.

That's the ethical consideration for sticking to my principle of nonaggression, but as a matter of psychology, I can tell you that I've seen people in this position, and the only thing they are thinking about is survival—until they slip beyond caring about anything at all. Those people are entirely too attached to their bodies. My view is that it's much more aesthetic to go out in a duel than wither away with a tube up your nose in some hospital.

L: Very well then. Whether or not Karma is real, the mental stench of blood on your hands can never be escaped. Now, let's talk about business ethics, which may be where the rubber really hits the road for many of our readers.

D: Okay, but you're really not going to like this.

Chapter 21

Doug Casey on Ethics: The Ethical Investor (Part Three)

July 7, 2010

Louis: Doug, you said at the end of our last talk that I wouldn't like what you had to say about business ethics. Given your two principles:

1. Do all that you say you're going to do.
2. Don't aggress against other people or their property.

Why would that be? Sounds like good business to me.

Doug: Well, as far as completing your contractual obligations and not stealing from—or intentionally harming—people you do business with, that's pretty obvious and we've already covered it. No need to discuss that further.

Unfortunately, though, when most people think of "ethical investing," it has nothing at all to do with ethics. Most people have been deluded into thinking it has to do with not investing in tobacco companies, gun manufacturers, miners, timber companies, oil companies, many drug companies, many agricultural and food companies—in fact, whatever is on the ever-growing hit list of the politically correct. Pretty soon the silly bastards will be saying you shouldn't invest at all, but give your money to NGOs.

L: Hey, you might be on to something there; if everyone gives their money to everyone else, everyone will get lots of money for nothing—free cash for everyone, what a great idea!

But let's come back to that in a moment. It's true that murdering your competitors is a rather short-sighted business strategy. It's also true that failing to deliver what your customers expect is an even shorter path to insolvency and dissolution of your business. And so forth. But a *lot* of businesses do things that are not ethical—or at least fall into legal gray areas that allow executives to claim they didn't do anything wrong. If that's such a bad idea, why do so many businesses do it?

D: I can't speak for other businesspeople, but you know that after hydrogen, stupidity is the most common thing in the universe.

I can say that in our own business, *reputation* is critical. We offer investment advice through our various publications. Why would anyone take advice from someone they don't trust? Of course we comply with all the laws and regulations imposed on our industry— even though I disapprove of any regulation—but we go beyond that. As you know, we not only do not sell the same shares we tell people to buy, we disclose when we already own shares of companies we recommend, and we let subscribers sell first when it's time to head for the exits. This may sound self-serving, and perhaps it is, but it remains true that people know that Casey Research can't be bought; companies cannot pay us to write them up.

We certainly have one of the best track records of investment results in the business. It's sometimes hard to know what to make of our competitors' claims. Some of our colleagues in the business are absolutely first class in every department, including ethics and competence. But others. . . .

Reputation is a strange commodity from a philosophical viewpoint. On the one hand, a good reputation is of high value. On the other hand, it's only an opinion held in the minds of others, and like

all opinions, it can be based on incorrect information or interpretation. I think we have a superb reputation, but as far as I'm concerned,
reputation is strictly secondary to our actually acting ethically.

I don't, however, worry about it. I almost never do, or don't do,
something because of what other people would think. The mob is
fickle, thoughtless, and easily swayed; the best proof of that is the type
of people elected to public office. Going back to a religious figure
mentioned earlier in this conversation, look how the mob turned on
Jesus when nothing had changed but perception.

I prefer to rely on reality. Damon Runyon was correct when he said,
gainsaying Ecclesiastes, that the bread may not go to the wise, nor the
battle to the strong, nor the race to the swift—but that's the way to bet.

L: So you adhere to ethical business practices because you adhere to ethical action in general, but for people without quite the same strength
to their ethical backbones, reputation can be a powerful market force
for the good. But still, there are companies that put out cheap, shoddy
products, relying on the fact that few people will complain or take
the trouble to return the items, and that the market is large enough
that they can make money for years before they run out of customers
who don't know how poor their quality is. Why doesn't reputation
seem to work in such cases? Is this a case of so-called market failure?

D: Well, there's a place for shoddy goods. People calculate costs and
benefits subjectively. Maybe junk is all the buyer can afford. Maybe
the buyer plans on just using it once and then discarding it. Maybe
it's just part of the buyer's learning process. For instance, I hate cheap
suits, but I've bought them when I didn't know any better. Cops
prefer them, however, since getting in a fight, which they often do, is
a sure way to ruin a good suit; and if they owned a good one, their
fellows would assume they were on the take.

My view is that I'd rather have one good suit than three crappy
ones. One good lawyer than a dozen shysters, one good doctor, friend,
whatever, than a dozen mediocre ones. Quality is what counts. But
it's a question of both having judgment in figuring out what "quality" is and having the means to procure it.

Of course, there are companies that take advantage of novices,
the unwary, the fools, and the greedy, by misrepresenting their wares.
But that's to be expected. Pareto's Law dictates that if 80 percent of

businessmen are honest, then 20 percent might be iffy, and 20 percent of that 20 percent are scoundrels. Generally, the scamsters prey on the fools, the greedy, the novices, and the unwary. It's a naturally balanced ecosystem. And if you try to protect idiots from themselves, even if you succeed, you just wind up filling the world with idiots.

And that's what government does. The problem, as is so often the case, is when the state sticks its nose into the situation, as when government regulators assure people that minimal standards are met. This gives companies an excuse for doing as little as they can get away with—and legal protection from claims in court—because they can show that they met the government's minimum requirements. That's why the FDA should be renamed the Federal Death Authority, because they kill more people every year (through vastly raising costs, distorting tests and usages, and slowing approvals, among other things) than the Defense Department does in a typical decade. The SEC should be called the Swindlers Encouragement Confabulation, since they don't just increase costs immensely, but make John Q. Public think someone is actually protecting them.

Regulation creates an environment in which reputation is less important because consumers think the government is protecting them. They think they don't have to worry about it, so they don't. If this weren't the case—if people knew they had to rely on their own judgment, experience, and expertise, as well as that of sources they trust—reputation would become much more important in all markets around the world. Having a reputation for striving for the highest standards of business ethics, as well as in quality of products or services, would become a powerful competitive advantage and regulating force. So government regulation doesn't protect the consumer, it really just makes things easier for the swindler.

L: Pretty grim. But I'm an optimist. As we progress into the twenty-first century, people and capital alike are becoming more mobile. That means that more and more people can essentially shop for governments, based on their reputations, tax rates, corruption, et cetera. You're doing it by moving to Argentina. Others are headed for Thailand, Panama, Switzerland, Costa Rica, et cetera. Eventually, it may dawn on even the densest politicians that they are going to have to compete for customers. Tax slaves evolve into voluntary fee payers.

D: In my dreams. At the moment, it seems things are going the other way: All over the world, people seem to be clamoring for the magic cornucopia of government to kiss things and make them better. They'll get what they deserve, good and hard.

L: One way or the other, we'll see as this century unfolds. But okay, back to ethical investing—like the fad for not buying shares in companies that did business in South Africa during the apartheid years. Or not investing today in companies that would ever, ever hurt cute furry creatures in the Amazon rain forest. That's what you mean?

D: Exactly, and I have to say that this type of ethical investing is bunk. To me, it's nothing but another form of political correctness, which we've already discussed. It's complete nonsense. It's the type of thinking that's resulted in Warren Buffett and Bill Gates encouraging other billionaires to give away half their money to charity while they are still alive. These people are idiot savants—excellent at their businesses, but fools outside of their narrow spheres.

L: And we all know what you think about charities.

D: That's the polite version. Conventional charitable giving is an entirely stupid, counterproductive, and perverse idea. If the goal is to improve the lot of their fellow human beings, conventional philanthropists are achieving just exactly the opposite by giving their money to charities, which only serve to dissipate that wealth so it can no longer be put to productive use.

Green investing is just as stupid, mired in the same moral morass. Investing with *any* criteria in mind other than maximizing return is, by definition, rewarding inferiority—or mediocrity, at best. Putting wealth to any use other than maximizing its growth is to squander it, to the detriment of the person who accumulated the wealth, all those he or she might employ, and humanity at large. And charity often damages its recipients even more, by making them feel entitled, just because they're poor, unlucky, incompetent, or whatever.

The best thing to do with your money—from an ethical, economic, and social point of view—is to deploy it in such a way as to make more money, that is to say, that it makes more wealth. When you increase the amount of wealth in the world, *everybody* benefits.

People who invest in these so-called ethical funds do so because it makes them feel good, perhaps assuaging their guilt if they've bought into the whole "money is the root of all evil" nonsense. Or, more accurately, hatred of the "love of money," which is actually even more pernicious. Maybe they actually believe it will save the planet.

L: I guess they didn't agree with George Carlin when he said the earth doesn't need their help.

[The video linked to above contains strong language.]

D: George Carlin was a genius; I love all his stuff on YouTube. But "green" investing is a *stupidity*, in the specific sense of that word I favor: an unwitting tendency toward self-destruction. It's absolute idiocy. It shows that these people know nothing about ethics or economics, or investing. Or the environment, for that matter. I'll go further. These people don't love the environment, so much as they just have a covert—and sometimes even overt—hatred for other people, no matter that they try to disguise it by mouthing benevolent sounding platitudes.

L: Okay, but it's their money. If so-called ethical investing is as stupid as you say it is—you could think of it as a self-imposed stupidity tax—doesn't that make it self-correcting? Anyone foolish enough to do this will deprive himself or herself (and his or her heirs) of the means for funding other really stupid ideas?

D: Maybe so; Darwinian principles should result in their being culled from the gene pool. They're certainly at its shallow end. But they've probably already passed on their genes by the time they're thinking of dissipating capital. The memes they promote, on the other hand, are even more virulent, propelled by squandered wealth. I'm not sure what you can do about that, other than have conversations like this and try to spread positive ideas around to nullify the destructive ones. It seems as if the good guys are losing the battle at the moment.

L: Well, the night before King Arthur's final battle with his son Mordred, when Arthur was in despair about the failure of his round table to improve society and prevent war, Merlyn told him that no one can really be saved from anything. The only thing one can really do to improve the world is to add to the pool of ideas. That way ideas conflict—with each other and reality—and over time the better ideas survive, raising the whole aggregate of the human condition.

[L is referring to T.H. White's version of the Arthurian saga, specifically *The Book of Merlyn*, part of the tale of *The Once and Future King*.]

D: I'll second that emotion. Looked at over the long term, there's cause for optimism, I suppose. Mankind has risen from the primeval ooze, and a world of 100 percent theft, to a reasonable level of technology and perhaps just 50 percent theft—if you look at the government's percentage of the GDP as a proxy for theft. The real problem seems to be the psychological aberrations seemingly ingrained in the human psyche. A pity, really. But the majority of human characteristics are good.

L: So, this might be a bit of a tangent from business ethics, but what the heck—it's interesting. What do you do when you're at the end of your rope? You're not going to give the money to charity, and you won't be around much longer to keep us producing more wealth. What do you do with it?

D: Well, you're certainly at liberty to disperse it to the four winds, with high living. But if you don't consume it all, you're going to have to put it under the management of *someone*. So, you'd better choose that someone as wisely as you can.

Obviously, that's almost *never* a foundation of any kind—especially not one of the big, popular foundations. They are bastions of politically correct stupidity, and the type of people who serve on their boards should never be given a lot of money to play with. They shouldn't even be given a little money to play with. Those types are generally just political hacks, highly conventional, mostly concerned with their position in the social pecking order. Wealth shouldn't be played with; it should be kept whole and focused on creating more wealth. At least if you care about other people and the future.

L: What about foundations with missions written out explicitly to honor the donor's intent, and created with sunset clauses that require the foundation to go out of existence after working on and spending (investing) the money into whatever the donors believe in?

D: It doesn't matter. First of all, who's to say the donor won't be as harebrained as Buffett and Gates? Anyway, entropy conquers everything. All systems have their flaws, and they all wind down. Once you're gone, the board will find legal loopholes to take advantage of; they will wrench the wealth away from fulfilling your intent. I suspect Ford, Rockefeller, and Carnegie—not that I consider them models—would roll over in their graves if they saw what was done with their wealth. Foundations are just not a good idea; most often, they are disastrous ideas. Their only redeeming feature is that they deny revenue to the state because of their tax-free status.

L: Okay. No surprise there. What about children? You don't have any, but most people do, and that's a natural thought for them.

D: Well, even if I did have kids, there's no guarantee I'd end up with one I trusted to run with the family business—or even with any I liked. I know several brilliant, successful people with children I wouldn't trust to run a lemonade stand. It's a total genetic and environmental crapshoot what you end up with.

And if giving money to a foundation that might drift from your instructions for the wealth is a bad idea, leaving your wealth to children who did nothing to create it, know nothing about how to increase it, and don't deserve to squander it, is just as bad an idea. Of course leaving it to your kids is ideal if they're worthy of it. My suggestion is that you at least make a proper education available to them to increase the odds they turn out right. But you never know. Look at Marcus Aurelius—his son was Commodus. Or Nero, who was tutored by Seneca.

Speaking of which, I like the Roman approach much better: Choose your heir from among those you know. Pick whoever you judge to be the most sound, ethical, and competent. You may not necessarily even like him. But if he's the one who'll do the best job of keeping the ball rolling and growing, he's the one you want.

L: Or her.

D: Or her. Or maybe, for lack of a better alternative, instead of giving it to anyone, invest it in a profitable company. You could buy the shares in a company that you really believe is creating wealth and has the best chances for continuing to do so, and bequeath the shares to the company in your will—a sort of free buyback.

The essence of the question is whether you're interested in improving the general state of the human race—really eliminating poverty, improving nutrition, education, medical care, and what have you—or just indulging your idiosyncrasies and playing big shot on the charity circuit. If it's the former, then you must invest money and make it grow; there's no other alternative that's even close.

L: You don't generally invest in big companies, so I guess you'd pick some entrepreneurial small company with management you really believe in. That's a bit like the Roman idea, again.

D: That's true. If you choose wisely, the small company will grow faster. As companies grow, they all eventually become victims of entropy and bureaucracy, and end up like General Motors: run into the ground by brain-dead suits. But that process can take decades and in the meantime can create a lot of wealth. But if you put it in a foundation, it's a guaranteed automatic write off. And, worse, maybe it will show a negative return, since most foundations are actually destructive, giving money to promote destructive memes and support human weasels and cockroaches.

L: So, it's all building sand castles in the surf.

D: Yes, it is. The good news is that in 1,000 years, what you do with your money won't amount to a hill of beans anyway. But that's the danger with taking a long-term view, I suppose.

L: But you know, if you build your sandcastle well enough, even if it's doomed, it can give you time to build the next one, even bigger and better, and that one can give you time to build the next one, and so on. So, progress is possible in the face of the ever-corrosive effects of entropy.

D: You may be right. In which case the second law of thermodynamics can be beaten, if only for a while. And we've got to fill those idle hours somehow.

Chapter 22

Doug Casey on the Morality of Money

February 8, 2012

Louis: Doug, every time we have a conversation, I ask you about the investment implications of your ideas, and we consider ways to turn the trends you see into profits. The assumption is that's what people want to hear from you, since you're the guru of financial speculation. But this, your known status as a wealthy man, the fact that you have no children, and other things may lead some people to form an incorrect conclusion about you—that "all you care about is money." So let's talk about money. Is it all you care about?

Doug: I think anyone who has read our conversation giving advice to people just starting out in life (or re-starting) knows that the answer is no. Or the conversation we had in which we discussed Scrooge McDuck, one of the great heroes of literature. However, I have to stop before we start and push back: If money were all I cared about, so what? Would that really make me a bad person?

L: I've grokked Ayn Rand's "money speech," so you know I won't say yes, but maybe you should expand on that for readers who haven't absorbed Rand's ideas.

D: I'm a huge fan of Rand; she was an original and a genius. But just because someone like her, or me, sees the high moral value of money, that doesn't mean that it's all that important to them. In fact, I find money less and less important as time goes by, the older I get. Perhaps that's a function of Maslow's hierarchy: If you're hungry, food is all you really care about; if you're freezing, then it's warmth, and so forth. If you have enough money, these basics aren't likely to be problems.

My most enjoyable times have had absolutely nothing to do with money. Like a couple times in the past when I hopped freight trains with a friend, once to Portland and once to Sacramento. Each trip took three days and nights, each was full of adventure and weird experiences, and each cost about zero. It was liberating to be out of the money world for a few days. But it was an illusion. Somebody had to get the money to buy the food we ate at missions. Still, it's nice to live in a dream world for a while.

Sure, I'd like more money, if only for the same genetic reason a squirrel wants more nuts to store for the winter. The one common denominator of all living creatures is one word: Survive! And, as a medium of exchange and store of value, money represents survival— it's much more practical than nuts.

L: Some people might say that if money was your highest value, you might become a thief or murderer to get it.

D: Not likely. I have personal ethics, and there are things I won't do.

Besides, crime—real crime, taking from or harming others, not law-breaking, which is an entirely different thing—is for the lazy, short-sighted, and incompetent. In point of fact, I believe crime doesn't pay, notwithstanding the fact that Jon Corzine of MF Global is still at large. Criminals are self-destructive. It's a subject I'm writing an essay about—evil, stupidity, sociopaths, and the fate of America— for this month's *Casey Report*.

Anyway, what's the most someone could take, robbing their local bank? Perhaps $10,000? That's only enough to make a wager with Mitt Romney, although I've always heard Mormons weren't allowed to gamble.

But that leads me to think about the subject. In the old days, when Jesse James or other thieves robbed a bank, all the citizens would turn out to engage them in a gun battle in the streets. Why? Because it was actually their money, not the bankers'. It was just being stored in the bank; a robbed bank had immense personal consequences for everyone in a town. Today, nobody gives a damn if a bank is robbed; they'll get their money back from a U.S. government agency. The bank has become impersonal; most aren't even locally owned. And your deposit has been packaged up into some unfathomable security nobody is responsible for. The whole system has become corrupt. It degrades the very concept of money. This relates to why kids don't save coins in piggy banks any more—it's because they're no longer coins with value, they're just tokens, essentially worthless. All of U.S. society is about as sound as the dollar now.

Actually, it can be argued that robbing a bank isn't nearly as serious a crime today as robbing a candy store of $5. Why? Nobody in particular loses in the robbery of today's socialized banks. But the candy merchant has to absorb the $5 loss personally. Anyway, if you want to rob a bank today, you don't use a gun. You become part of management and loot the shareholders through outrageous salaries, stock options, and bonuses, among other things. I truly dislike the empty suits that fill most boardrooms today.

But most people are mostly honest—it's the 80/20 rule again. So, no, I think this argument is a straw man. The best way to make money is to create value. If I personally owned Apple as a private company, I'd be making more money—completely honestly—than many governments, and they are the biggest thieves in the world.

L: No argument.

D: Notice one more thing: Making money honestly means creating something *other* people, not you, value . The more money I want, the more I have to think about what other people want, and find better, faster, cheaper ways of delivering it to them. The reason someone is poor—and, yes, I know all the excuses for poverty—is that the poor do not produce more than they consume. Or if they do, they don't save the surplus.

L: The productive make things other people want: Adam Smith's invisible hand.

D: Exactly. Selfishness, in the form of the profit motive, guides people to serve the needs of others far more reliably, effectively, and efficiently than any amount of haranguing from priests, poets, or politicians. They tend to be profoundly anti-human, actually.

L: People say money makes the world go around, and they are right. Or, as I tell my students, there are two basic ways to motivate and coordinate human behavior on a large scale: coercion and persuasion. Government is the human institution that is based on coercion. The market is the one based on persuasion. Individuals can sometimes persuade others to do things for love, charity, or other reasons, but to coordinate voluntary cooperation society-wide, you need the price system of a profit-driven market economy. That's how money makes the world go around.

D: And that's why it doesn't matter how smart or well-intended politicians may be. Political solutions are always detrimental to society over the long run, because they are based in coercion.

If governments lacked the power to compel obedience, they would cease to be governments. No matter how liberal, there's always a point at which it comes down to force—especially if anyone tries to opt out and live by their own rules. Even if people try that in the most peaceful and harmonious way with regard to their neighbors, the state cannot allow separatists to secede. The moment it grants that right, every different religious, political, social, or even artistic group might move to form its own enclave, and the state disintegrates. I'd say that's wonderful—for everybody but the parasites who rely on the state—which is why serious secession movements almost always become violent.

I'm actually mystified at why most people not only just tolerate the state, but seem to love it. They're enthusiastic about it. Sometimes that makes me pessimistic about the future.

L: Reminds me of the conversation we just had on Europe disintegrating. But let's stay on topic. So you're saying that money is a positive moral good in society because the pursuit of it motivates the creation of value, because it's the bridge between selfishness and social good and because it's the basis for voluntary cooperation, rather than coerced interaction. Anything else?

Doug: Yes, but first, let me say one more thing about the issue of selfishness—the virtue of selfishness—and the vice of altruism. Ayn

Rand might never forgive me for saying this, but if you take the two concepts—ethical self-interest and concern for others—to their logical conclusions, they actually are the same. It's in your selfish best interest to provide the maximum amount of value to the maximum number of people—that's how Apple became the giant company it is. Conversely, it is *not* altruistic to help other people. I want all the people around me to be strong and successful. It makes life better and easier for me if they're all doing well. So it's selfish, not altruistic, when I help them.

To weaken others, to degrade them by making them dependent upon generosity, as we discussed in our conversation on charity, is not doing those people any good. If you really care about others, the best thing you can do for them is to push for totally freeing all markets. That makes it both necessary and rewarding for them to learn valuable skills and to become creators of value, and not burdens on society. It's a win-win all around.

L: That'll bend some people's minds. So, what was the other thing?

D: Well, referring again to our conversation on charity, the accumulation of wealth is in and of itself an important social as well as a personal good.

L: Remind us.

D: The good to individuals of accumulating wealth is obvious, but the social good often goes unrecognized. Put simply, progress requires capital. Major new undertakings, from hydropower dams to spaceships to new medical devices and treatments, require huge amounts of capital. If you're not willing to extract that capital from the population via the coercion of taxes (i.e., steal it), you need wealth to accumulate in private hands to pay for these things.

In other words, if the world is going to improve, we need huge pools of capital, intelligently invested. We need as many obscenely rich people as possible.

L: Right then. So, money is all good—nothing bad about it at all?

D: Unfortunately, many of the rich people in the world today didn't get their money by real production. They got it by using political connections and slopping at the trough of the state. That's bad. When I look at how some people have gotten their money—Clinton, Pelosi, and all the politically connected bankers and brokers, just for a start— I can understand why the poor want to eat the rich.

But money itself isn't the problem. Money is just a store of value and a means of exchange. What is bad about that? Gold, as we've discussed many times, happens to be the best form of money the market has ever produced: It's convenient, consistent, durable, divisible, has intrinsic value (it's the second-most reflective and conductive metal, the most nonreactive, the most ductile, and the most malleable of all metals), and can't be created out of thin air. Those are gold's attributes. People attribute all sorts of other silly things to gold, and poetic critics talk about the evils of the lust for gold. But it's not the gold itself that's evil—it's the psychological aberrations and weaknesses of unethical people that are the problem. The critics are fixating on what is merely a tool, rather than the ethical merits or failures of the people who use the tool and are responsible for the consequences of their actions.

L: Sort of like the people who repeat foolish slogans like "guns kill," as though guns sprout little feet when no one is looking and run around shooting people all by themselves.

D: Exactly. They're the same personality type—busybodies who want to enforce their opinions on everyone else. They're dangerous and despicable. Yet they somehow posture as if they had the high moral ground.

L: Okay, so even if you cared only for money, that could be seen as a good thing. But you do care for more—like what?

D: Well, money is a tool—the means to achieve various goals. For me, those goals include fine art, wine, cars, homes, horses, cigars, and many other physical things. But it also gives me the ability to do things I enjoy or value, like spend time with friends, go to the gym, lie in the sun, read books, and do pretty much what I want when I want. Let's just call it as philosophers do: "the good life." It's why my partners and I built La Estancia de Cafayate. We're having several events down there in March that I'd like to welcome readers to.

But I don't take money too seriously. It's just something you *have*. It's much less important than what you *do*, and trivial in comparison to what you *are*. I could be happy being a hobo. As I said on that in the conversation on fresh starts, there have been times when I felt my life was just as good and I was just as happy without much money at all. That said, you can't be too rich or too thin.

L: Very good. Investment implications?

D: This may all seem rather philosophical, but it's actually extremely important to investors. What is the purpose of investing or speculating? To make money. How can anyone hope to do that well if they feel that there is something immoral or distasteful about making money?

Someone who pinches his or her nose and tries anyway because making money is a necessary evil will never do as well as those who throw themselves into the fray with gusto and delight in doing something valuable—and doing it well.

L: The law of attraction.

D: Yes, but I don't view the law of attraction as a metaphysical force— rather as a psychological reality. If you have a negative attitude about something, you're unlikely to attract it, even if you try to talk yourself into thinking the opposite.

L: Okay, but that's not a stock pick.

D: Sure. We're talking basics here. No stock picks today, just a PSA: If you think money is evil, don't bother trying to accumulate wealth. On the other hand, if you want to become wealthy, you'd better think long and hard about your attitudes about money, work through the thoughts above and those you can find in the rest of our conversations via the links we provide. Cultivate a positive attitude about money, which is right up there with language as one of the most valuable tools man has ever invented. Think about it, and give yourself permission to become rich. It's a good thing.

L: Very well. Thanks for what I hope will prove to be a very thought-provoking conversation!

D: My pleasure. Talk to you next week.

Chapter 23

Doug Casey:
Bah! Humbug!

October 13, 2010

Louis: Happy Canadian Thanksgiving, Doug. But you're an atheist, and you pay for your own meals, so whom do you give thanks to, if anyone?

Doug: Yes, I guess it's getting to be that time of year. Holidays can be fun, regardless of one's beliefs, and for the record, neither you nor Bob Cratchit have to work Christmas Eve.

L: I probably will anyway. I celebrate the New Year, and sometimes raise a glass to Sir Isaac Newton, whose birthday was December 25, but not Christmas.

D: Why is that? I know you're an atheist as well, but you also call yourself a student of the carpenter of Nazareth, so why not celebrate his birthday?

L: You're right. I'm what you might call an Atheist Christian; I don't believe in any gods, but I do find great value in what Jesus actually said and taught, which was to love, forgive, and let live. That's quite different from what many modern churches teach, which is to fear and to try to control the behavior of others. Such people often have no qualms about employing the coercive machinery of the state to impose their values on others, which Jesus never did nor advocated—his slate was clean, and yet he cast no stones.

But to answer your question, ever since I was a teenager, I've thought Christmas, at least as practiced in most of the West, is a bad idea. It all revolves around a massive conspiracy of lies aimed at controlling children. I never wanted to control my children; I wanted to help them learn self-control. I decided long before I had any children that I would never lie to mine. That's bad psychology. I wanted my children—whatever else they might come to think—to always regard me as a reliable source of information. And 23 years after the first was born, they all still do.

Plus, if you think about it, Santa Claus is basically God on training wheels. He's omniscient—knows if you've been bad or good—and punishes or rewards you accordingly. If I believed in a god, this would seem like a bad idea to me, as children come to first discover that Santa does *not* know everything, and then find out the whole thing is a scam. The collapse of the Santa conspiracy sows seeds of doubt as to the supernatural, not to mention distrust of parents.

D: But you didn't send your kids back to school having to confront their peers after receiving no presents.

L: Of course not. We enjoyed the holiday songs and stories, I just never told my children they were *true*. They were fun fantasies like Curious George or Batman. I buy trees and decorate them, but I call them New Year's trees, and we give each other presents on New Year's Eve.

Later, when I started making friends in former Soviet countries, I found that the Soviets had done essentially the same thing; Marx said religion was the "opium of the masses," after all.

It was a slightly embarrassing discovery for a staunch capitalist to make, but a good joke on me. At any rate, we're here to talk about *your* take on all this. Are you a Grinch?

D: I've never read that story, nor watched the cartoon all the way through, to be honest with you.

L: But you've heard of *How the Grinch Stole Christmas!* by Dr. Seuss? You know what I mean by Grinch?

D: Yes.

L: So, are you a Grinch? What do you do when you're visiting someone during the holidays and they bow their heads to say grace?

D: I listen respectfully, but then I always ask if I can say grace, too. They usually say, "Well, of course!" And the grace I usually say is either to Odin, who's a favorite myth of mine, and sometimes to Crom, who was the god of Conan the Barbarian. "Oh Crom, help us to slay our enemies, ravish their women, burn their houses and enslave their children—and if you won't help us, then to hell with you." That always sets the tone for an excellent dinner conversation.

L: I've actually been present at a nice dinner in an expensive restaurant when you did this, and it was in the predominantly Catholic country of Argentina. But, to be fair, the dinner was with old cronies of yours, who know very well how you like to stir things up. Have you ever actually done that in a group of total strangers?

D: Yes, I have, with entertaining results. As you know, I'm a great believer in entertainment and refuse to waste much time talking about the weather and the roads. The next subject is philosophy. But abstract, theoretical philosophy is not very entertaining, so that leaves practical philosophy: politics and religion.

L: The two forbidden subjects. I should have known. But you know, in addition to people who wrote after our last conversation to say that you are wrong about the Tea Party, we got letters from people who said that you contradicted yourself, saying you don't make fun of religion, and in the next breath speaking of parroting and chimpanzees. I replied that if they would look carefully at what you said, it was not the religion you were poking fun at, but at dogma, at the religious-flavored groupthink that can be so dangerous. I don't think I've ever heard you criticize Jesus or his teachings. Churches are another matter entirely. Churches are *human* organizations, run by fallible human beings, with their own ends in mind. Churches can and should be held up for scrutiny and criticism, just like any other human institution.

D: I admit that many of Jesus' words were very wise. But Paul took over as his promoter after Jesus died, and many of Paul's ideas were very different from Jesus's. Paulism is really an entirely different religion from Jesusism, though they've become conflated in modern Christianity.

L: I agree, and Jesus also brought a "new covenant" that set aside much of the Old Testament, so the frequent citations of the Old Testament as grounds for persecuting homosexuals or other religions also run counter to the teachings of Jesus, in my view. I like looking at what Jesus is reported to have actually said and done, himself—not Paul, and not Moses.

D: Some readers might be surprised to know that I've actually read the Bible and made a study of many religions. The more I learn of them all, the less I'm inclined to believe any one of them. However, if we define religion as a quest for some form of spiritual reality, I certainly don't in any way denigrate or make fun of religion. Unfortunately, that's not how most people approach religion; for many, it's a balm for their fears and miseries, rather than a possible path to enlightenment.

L: I can see that. But we digress. The topic today was holidays. So, if you don't believe in holiness, what do you do on holy days, and why?

D: I'm a big fan of the winter solstice and the summer solstice. Those are important turning points for life on this planet, and worth celebrating. Presents are nice; it's fine to give things to people you like. Even the shared traditions of society can be nice, though I have to say that the religious significance of many of these holidays has been totally lost to the commercial events they have become. In point of fact, by Christian tradition, Easter is the holiest of holidays, not Christmas, but all most people think of at that time are bunnies, chocolates, and colored eggs.

L: So, you're not a Grinch. Reindeer and blinking lights are okay?

D: You can even find them in some predominantly Muslim countries, and that's fine. It's good wintertime fun.

L: I suppose societies need periodic celebrations, in one form or another.

D: Yes, but there's a dark side to what we call the holiday season in the West, at which time people are supposed to celebrate happiness. That's a problem for unhappy people.

L: Which is why there's said to be so much trouble with alcoholism, increased suicide rates, and such during the holidays.

D: Yes, and even generally happy people can feel increased stress from the increasing financial demands of the season. It's becoming like the potlatch tradition of the Northwestern Indians, where gift giving is a very strong social expectation. That can be problematic in hard times, when extra cash for buying nice presents for others can be tough to come by. In Dickens's days, there was no expectation that you'd buy presents for everyone you know if you were a Cratchit. Today, it's becoming an embarrassment to go see anyone during the holidays without a gift in hand.

L: Some people might rather stay home, not wanting to seem like a Scrooge.

D: Now there's something I do object to: Scrooge has become a power-fully destructive meme loose in society. Dickens was a social critic of the Victorian age, perhaps rightly so in many ways, but his attack on the creative power of wealth in the form of his caricature, Scrooge, is misleading and harmful.

L: There was great injustice in the Victorian era, and to all accounts much inhuman treatment of poor people by the wealthy, though that was hardly a Victorian invention. But the wealthy, back then, were also usually the aristocracy, with hereditary titles and power. I've long thought that the problem lay in the legal power—coercive power—the wealthy had over others, not their wealth, per se.

Since then, there have been changes, including a huge though incomplete separation between the noncoercive power of money and the coercive power of the state. But people still conflate wealth with coercion and various personality traits that have nothing to do with wealth.

D: Such as?

L: Many people believe stereotypes, reinforced by Hollywood and other cultural sources, that rich people are obsessed with money, care only about money, are greedy, and [are] completely lacking in generosity. Nice people don't care about money. Rich people are mean, and being mean is how you get rich.

But it's not true. I've made a study of this. All the really wealthy people I know got that way by creating enormous value. I know one of the first guys to set up "sweatshops" in China, enabling peo-ple who had few choices other than prostitution and destitution to work in clean buildings—albeit for long hours—at better pay than they could get anywhere else. I know another fellow who saw a trading pattern and developed a system to take advantage of it and then sold it to Goldman Sachs for $125 million. And more—all were passionate about creating something of value, and that's what led to great wealth. Most started with nothing more than anyone else, and even the few that were born with silver spoons in their mouths took the money they started with and turned it into a *lot* more money. And none of them think the most fun thing to do on weekends is to evict poverty-stricken people from their homes.

I found that rich people do think about money; they understand it, invest it, put it to work for them. But it seems to me that poor people spend a lot more time thinking about money, precisely because they have so little of it; managing every penny is critically important. Poverty is not bliss, which is why people struggle so hard to escape it. They are not idiots fooled by Madison Avenue advertising executives; they're *poor*, and they know that's no fun.

D: That's right. As you know, I've pointed out in all my books that the key to accumulating wealth is to pay attention to these very things. Produce more than you consume, so you have money to invest in creating more wealth. Maybe the Calvinists were on to something, with their notion that visible wealth was a sign of inward grace; they figured God must think you're doing something right if he rewarded you with wealth.

That brings my mind back to Scrooge, not Dickens's Scrooge, but Uncle Scrooge, who, in my view, is a totally sound character.

L: I'm familiar with Scrooge McDuck, but not all of our readers might be, so perhaps you should fill them in on the Disney reference.

D: Donald Duck is better known, but he had three nephews and a phenomenally wealthy uncle of his own, named Scrooge McDuck. Uncle Scrooge is one of the great heroes of Western literature. He's a miser, but he's innovative and an adventurer, with a very good heart. That's shown in all of the stories about him. He didn't have to be transformed, as Dickens's Scrooge had to be; rather, it was an essential part of his character. I remember one story in which he took Donald and the boys on an adventure to Alaska—he was always taking Donald and the boys on fantastic adventures all around the world—and had to make a choice between saving his sled dog, Barko, and saving the sled, which had a treasure on it. He chose the dog, which was typical of him.

This is a positive image, one I wish was much more celebrated than Dickens's caricature.

L: And he created value. How many jobs did Scrooge McDuck create, feeding families all around the world? He had mines, as I recall, and factories and office buildings—always clean and modern.

D: That's exactly right. Scrooge McDuck embodies the true, creative, life-giving spirit of the holiday, if you ask me.

L: [Laughs] You don't have children—do you actually deck the halls?

D: Well, I'll be in Buenos Aires this time, and it's a bit odd to decorate a tree with tinsel or fake snow in the middle of South American summer, but sure, I'll get a tree. Why not?

L: So, when people sneer at you for being a rich Scrooge, your reply, with pride, is: "Yes, but Scrooge McDuck!"

D: Right. The right Scrooge, the sound one, is my model.

L: And, in a way, that's exactly what we strive to help people achieve in their own lives, through our newsletters. _The Casey Report_ sets out the sound philosophical and economic basis for everything, plus investment ideas. The energy, technology, and metals letters offer even more specific guidance for accumulating McDuck-like wealth. We're the Scrooge Academy.

D: The more the merrier.

L: Okay then, that's what I'm giving thanks for this year: Scrooge Academy.

Chapter 24

Doug Casey on Art
(Part One)

January 12, 2011

Editor's Note: Skype rings, I answer. It's Doug, calling from Punta del Este.

Louis: Doug, how are you? And how were the holidays? Was Punta hopping?

Doug: Actually, yes. Especially Christmas. I went to Christmas dinner at the house of a Jewish friend down here. At midnight, even though dessert hadn't been served, we went out to his backyard, where he set off a professional quality fireworks display—skyrockets, explosives, the same stuff you see at stadiums in the United States. Then one of his next door neighbors started, then another, then another. Everyone was in competition for the best display.

L: What? In their backyards?

D: I love the smell of gunpowder on Christmas; it's the smell of a free country. I like a place where everyone is expected to have stuff that they'd call in a SWAT team for in the United States. But that's just some local color; everybody from Buenos Aires comes over to go to the beach this time of year. But, actually, I called to talk about art. Partly because Punta has scores of art galleries.

L: Well, last week I said we should talk about something more positive, but why art?

D: Perhaps because art is one of the most positive things about life itself. It's really about aesthetics, a very important part of human existence. We talk a lot about philosophy here, and that's important. Aesthetics is actually a division of philosophy, and art can make philosophy . . . concrete. If one picture is worth 1,000 words, then art can visually describe the way you see the world. The kind of art you like can describe the way you think the world is, or should be. A good sense of aesthetics is as important as having a well-developed intellect, in my opinion.

L: Or it should be. Okay, let's start with a definition. My Webster's says aesthetics is the branch of philosophy that deals with the nature of beauty, art, and taste, and with the creation and appreciation of beauty. Why is this so important now, with the world in a deepening crisis of historic proportions?

D: Humans have always placed a high value on aesthetics, even in the worst of times. There's plenty of evidence the hunter-gatherers of prehistory took time out of their fight for survival to create art, and that has continued throughout history and continues today. This pursuit of beauty is a defining characteristic of what it means to be human. One of the main purposes of being wealthy is to be able to live in an aesthetic environment. The reason notorious misers like Hetty Greene are considered so shameful and bent is that they didn't have a clue what to do with their money; they confuse the means, money, with the end: an aesthetic life. Warren Buffett is almost in that class; he's an idiot savant generally, but he certainly appears to have no sense of aesthetics. On the other hand, some of the poorest people in the world strive to be as beautiful as they can, and to own what small pieces of beauty they can; this alone makes them worthy of respect. A brute with no sense of beauty, nor appreciation for it, can barely be called human.

Really good art distills an intense experience or emotion. The ongoing crisis will create many intense experiences for many artists, and may result in some very powerful works of art—although that's just conjecture on my part. I'm not sure what correlation actually exists between various world crises and great art. A sure bet, though, is that the Greater Depression will probably put all sorts of art on sale, as belt-tightening cuts nonessentials from peoples budgets. Maslow's hierarchy will become much more apparent than has been the case in recent years.

Food and shelter are essential, of course, but art is also essential. If you don't have any beauty in your life, what's the point?

L: I'm with you there. Life without beauty would be a torture. Death would seem like a reprieve, in comparison. So, do you consider yourself an artist? Or just a connoisseur?

D: The latter. I've always been interested in art, though I don't have any real skill at producing it. I wish I did! I've taken art lessons—painting—from several teachers both in the West and the Orient, but I'm not at all satisfied with my technical ability. A man's got to know his limitations.

L: So, what makes one a connoisseur? Isn't it a bit presumptuous to say what's "good art" and what is not? In speaking about movies, books, and especially music, we've said that art is a highly individualized experience. Doesn't it rub your anarchistic soul the wrong way to have some snooty expert from the Louvre or the Royal Museum tell you what's good art? Some of those clowns pay huge sums of money for blank canvases—or ones literally smeared with shit.

D: There's a lot of genuine garbage out there masquerading as art, but that tells you right there that there is such a thing as "good art." Going to school to study art or art history is a complete and total waste of time and money; these are things that you can, and should, be able to teach yourself, through reading and observing. As we observed in our discussion on education, there are very few Aristotles teaching in colleges today. So-called "higher education" is a veritable magnet for second-raters and actively destructive parasites bent on promoting unsound ideas to the inexperienced and gullible. They concentrate in areas like social studies, literature, and art—where opinion reigns supreme. And I find their opinions almost universally appalling.

I would never tell you what *you* must see as good art. *De gustibus non disputandum est.* Although I'd bet you and I would agree on most of it, simply because we share a very similar view of life, and what's important. It bears repeating that aesthetics is a division of philosophy, so what a person finds appealing usually offers a window into their soul. That means something. Every educated person should cultivate a practical education—familiarity, background, understanding, judgment—in various types of art. We've spoken about the value of literature, film, and music, and this includes visual arts, like painting and sculpture.

L: I remember looking at Picasso's Cubist paintings of women, as a child, and thinking they were ugly and Picasso was overrated. I liked da Vinci more, and romantic nineteeth-century painters even better. My dad is a real art-lover, and for some time, we used to go to art galleries almost every weekend; this resulted in my teachers' great astonishment in high school, when I could identify a Picasso, a Miro, or a Giacometti on sight. Anyway, I later saw some of Picasso's early drawings, done in simple pencil, but with photorealistic detail and perspective. Could have knocked me over with a feather—the man really did have talent, he just chose to use it to express something that was over my head, when I was a child.

D: He had immense talent and versatility. That said I'd never pay the premium to own a Picasso; like everything else in the material world, it's a matter of value, and cost/benefit ratios. The point is that if you know enough about art, you can start separating the poseurs from the real artists. After that, it gets pretty subjective.

L: So, what do you like?

D: I'm very particular about the art I buy. I personally like things that have a message of some significance, that tell me something about the way the world works. I've great respect for high technical ability as well; if the artist doesn't have excellent technical skill, he doesn't make the first cut. But technical skill alone is not enough. There are draftsmen, graphic designers, and commercial artists with excellent technical skills, but they're not actually artists worth buying, because they don't make a philosophical statement, they're not really trying to tell you how the world works, or ought to work. They're not taking a metaphysical position.

What this means, in practical terms, is that I tend not to buy landscapes, or simple portraits—things that could be done better by a skilled photographer. Which is not to say that a photographer can't also be an artist, but he has to capture reality, as opposed to create it from whole cloth.

There's no limit to the amount of art you can buy, other than your pocketbook and your storage space. So you usually wind up specializing. I've always been drawn to, and specialize in, surreal art, with a smattering of other approaches.

I've accumulated so much of this stuff over the years, I have a trailer full of it headed to Argentina right now. I've got lots of tall walls in all my places down here, so I've finally got room to display my art. I'm really looking forward to opening the container; it's going to be like discovering the art and buying all over again. Although I'm sure some will turn out to be disappointing, since I've become more discriminating over the years, and I no longer have to really look at the right side of the menu. Although, it must be emphasized, there's only a limited, even accidental, correlation between quality and price.

L: You get the excitement twice. Did you have this in mind, as you bought or built homes—you need lots of hallways or extra walls, just to have room to hang art?

D: I'm not big on hallways, but all my places have 12- to 14-foot ceilings, and wide open walls. Most of the paintings I have tend to be large. They probably average three by four feet, or larger. I hate little kitschy things.

L: Bathroom art?

D: Yeah. Small stuff tends to be nondynamic and kind of cheap-looking. Clutter. I like to go big or go home, generally, and in art too. I prefer things that I can look at from a distance, rather than be forced to scrutinize like a postage stamp.

L: Let's take an example. In the living room of your flat in Buenos Aires, you have a painting we've referenced before, the war painting. What's the story there?

D: I bought that in BA, a few years ago, just after the height of Argentina's financial crisis. I don't know the artist, and don't really care who he or she is. Although the price was absolutely right, that wasn't a factor, as I didn't buy it for an investment. And certainly not because I'm a fan of war. I do tend to like things that are intense, even disturbing. You'll never find one of those mass produced paintings of a house with a chimney in a forest vale—Thomas Kinkade—in my collection. The guy gets like $25,000 for them. Not because they're any good—I suspect even I could replicate them—but because he's a great marketer. Selling art isn't nearly so much about quality as it is about marketing. The same is true about investment advice, or almost anything.

L: I don't think anyone could look at that image and think it was pro-war. But that's interesting about art and marketing.

D: An observation I want to make about buying art is that the price of art is totally arbitrary. The cost of production of something like that war painting, which is about five by five feet, including the canvas, wood, paints, might be a couple hundred bucks—simply not significant compared to what you pay for it. But when you sell it, it's all about how badly the buyer wants it. You can sell a piece like that for anywhere from less than the cost of materials to over a million dollars.

L: So, why pay millions for a Picasso, when you can buy something by an unknown for 1,000 bucks that makes you feel just as strong a response?

D: Exactly. Especially for me, in that I really don't give a damn what the public in general, or art critics in particular, do or don't think. I, therefore, generally don't buy established artists. People who reflexively buy recognized artists impress me as the same kind of people who buy Ralph Lauren shirts, just to show they can afford Ralph Lauren shirts. Or, Goddess forbid, buy Tommy Hilfiger crap, where he displays his name boldly, because they somehow think it shows they have good taste—which, in my opinion, is just the opposite of the case.

L: Do you ever buy art as an investment?

D: No. Art prices are, much more than the prices of almost anything else, arbitrary and subject to fashion, promotion, and chimerical opinion. I don't buy art to make money on it; that's a real long shot. I buy from unknown artists whose work I just like. I'll never, ever be able to resell the stuff unless lightning strikes and the artist becomes popular, which usually happens because some clever gallery decides to promote him or her. It's a lot like buying real estate, but much worse. Even though it has speculative potential, I really only buy stuff I like myself. You can never be sure of a sale, so you better take pleasure just in owning it.

That actually applies to almost anything, even stocks. Don't buy something because you hope a greater fool will materialize. You must already know exactly who the fool is, in advance. It's like a poker game: If you can't pick out the fool at the table in five minutes, then you're the fool. It's very dangerous to buy on the "greater fool" theory; it's almost always much easier to buy just about anything than to sell it.

The last large purchase of art I made was in Zimbabwe, a couple years ago. I bought about 30 Shona stone sculptures, a small shipping container full of them. The Shona are renowned for their tradition of stone sculpture. Not marble, more like soapstone, but harder, and these are large pieces, typically a several hundred pounds. I paid about $30,000 for those 30 pieces, including shipping. That's a great price—I got 'em dead flat at the bottom when Zimbabwe's currency collapsed. What could I sell them for? Who knows? I could ask anything—put on a show, tell the story of the artists; if they caught on, they could easily go for $15,000 each. I could turn my $30,000 invested in Zim into a few hundred thousand dollars. But I'm not going to do that, because I actually like them. And I don't want to get into the business of hawking art, if only because I hate dealing with the public. Although, I have to admit that I don't have enough room to put 30 large sculptures.

L: Maybe you could add a sculpture garden to your new house in Cafayate?

D: Maybe. In fact, definitely. And some will make extraordinary gifts for certain friends. Another thing I did, which is usually a very bad idea, was to commission a work of art from my friend Barry Johnson in Washington, DC. He's a very competent classical sculptor, and some years ago, I had him sculpt a three-foot image of Lilith, and one of Icarus rising, gripped by a female figure who represents Mother Earth. Both in bronze, really beautiful. I paid about $1,000 for one, and $3,000 for the other, which was a lot more money then than it is today. Now, today, just casting costs would be several times as much, never mind his fee.

I remember buying a couple of paintings by a well-known Brazilian artist about 15 years ago, when Brazil was in one of its cyclical lows, back when you could also buy a nice apartment on Ipanema for $50,000. Brazil is in a boom now, incidentally, and I wouldn't touch it—it's unlikely to stay up where it is for long—but that's a discussion for a different day. I bought two large paintings, about four by four, for $1,000 each, including shipping to Colorado. I really love those. And they were a tremendous bargain, almost as good as one of those Ipanema apartments. You can find great art cheap, if you go look for it. It's best to go to a country in economic crisis.

These people who sit in New York and bid hundreds of thousands of dollars against each other, sometimes for total crap, are just not right in the head. They're unsophisticated buyers with no taste, but too much money, too recently acquired.

L: But it's trendy crap.

D: Very trendy crap. And a lot of it that doesn't end up in a landfill, should. Actually, it will. And I don't say that just because eventually everything gets folded into the mantle. And that's before the planet itself is subsumed into the sun. It's simply good to keep these things in perspective.

L: Okay, but these are unrealized gains. Have you ever actually sold any of the art you've bought?

D: No, even though I have enough to open a gallery. But I've never actually tried, if only because it would likely be futile for the reasons we've just discussed. I thought about it, however, and not as just a small scale hobby, but as a substantial business. Many years ago, the early 1970s, before the government totally destroyed Haiti—which happened well before the earthquake destroyed the government— Haiti was a famous source of great, cheap art. Most of it was crap, of course—Pareto's Law is always with us—but also good stuff, and the good stuff was very good. My idea was to use this supply as a source for restaurants that wanted real art in their décor. That would provide distribution on a scale to make a business that mattered. Now it's commonly done.

One other thing, from a business point of view, is that when I go to a city for the first time and need to get to know it and the key players in town, I check out the art galleries. I'm interested in art anyway, and knowledgeable, so I'd go to the galleries, meet the local people, and it was a very good way to get introduced to the local culture and the local movers and shakers in society. But this only works if you have a sincere interest in art.

This was part of my standard MO when I didn't know anyone in a city, which isn't true for many cities of any size or significance anymore. The other things we've talked about before include making appointments with lawyers, who were always happy to talk to foreign investors, real estate brokers, and, of course, I'd always go to the polo club. That pretty much covered all the bases. After a couple days, I knew all the people I'd need to know to move to any of those places and live comfortably, if I'd wanted to.

L: Makes sense. But let's back up a bit: Why is it a mistake to commission art?

D: Because you never really know what you're going to get, or if what you're hoping the artist is going to deliver is what's actually on his or her mind.

Chapter 25

Doug Casey on Art (Part Two)

January 19, 2011

Louis: Why is it a mistake to commission art?

Doug: Because you never really know what you're going to get, or if what you're hoping the artist is going to deliver is what's actually on his or her mind. These things shape themselves as they come into being—at least if you're dealing with a competent artist, and not just a craftsman. Unless you're a Medici dealing with a Michelangelo, and the sky's the limit, you just don't know if the result is going to appeal to you. I've been lucky with the pieces I've commissioned, like the two bronzes Barry Johnson made for me, but it's been pure dumb luck.

L: Perhaps so, and I don't have anywhere near the level of experience you do, but I have commissioned several works of art, including a jewelry box I had made for a lady once. The size and shape of the piece totally surprised me, but it was gorgeous, worked with stones, shells, and etched images that represented the two of us. It wasn't what I'd asked for; it was better. I've also commissioned paintings with similar results.

D: You were lucky too, then.

L: Is that really so? If you ask an artist whose work you love to do something on a theme that moves you, aren't you stacking the odds heavily in your favor?

D: Now that you mention it, I commissioned another sculpture I'm very pleased with. I once had 1,000 ounces of silver lying around, which I'd bought at about the $4 level, and I had a friend in Aspen, Charles Savione, who's a very competent sculptor and very into Buddhism as well, partly due to his martial arts background. So I asked him to turn my 1,000 ounces of silver into a Buddha. Which he did, and he gold-plated it as well. I really like it. He also made a series of bronze statues of the goddess Eris, mementos of the Eris Society.

So I suppose you're right; if you pick the right horse and jockey, you shouldn't be too surprised to do well in the race. But you never know—you just can't control the process once you initiate it. I know many people who've been very disappointed commissioning works of art. Maybe I'm just easy to please. It's safer just to buy completed works that you know you like. And there's such a vast amount of art out there, you don't really need to commission any.

L: Hm. Is there a difference in cost? As in, if an artist has a bunch of stuff gathering dust in his attic, she may sell it cheaper than if you ask her to make something—then she knows you really want it.

D: That's true. The price is set by supply and demand; Paul Gauguin and Toulouse-Lautrec were starving artists. An art speculator could have made millions buying their stuff when they needed some food or drink. Apart from that, there are norms in the business. For sculpture, unlike painting, material costs are significant, and the artist usually charges a fee equal to the foundry costs. In the case of my Buddha, a very nice piece of work, I've got about $15,000 in it. What could I sell it for? Who knows? What would someone pay for a large gold-plated, solid silver Buddha, if that's what he really wants?

L: Not to digress too far, but why the heck would you gold-plate something made of solid silver? Doesn't that sort of defeat the point of it being solid silver? Might as well gold-plate a Styrofoam Buddha; it would look the same.

D: Well, remember that silver tarnishes.

L: Ah, of course!

D: That was why we did it, but in retrospect, it was a mistake. For technical reasons, it's actually very hard to gold-plate silver. You have to lay down a layer of nickel first. More important, if some criminal saw that Buddha, it might just look and feel enough like solid gold that he might want to kill me for it. If he knew it was just silver, the cost/benefit ratio of committing a capital crime might not be as appealing—cost/benefit, risk/reward. It's a good thing most criminals are so stupid that the TV and the stereo would be higher on their "must steal" list.

L: So, you generally don't commission, you buy . . . what's in galleries? Don't they charge more?

D: Galleries usually mark up the art they are selling by a factor of about two or three. So, if you negotiate with the gallery, you can usually get about a third knocked off. That's especially so if you establish yourself as someone who knows his or her way around the art world. If a gallery doesn't want to negotiate, a good gambit is to go to a friend who owns a gallery, and have him buy it. Galleries will typically offer a 30 percent discount to each other as a professional courtesy.

L: Is it a buyer's market now with the global economy in the dumps? Nobody *has* to buy art, so it would seem that demand must be dropping well below supply these days.

D: It depends what and where. This, however, is an advantage of buying "name-brand" artists—there's a reasonably liquid market for well-known, expensive artists. But like I said, it's a very dangerous game to try to invest in art; you should treat art as a consumer good, and assume that once you buy it, you'll never be able to sell it.

That said, try not to buy, ever, when and where there's an economic boom going on. When money really starts flowing, a lot of it flows into the hands of artists, and when it stops, artists starve—that's the time to buy. I bought Chinese art 20 years ago; I wouldn't touch it now. Here in South America, where I am at the moment, high soybean, sugar, cotton, even cattle prices are producing a wave of increased prosperity, and people are buying art. Brazil in particular is a terrible place to buy art at the moment, and Argentina and Uruguay aren't much better.

L: Where would you go to buy art today?

D: Zimbabwe is still in the dumps; I'd go there if I needed more Shona sculpture, which I don't. But places like that. I have one friend, a World War II vet, who bought hundreds of pieces of old—seventeeth to nineteeth century—Spanish furniture during the Franco years. At the time it was considered unusable junk and cluttered barns; now it's viewed as irreplaceable antiques. Jean-Pierre Hallet describes in his book, *Congo Kitabu,* how he bought literally tons of Congolese sculpture during the 1950s, when nobody cared about the stuff. The problem is that the world has become much wealthier and more sophisticated over the past few decades. Russia had spectacular bargains after the fall of the Soviet Union. There are now few stones left unturned. If you want to speculate, I suggest waiting until the Greater Depression bottoms. That will be some time from now.

L: Where to look today—maybe Detroit?

D: Maybe, but it's hardly an epicenter of artistic activity, unless you want to count spray-painted walls on abandoned buildings. One place that isn't overly inflated is Cuba, where I've bought a number of paintings that are decorative, although nothing cosmic.

I'll tell you what the best single—very recent—place in the world for great, cheap art used to be, though I suspect it may be doing too well for that to be the case now: Vietnam, especially the north. It's certainly among the most art-oriented places on earth, in my experience—and excellent quality. You can go there and get extremely competent student artists to replicate great works—Raphael, Monet, Van Gogh, El Greco, you name it. They'll turn out a technically excellent copy on a price-per-square-inch basis.

This leads to an interesting philosophical question: Is it true that a difference that makes no difference is no difference? In other words, I'd love to own Van Gogh's *Irises,* but even if I had $100 million to buy it, how could I possibly display it? Why not have a Vietnamese duplicate it for $1,000? It would be almost as pleasant to look at, which is really why I'd want it. I'm sure some fool will accuse me of being a philistine for even having the thought, though, so perish the thought.

But that gets us into the area of art forgery, which is a real problem with expensive works, especially of recent vintage. It's often actually impossible to tell the real thing from a forgery. In that case, you're actually paying for the provenance, not the work itself. The whole area has become not only esoteric, but corrupt. It impresses me as ridiculous. The point of owning art is to be reminded of what life is about, and to be surrounded by beauty, not to have to be assured of reality by some expert's opinion.

L: As a matter of technical achievement, have you seen artists breaking new ground in the twenty-first century in a way you think has merit?

D: There may be some good new stuff out there, but nothing I find interesting, frankly. Performance art, for instance, is only entertainment. I knew a guy in Aspen—a very famous art collector. He showed me his collection, which included among his favorite pieces something very expensive, and hard to describe. It was like a big plastic cushion. You plugged it in and it blew up, and then it deflated again. That was it.

It reminded me of that movie, *The In-Laws*, with Alan Arkin and Peter Falk. In the movie, they visit a Central American dictator, and the guy is showing them his art collection. The dictator proudly tells them he paid $50,000 for one piece that was one of those black velvet things you buy at a gas station.

L: Jesus or Elvis?

D: Just like that—it was very, very funny. Frankly, most unconventional artwork is a scam. I'd definitely put Jackson Pollock, Andy Warhol, and Willem de Kooning in that class. But then again, I'm rather amused by Fernando Botero's stuff; it doesn't fit my philosophical definition of art very well, but everyone has idiosyncrasies. I definitely would have bought his stuff if I'd found it before it became so beastly expensive.

L: So, you only buy it if you really want to look at it.

D: True enough. And while it doesn't necessarily take a lot of money to buy good stuff, it does cost money, and it takes experience and some technical education to be able to identify really good art. I mentioned taking lessons, which I've done in Hong Kong and several places in the United States, Canada, and Spain, in part because I wanted some reality on the technical skill involved. If you're going to get into art, I think you owe it to yourself to educate yourself in such a way first.

L: So, when you said that studying art was a waste of time, you meant theoretical study, in a classroom, not technique, which you do recommend studying to those who want to become connoisseurs?

D: Yes. It's the difference between seeing and doing. Instruction is very helpful when it comes to learning how to do things, though I'd say that you could discover most techniques on your own, if you were patient and diligent enough. But why try to reinvent the wheel?

L: My two sons who are artists would agree. I offered to send them to art school and they didn't want to go; they wanted to develop their own styles, not be taught to mimic others'. They wouldn't even consider classes on basic technique. That seemed like reinventing the wheel to me, as you say, but they wanted to do their own thing, and they did. As a result, both have developed powerful styles of their own and have made commissions.

D: I've seen some of the younger one's work, and I'd say he proves the point, although it's helpful to stand on the shoulders of giants.

L: Okay. Hm. Pulling back to the larger world we live in, it seems that your art-buying has been a contracyclical thing. Do you ever use art prices as a contrary investment indicator?

D: I've never made a study of that, but I've no doubt that there's a correlation. And if I'm right about the Greater Depression being even worse than I expect it to be, you're going to be able to find lots of quality art going for less than cost of materials. I'm sure there are many thousands of people like myself who have so much art in storage, they can't even remember everything they have; a lot of that could hit the market at fire sale prices at some point.

This is absolutely true of museums too, by the way. People donate their collections to museums, and most museums have large storerooms—warehouses—packed with the stuff. There's a gigantic inventory overhanging the market. So I would not buy art as an investment on any basis now. I don't care if we're talking old masters, or modern fads, any of it. Quality art has been a good investment in the past, but I can't see it being a good investment for years to come.

Everything has become a piece of collectible art—cars, for instance. People are inventorying the things. I love cars, but the time will come when you will be able to buy exotica that's been sitting in a barn, with a dead battery and flat tires, on the cheap. In the 1940s that was how some people found Duesenbergs, Packards, and Cords.

Modern coins are another thing I don't think make sense; they're really just mass-produced government tokens. I used to collect ancient Roman coins. Each is an individual piece of art, and very historically instructive. And there's no popular interest in them, which makes them an excellent value.

L: It'd take some guts and vision to start buying art, if you live in one of the world's leading economies when they really start falling apart.

D: That's what separates the real speculators from the day-trader wannabes. As we've discussed, especially in our talk on technology, the longest trend in history—and beyond—is the ascent of man. That's likely to continue. That said, I'm firmly convinced that the Greater Depression is going to irrevocably alter the global economy, the lines on the maps, and entire ways of living for millions of people. But when the dust settles and this era is well and truly behind us, the world will be a better place. There will be a tomorrow, so when things crash, you've got to see it as an opportunity to buy low.

L: Understood. One more question. Speaking of masters, who would you say are your favorites? Given what you've said, not da Vinci—you wouldn't want the *Mona Lisa* on your wall, even if it was given to you. And you've bought a lot of unknowns. But are there any famous artists you like our readers might recognize?

D: Well, I wouldn't go that far about the *Mona Lisa*, even though it's just a small portrait. My favorite painters among people who are well known definitely include Salvador Dali, Hieronymus Bosch, Albrecht Dürer, William Blake, and Pieter Bruegel the Elder. But they're unaffordable, unless you have a Vietnamese knock-off commissioned.

L: My oldest artist offspring is a huge fan of Dali. I like him, but am more partial to the Russian painter Mikhail Vrubel.

At any rate, summing up your view, then: Forget about investing in art for the foreseeable future, but if you like it, watch for buying opportunities to come. Art itself is best seen as an expense that enhances quality of life.

D: I would say that's just about it.

L: Thanks Doug. 'Til next week.

D: My aesthetic pleasure.

Chapter 26

Doug Casey on Second Passports

January 26, 2011

Louis: Doug, a lot of our readers have asked about getting a second passport. I realize this is a large and complex issue—several issues, actually—but would you care to go over the basics of where to go and what to do? And for those not already thinking about this, why?

Doug: Sure. We've talked quite a bit about the increasing urgency of getting some of your assets out of your home country, especially if it's the United States. We've talked about having stores of precious metals in safe places abroad, and setting up bank and brokerage accounts abroad as well. I've said that the safest way to store wealth abroad is to buy property, which can't be seized by your home country without an act of war. The purchase of real estate solves several issues all at once.

But that's all about protecting assets; to protect yourself, getting a second passport is unfortunately very important.

L: Why unfortunately?

D: Because you shouldn't have to need government papers to live as you please. It used to be that a passport was a document that a ruler of one country would give to a traveler to ask the rulers of other countries to assist him in his travels. Now, instead of a convenience, it's become a required permit for travel. It's degrading and actually runs counter to the whole idea of the thing. The original purpose of a passport has been turned upside down.

L: Passports are becoming a world ID card—and they will be, once the governments all link up their databases.

D: That's exactly what they are, and I'm sure it's going to get worse. It's funny the way people treat these things like some sort of holy relic, or magical object; they are nothing but another government ID. But since they are necessary in today's world, you ought to have several of them, for your own convenience. If nothing else, it prevents any one government from basically placing you under house arrest by taking your passport away from you.

L: Do you really think of it mostly in terms of convenience? Or do you sometimes think about the potential for physical danger, should you find yourself in an Achille Lauro–type situation in which violent people who hate Americans select U.S. passport holders for abuse?

D: That's definitely a good reason for Americans to have a second passport, and increasingly for others, now that the war with Islam is underway. If you ever get caught in harm's way, it helps that nobody starts by shooting all the people from countries they've never heard of.

L: Round up all the Uruguayans!

D: Right—that just doesn't happen. Another reason, certainly if you're an American, is that *nobody* anywhere in the world wants to open a bank account or a brokerage account for you. It ranges from impossible to hard and inconvenient. It's a subtle and indirect form of exchange control that the United States has already imposed. I have no doubt controls will become much more formal and serious in the near future.

L: Are you saying that if I go to Switzerland, and I look and sound like an American, but have a Mexican passport, they'll open a bank account for me?

D: It depends. Here in Uruguay, where I'm still hanging out on the beach, I went with a friend from South Africa to open a bank account, using her South African passport. I didn't say a word, so I could have been a South African too, for all they knew. Still, the bank officer asked her: "Are you also a U.S. citizen?" and "Are you resident in the U.S.?"

L: The long arm of Uncle Sam keeps getting longer.

D: It really is getting harder and harder. Banks really don't want the aggravations that come with dealing with "U.S. persons" and their bullying government. Of course, it's all going to eventually backfire on the United States, but in the meantime, it's going to get worse.

L: So, how have you dealt with this problem?

D: Well, when I first started on this, I got a travel document from the World Service Authority in Washington, DC. That organization was started by a guy named Gary Davis, who was a bomber pilot for the United States during World War II. He got so fed up with war and governments that he renounced his U.S. citizenship while in Paris after the war. That was a big deal, because he was also the son of Myer Davis, who was a famous bandleader during the war.

Anyway, after he renounced his citizenship, he found he couldn't leave France, because he had no passport. So he created the World Service Authority and printed up a very nice-looking passport that looked a great deal like the UN passport. It was the same color, has a globe on the front (though a bit different from the UN's globe), was printed in some five languages, and had quotations from the appropriate parts of the UN charter.

I have one that I got directly from Gary, himself, back in the 1970s, and have had some very interesting adventures with it. I've used mine successfully in Iceland, French Polynesia, Honduras, Costa Rica, and Peru. It worked in some other places as well, but I'd have to look at the stamps to list them all.

L: Are those still available?

D: Yes, they are, but with all these governments linking up and sharing data, prompted mainly by the U.S. government, it doesn't work nearly as well as in the past. Unfamiliarity used to be your friend. Now, if you go to a country and the immigration officer doesn't recognize your passport, he'll look it up on a list. But even in the old days, it didn't always work. A Swiss border guard got very affronted with me over it. When I used it in Rhodesia, during the war, I got sent to the back of the line and got a big lecture. When I used it in

Egypt, it meant an hour in the back office, because someone had used one the week before when he assassinated their ambassador to Malta. In Senegal, 30 years ago—a place so backward you'd think they wouldn't even know—they laughed good naturedly and said it was out of the question.

The most interesting adventure was in Morocco, where the officer immediately called for a supervisor, and the supervisor had me taken to a back office—something worth being a little nervous about back then, and maybe even more nervous about now. At the time, my French was still pretty competent, and I was feeling my oats that day, so I was hanging tough and arguing with the guy in French. In the end, I said to him: "Okay, so what am I supposed to do?" He replied with an absolutely perfect Gallic shrug. He could have been an actor in a movie. So, I took out my U.S. passport and he took me back to the front of the line.

L: David's right. You must be missing the gene for fear. Most people wouldn't even have tried such a thing back then, and most who did, probably gave up after wetting their pants in the first encounter you call an adventure.

D: Perhaps so, and now the point may be moot. But even with all these governments linking together, it's still worth getting a World Service Authority travel document, because in some countries you have to turn in your passport at hotels and other places.

L: Yes, I don't like it when they ask for my passport at hotels, and I hate it when they say they have to keep it.

D: As well you should, for all kinds of reasons. You never know how good the security at the hotel is, and the inconvenience of a lost or stolen passport is substantial. I'd say a second one is a good thing to have, just on principle. An alternative would be to get documents from some of those people trying to set up new countries, like Sealand, the World War II gun platform off the coast of England taken over by Roy Bates and recognized by three countries. I spent an afternoon with him once, but foolishly never signed up as a citizen. Oh well. Other outfits sell reproduction passports of defunct or renamed countries like Rhodesia and British Honduras.

L: I shudder to think of what "inconvenience" means to a man who finds it amusing to argue with immigration officials in back rooms in flyspeck countries. But at any rate, mentioning purveyors of passports from defunct countries underscores the importance of telling our readers that there are a lot of scams out there, and that it pays to be very skeptical of websites that claim to be able to set you up with documents, corporations, and bank accounts overseas. There are freelance thieves to worry about, and worse—governments trying to entrap so-called tax evaders and money launderers. There's no need to take such risks when you can go to any of the many countries that encourage immigration and permanent residency, and acquire government-issued documents legally.

D: Yes, these are indeed shark-infested waters. You really have to do things in a totally correct and proper way. For instance, there always seem to be people running around who have passports stolen from the issuing agency, and some fools buy them, not realizing they'll not only lose their money, but might wind up in jail besides. But, even among perfectly legitimate documents, not all passports are created equal.

L: Why would that be?

D: The defining characteristic of a "good" passport is how much visa-free travel it allows. And by that I really mean visas that have to be applied for, and approved, before the trip begins, as opposed to those issued at the border. Avoiding those is the real key value.

In spite of its reputation, a U.S. passport is by no means the best one to have. First, if you have one, you're a U.S. taxpayer, which is *very* inconvenient, but it also means you need visas for a lot more countries than you would with some other passport. Argentina, Chile, and Brazil, for instance, all charge Americans about $150 to issue a visa. It's a perverse form of reciprocity, as that's what the U.S. government charges their citizens. It's the same kind of thinking that starts trade wars, and I expect more of it in the years to come—but that's another subject.

Speaking of South America, two passports that are relatively quick and easy to get are those from Uruguay and Paraguay. Both countries are members of the Mercosur group of South American countries, which offers some additional advantages to their nationals. Panama also offers citizenship with very few hassles.

One of the best, I'm given to understand—and this is constantly changing—is a Singapore passport. I also understand that Singapore has a number of ways to become a citizen in a relatively short period of time.

L: What are some of the shortcuts to second citizenship?

D: One of the best is if you have parents or grandparents from a country that will give you citizenship on that basis. Ireland and Italy are known for this. It's true, under some circumstances, for the UK, Poland, and Lithuania as well. Saint Kitts is a relatively easy place to get a passport quite quickly, but it involves a significant investment that adds up to a couple hundred thousand dollars. Selling IDs is a significant source of income for the island.

And of course, in a number of countries you can obtain citizenship, and hence documents, relatively easily by marrying a national. Brazil is one, and a Brazilian passport is not a bad one to have.

There's information on this out there, but there have been scam reports done on this subject and many other sources that are simply unreliable, so watch out. I don't think there's ever been a truly definitive study done on all the ways, in all the 200 or so countries in the world. I believe my book, *The International Man*, was the first to really explore the ground, but it's long out of date. Even if there were a current book, it would have to be updated monthly to be of real value; governments are always changing their rules. And when it comes down to the particulars of a given situation, you'll want to hire a tax attorney and maybe an immigration one as well, to make sure everything is done correctly. That said, our team did put together a special report for people considering expatriation, called "Going Global" (click here for details).

It's generally better not to try for short cuts, but to move to a place you like living in, at least part of the year. Operating through the established, legally recognized channels, you can get a passport in two to five years.

L: Okay. And, to be clear, the U.S. allows second citizenships?

D: Yes. Many countries don't, and are strict about it. Others don't, but look the other way. You may feel you want to keep your U.S. documents for various practical reasons, but remember that keeping your U.S. citizenship means remaining a U.S. taxpayer, which is most undesirable.

L: I read that if your income is less than $100,000 per year and you live abroad, it's not taxed, so maybe the tax issue is less important to people who earn less than you?

D: That's true, but that exemption only applies on income earned outside the United States. You still pay capital gains taxes, and taxes on U.S.-sourced income. I also understand that under current law, until 2013, there's a $5 million exemption on appreciated expatriated assets. That means there's a window closing soon on some of the benefits of getting rid of your U.S. citizenship.

L: Any reasons other than taxes you'd want to get rid of your U.S. citizenship? If I was young enough, I'd worry about conscription, for example.

D: That's a very good reason. More generally, as long as you're a citizen of a country, that country's government is going to treat you like its property. So, if you are going to be a citizen of any place, which is unfortunately necessary, it's better to be a citizen of a small and backward country, or one that just doesn't have the ability or interest to monitor all of its citizens like prison inmates, as the United States does.

L: I hear that. It's such a pity that America the beautiful has turned into the United State and is rapidly marching down the road to serfdom. I really loved America.

D: Nothing lasts forever, Lobo. It's suicidal to let sentimentality blind you to reality. But, eternal optimist that I am, it's always good to look at one of the major bright sides of the ongoing financial and economic collapse. Namely that the governments of most advanced nation-states are bankrupt. There's a chance that some of them will be forced to cut back on their most noisome activities. There's even a chance that one or two will be completely hollowed out and will exist mostly in theory, like Rome in the late fifth century.

It's very hard to predict what will happen, so it's best to have a plan B. And a plan C. Unfortunately, most people have a medieval serf mentality—although they don't know it, and probably wouldn't admit it even if they did—and have no plan at all, because they think everything is fine.

L: I agree. And you know I'm diversifying out of the United States as well. Any other essential points?

D: Yes, remember that getting a second passport is just part of a larger "permanent traveler" strategy. The ideal is to live in one place, have your citizenship in another, your banks and brokers in other jurisdictions, and your business dealings in yet others. That makes it very inconvenient for any one government to control you. You don't want all your eggs in one basket—that just makes it easier for them to grab them all. I understand it may not be easy for most people to structure their affairs that way. That's exactly why most serfs stayed serfs; it was hard and scary to think of anything other than what they were told they should do.

L: Understood. Thanks for the guidance.

D: You're welcome. Maybe we should talk about Obama's state of the Union address next week, but that means I'd have to actually listen to the thing, and that would be painful.

L: Ugh. Maybe Mr. Market will provide us with something more entertaining to talk about. Well, we'll see. *Buenas noches*, Tatich.

Chapter 27

Doug Casey on Fresh Starts

November 23, 2011

Louis: Doug, we've had a lot of requests from younger readers asking for advice on how they should tackle the world, starting out amidst a crisis. We've also had questions from older readers asking what you might do differently if you were 21 again, or if you were suddenly unemployed and had to start from scratch. What do you think? Can you stroke your long, white beard and give us some practical guru wisdom for today's world?

Doug: I keep telling people I have no crystal ball, but they don't listen. Nobody has a crystal ball. But, perhaps paradoxically, I also keep giving people advice because they ask; and like anyone, I'd like to help—but those people rarely listen either.

Giving advice is temporarily gratifying to the giver, because it makes him feel like he knows something—for that moment. But it's ultimately frustrating because few receivers ever use advice. People generally have to make their own mistakes. I believe it was Stalin who said that even those few people who learn from their own mistakes weren't all that smart; he preferred to learn from other people's mistakes—not that Stalin should be considered a generally sound source of advice. It's odd, actually—one of history's great sociopaths dispensing words of wisdom.

L: I wouldn't say people *never* listen; last time we were together here in Cafayate, I introduced you to one of my students who took your advice to leave Eastern Europe and travel the world gathering experiences. Another one just did the same thing and went to India. And another one quit his job and started his own business.

D: [Blinks] Okay, okay. For the few, then. Some who have ears do in fact not only hear but listen. But of course, there's never a guarantee that the advice you're going to get is worth anything. Some poor fool might ask economics Nobel Prize–winner Paul Krugman a question on economics and god forbid, take the answer seriously.

At any rate, like most of those I expect Krugman hears, most of the questions I get center on money. Well, I've been quite fortunate in that I've been able to accumulate a fair amount of capital. So, although I've written a lot about the airy, theoretical aspects of the stuff, I guess I've also shown a degree of practical expertise in dealing with it.

Let me start off by stating the obvious: It's definitely better to have more money, more assets, more capital, because it gives you more options, more flexibility, more control. Building that pile of capital can give you those things, and you're going to need them. Having capital is critical, and given where the global economy is headed, the faster you can get it, the better. Strive to create more value—something very few wage earners ever think of. Everybody understands, at least intuitively, that if you want to build capital you have to spend less and save more, but very few have the self-discipline to actually do it. And of course, once you have sufficient savings you have to invest wisely, but most people only invest conventionally.

The bottom line is that one of the things—and I emphasize it's just one—a young person should do is grub for money now, in order to avoid having to grub for roots and berries in the future.

L: Money is power. But—contrary to popular, sloppy thinking—not all power is necessarily bad. The coercive power of the state and other forms of power based on force are destructive in their essence, and the outcomes of their application tend to be negative. When you offer someone money for a service or good, you are motivating cooperation, and the transaction only closes if both sides feel they are getting more than they are giving. Win-win. That makes the power of money essentially constructive, and the outcomes of its application, absent the corrupting influence of force, tend to be creative.

D: Yes. And people are going to need all the power they can muster to survive the coming storm. Power also comes from having lots of good relations, connections, with worthwhile people. It comes—as the Boy Scouts at least used to know—from being physically fit, mentally awake, and morally straight. It comes from having lots of both intellectual knowledge and practical skills. These are the things that separate the wheat from the chaff among people.

That said, I want to stress that people should not get too attached to wealth and money—that's a huge mistake on all levels. Wealth is a normal consequence of excellence in other areas of life. But it's only a consequence, a significant side effect, or an aid. It's not an object in itself. You can only pity the fool who confuses what he is with what he has.

L: Yes, Mr. T.

D: I'm a happy man. Right here and now, I'm living in the lap of Argentine luxury, smoking a mellow Cuban cigar, building my own polo club, growing my own grapes for a great wine, driving high-performance cars, and so forth—things that require money. But that said, some of the times when I've been happiest in my life have been times when I had no money whatsoever.

I remember a trip I took from Bern to Istanbul with a couple of buddies, back when I was a penniless student in the 1960s. None of us had any sense of financial planning, so, for the last three days, on our way back from Istanbul, we had absolutely no money. Zero. Not even small coins. We were riding third class, bumming cigarettes and morsels of food from gypsies on the train. I kid you not. But it was a great adventure, and we were very happy hippies.

More recently, I spent some time living as though I had no money. A friend and I hopped a train in Grand Junction, Colorado. It took us three days to get to Portland, sleeping in rail yards, eating in missions, living like bums—or, more accurately, hobos. Another time we went to Sacramento, which also took three days. A measure of cheap thrills and chills and a tad of danger are good spices in life. Both times were a lot of fun, and I didn't really need, or use, any money at all. Doing things like that is salubrious and therapeutic. It puts you into a new reality.

Living the vanishing middle class American dream in ticky-tacky little boxes is an illusion of security. You don't need any of that stuff to be happy. Actually, it can make you unhappy, because it starts to own you, more than you own it. You get involved in the "rat race," and before you know it you're old, tired, and relying on Social Security or the kindness of others. Grubbing for roots and berries is only fun—at least once you've reached a certain age—when you don't really have to do it.

L: Well, I appreciate the wisdom of not getting too wedded to stuff. It's not just Eastern mysticism; it can greatly increase your enjoyment of life not to get all stressed about keeping up with the Joneses, taking on more debt to buy more toys, and such. When piling up money becomes the sole focus of life, it's easy to forget that life is the reason to accumulate money in the first place. But unless you do want to become a vagabond and exist to some degree on the charity of others, or a hermit eating grubs in the woods, you have to have money.

It's fine for you to play hobo on a train for a few days, but if you have children, they need to be fed, and that takes money. If you can't feed your kids properly, that is *not* a happy thing, and if they get sick and need to see a doctor, that is not a fun adventure.

Money is the power by which we acquire the things we need in life, not just a meaningless scorecard for competing with the Joneses.

D: Sure; and it's easy for me to say that money is no big deal when my biggest problem right now is that my Cohiba just went out. I'm not in the position of having no money. Look, money is like any other tool; it's better to have it and not need it, than need it and not have it. But I really don't worry about it too much.

L: So how do you get to where you don't have to worry about it?

D: Remember: Everyone in the world—everyone—has an infinite capacity to desire goods and services. Everyone wants more—it's a survival trait for all species to gather while the gathering is good. This unlimited appetite means that there are unlimited opportunities to earn a living. On the most fundamental level, all you have to do is look around and figure out what people need and want, then put yourself in a position to provide it to them. There's wealth in the world, a lot of it; your task is to figure out what you can offer people that will persuade them to voluntarily give you some of what they have. When what you give them makes them better off, it's a creative, win-win process, just as you said before.

When I used to land in some third world country where I knew no one and had no connections, what would I do, sit in my hotel room and watch TV? No. I'd open up the Yellow Pages for that city—it'd be online today—and look at the different kinds of businesses listed and think of ways I could offer some value to those people in those businesses, such that they would be willing to give me money in exchange. I always started with the people who tend to be centers of power—lawyers, real estate agents, and the like. In most places, they either have the money or know the people who do. I'd call them up and arrange an interview.

L: They'd give time to a perfect stranger?

D: Here it's an advantage to be in a different town, preferably in a different country. They don't know who you are; for all they know, you're an eccentric billionaire, looking for opportunities. You're interesting, simply because you're from elsewhere. With some of them, you'll establish a rapport, and next thing you know, you're being invited home for dinner, you meet some of their friends, you keep your eyes and ears open, one thing leads to another, and you can find some great opportunities.

This technique works best for people who have a wide array of knowledge and other connections. If you've done nothing significant with your life previously it's a waste of time—why should these people want to talk to you after the first five minutes, when they're sizing you up? Hitting the ground in a strange, foreign country is doing something significant—an excellent start. It both allows you to see opportunities that most people don't (stuck as they are in their medieval serf mentality), and to bring some new intellectual capital to the party—a reason for those with the money to deal you in.

You never know what the opportunity might be, but it will present itself. Ted Turner was absolutely correct when, in response to a question about how to make a fortune, he answered that you should go to where the action is and throw yourself in the middle of it. The law of large numbers will work, and some of the wealth will start coming your way.

L: You make it sound easy, but most people are afraid to do this. They'd feel more secure getting a well-paid job wherever they went. Preferably before they went.

D: The worst thing to do is to look for a job. That means you're looking for someone to pay you for some of your time, usually in a time and place where there are others willing to trade theirs for less. That's totally the wrong mindset. Don't be a supplicant. You're then setting yourself up as the effect of someone else's cause. What you should do is work to put yourself at cause over the situation, which works best if you've spent the time preparing yourself in previous years. You want to look for people who will trade things you want for what you can give them, or help them get. Not wages, deals. That's the critical thing to get straight in your mind. It's so obvious, but most people completely overlook it. You shouldn't look for employment; you should look for business.

Part of it is how you relate to the universe. Personally, I only relate to other people as equals; I don't talk up nor talk down. I don't kowtow to the rich and famous; I treat them with respect and courtesy, but only the amount due to any decent human. And if I don't consider them decent, I give them only that much respect. On the other hand, I never talk down to "inferiors." For all you know, that Chinese houseboy is actually the head of a triad. For all you know, that skinny, nerdy kid is the next Steve Jobs. Of course, after enough time—anywhere from five seconds to five years—you will determine with adequate certainty who you're really dealing with. People should be treated with the respect they deserve, regardless of how high or low their station in life. The key is figuring out how much they deserve.

L: I hadn't really thought of it this way before, but there have been two times in my life thus far when I personally had major financial crises—total meltdowns, with heavy obligations and no way to meet them. Both times, the fastest and easiest way I could think of to get some cash flow going was to create a business, so that's what I did.

D: Absolutely right. In my situation, it's rarely been that urgent. I don't really have a family. I'm married but have no children. I'm independent and can walk away from just about everything with no obligations.

L: What about Roscoe Studmuffin and·Moxy Crimefighter?

D: My poodles, the football star and the supermodel? Well, maybe I do have a family—I couldn't let them starve—although they wouldn't, because they're extremely competent gopher hunters. But apart from that, I've always looked at things as an individual and evaluated risk, effort, rewards in terms of my own needs and happiness. It's different, I grant, if you have a family. I understand that.

But most of the inquiries about how to make the most of one's life seem to be from people who may be in college (which is a big mistake for most people, who turn themselves into indentured servants with student loans that can't be defaulted on, while cluttering their minds with useless or counterproductive thoughts). If I were 18 or 21 again, what I would do is get *some* money—borrowed from grandmother, saved from moving lawns, withdrawn from the college fund, raised selling possessions, whatever—and use that grubstake as seed money.

L: Or get a job if you really can't find any other source of funds short of stealing. But then, for cryin' out loud, *don't spend all you make*, so that you can accumulate start-up capital.

D: Yes, exactly. You have to start someplace. Most people could learn something from the average Chinese. As a culture, they've really been through the meat grinder over the last century, and know how important it is to save.

Anyway, I would take that grubstake and hit the road and go someplace new, as different as you can get from wherever you start. That way you're new, fresh, unique. If you're American and you stay in the United States where there are masses of people just like you, no one has any special reason to hire you; you are—at least at first blush—just one of millions with similar backgrounds. Better to go to Honduras or Bolivia or Laos or Nigeria, where you'll stand out from the crowd and have something to contribute that others do not. Do like the students you mentioned at the beginning of this conversation—they are to be greatly admired for what they've done.

L: If nothing else, when you do that, you're interesting.

D: You're interesting, and that opens up opportunities. And how interesting you are is a function of how many books you've read, how much thought you've put into things, how widely you've traveled, how many skills you've mastered, how many people you know. It's completely up to you. But you've got to get out of your comfortable and safe-seeming hometown, otherwise you're no better than a medieval peasant, chained to the dirt his ancestors toiled over and were buried in, for generations. Your chances of getting anywhere that way are slim and none.

L: And Slim's out of town.

D: [Chuckles.]

L: I've told you about my brother before. He was injured on the job and couldn't work at about the time the crisis hit, then just couldn't find new work. Month after month, then year after year. So I bought him an airplane ticket, and he came out here to where I live, and within a month got a job. I know we're not trying to encourage people to think in terms of jobs, but even on that level, it helps to escape what you call the "medieval peasant" trap of thinking only in terms of the place you happen to be. We have feet. If we can't find opportunities around us, we can go to where there are opportunities.

D: Sure. On whatever level you're able to, you've got to grab the bull by the horns.

This highlights the truly shameful results of U.S. government policy and programs over the last few generations, especially since the New Deal. They've totally corrupted the average American, who used to ask for no more than an opportunity to work hard and benefit from the fruit of his own labor. Now the average American thinks that the U.S. government not only should, but actually can serve as a magic cornucopia, assuring him of all the good things in life.

L: You mean we don't have a human right to cars, air conditioning, widescreen TVs, and mocha lattes? Doesn't it say so in the Constitution?

D: [Chuckles.] This is why I see no way out for the United States that doesn't send the whole society through the wringer.

I remember my friend Barry Reid, who started a company called the Eden Underground Press. Barry was in the marijuana business in the 1960s. He got caught, did three years in jail, and returned to society a felon. Didn't stop him. He started his publishing company and became very successful. But he made a wrong move when he started printing "private identification documents" that looked almost exactly like state-issued drivers' licenses. The cards didn't say they were drivers' licenses, but you'd have to look carefully to see that. So he did another three years' time. Did that stop him? Absolutely not. Barry always said: "For every door that closes, there are two that open." That's the proper attitude.

L: That's interesting. Did I tell you that in 2009, before the impression of renewed growth spread through the U.S. economy, I had three former students from the Republic of Belarus visit my family? At the time, "everyone knew" there were no jobs, and many Americans were sitting home, not even trying to find them. But my three friends got on the bikes I gave them and rode into town every day, going door to door, asking at every single business they came across, until they got jobs—two got jobs at a supermarket 10 miles away and rode their bikes there every day.

D: Never surrender; it's bad karma. Getting a job like that can help you save some money and put some rice on the table, but the real value is that it gets you out in society. You're active, meeting people, finding opportunities, and that's not going to happen if you sit at home, collecting your welfare check, cementing your bad habits in place, and degrading your psychology.

L: And I'm sure it helped that my students were not American—they were different. They were interesting, from a place most people have never heard of.

D: Sure. And it's not easy for Belarusians to travel to many places. Americans and Europeans have a huge advantage in being able to travel to many places with no visas. They can go to places where their experiences and even simple language skills set them apart from billions of other human beings, all looking to get ahead.

I have two different friends who didn't know each other, but both with connections with The Discovery Channel. They both thought I should make a proposal to The Discovery Channel for a documentary in which I would drop in on some nothing, nowhere country and do exactly as I've described. Start with the phone book and see if I could be sitting down with the president by the end of the week, pitching him on some deal.

L: Casey Reality TV. Some readers may not know that this is actually a hobby of yours. I've seen you sit down with a president—now the former president of Panama—and pitch him on how rich he could get putting the country back on a gold standard.

D: [Laughs.] Yes. And if I could do it, so could anyone. You know, I've actually pitched nine other presidents or military dictators on various deals, usually trying to privatize most or all of the government. In many cases, I believe I could have made it happen, but I would have had to move to the country and make the project the center of my life. I was never willing to go that far. Why should I, given all that I have in my life? Entirely apart from the fact that, if I succeeded, no good deed goes unpunished—at least in the realm of politics.

But, if I were 21 and didn't have much money, I'd do the same thing and stick with it as far as I could take it.

Actually, I learned something very important when I was . . . maybe 23: I met an Israeli guy named Yahuda ben Yahuda. After talking with him for a while, he said, "You know, Mr. Casey"—he was very kind to address the young punk I was as Mr. Casey—"if you go to the Gold Coast, and you stay there for five years, you'll have 5 percent of everything going in or out of the country." I've always remembered that, because he was right. It's what he did when he came to America.

L: Is that always the right thing to do, Doug? Take the path less traveled?

D: When you come to a fork in the road—

L: Take it.

D: Take it. Whether you go left or right, your whole life will be different, and you never know which will be best. It's part of why I'm a solipsist, and am also very sympathetic to Taoism. At least once a day, if you turn right instead of left, if you say yes instead of no, your whole life could change totally and unrecognizably. I, for one, am on a quest for Alice's rabbit hole, or her looking glass.

The most important thing is to have the right attitude, so you can see opportunities when they present themselves, and be willing and able to take advantage of them when they do. You can help prepare yourself for that by reading a lot, associating with other interesting people, and securing a real education for yourself, rather than relying on teachers to tell you what you should think.

L: Attitude is everything. That's something I teach my students.

D: Just so. It's why a determined little dog will beat an unmotivated big dog in a fight 90 percent of the time. It's why Joe Pesci could probably have been a mob boss in real life.

L: Okay. Well, this conversation doesn't lend itself to new investment insights, so I guess we'll just leave it as a Public Service Announcement.

D: Sure, though I might add that while getting a job may be a necessary first step toward accumulating capital, and while it's better to be a business owner, what you really want is to move up the food chain and become an investor as soon as you can. Put your money to work for you, instead of working for money. The creative peak of capital accumulation, of course, is to become a speculator.

L: I teach that too—or try to—to my readers as well as my students. Very well, thanks for your insights.

D: My pleasure, as always.

Chapter 28

Doug Casey on Getting Out of Dodge

December 21, 2011

Louis: Doug, a lot of readers have been asking for guidance on how to know when it's time to exit center stage and hunker down in some safe place. Few people want to hide from the world in a cabin in the woods while life goes on in the mainstream, but nobody wants to get caught once the gates clang shut on the police state the United States is becoming. How do you know when it's time to go?

Doug: Well, the first thing to keep in mind is that it's better to be a year too early than a minute too late. David Galland recently read *They Thought They Were Free: The Germans, 1933–45*, by Milton Mayer. He quoted a passage in his column of last Friday. It goes a long way in explaining why Americans appear to be such whipped dogs today. They're no different from the Germans of recent memory. For those who missed it, let me quote it:

"You see," my colleague went on, "one doesn't see exactly where or how to move. Believe me, this is true. Each act, each occasion, is worse than the last, but only a little worse. You wait for the next and the next. You wait for one great shocking occasion, thinking that others, when such a shock comes, will join with you in resisting somehow. You don't want to act, or even talk, alone; you don't want to 'go out of your way to make trouble.' . . . In the university community, in your own community, you speak privately to your colleagues, some of whom certainly feel as you do; but what do they say? They say, 'It's not so bad' or 'You're seeing things' or 'You're an alarmist.'

"These are the beginnings, yes; but how do you know for sure when you don't know the end, and how do you know, or even surmise, the end? On the one hand, your enemies, the law, the regime, the Party, intimidate you. On the other, your colleagues pooh-pooh you as pessimistic or even neurotic . . . the one great shocking occasion, when tens or hundreds or thousands will join with you, never comes. That's the difficulty. If the last and worst act of the whole regime had come immediately after the first and smallest, thousands, yes, millions would have been sufficiently shocked. . . . But of course this isn't the way it happens. In between come all the hundreds of little steps, some of them imperceptible, each of them preparing you not to be shocked by the next. Step C is not so much worse than Step B, and, if you did not make a stand at Step B, why should you at Step C?"

The fact is that the United States has been on a slippery slope for decades, and it's about to go over a cliff. However, our standard of living, while declining, is still very high, both relatively and absolutely. But an American can enjoy a much higher standard of living abroad.

On the other hand, if I were some poor guy in a poverty-wracked country with few opportunities, I'd want to go where the action is, where the money is, *now*. Today, that means trying to get into the United States. The United States is headed the wrong direction, but it's still a land of opportunity and a whole lot better than some flea-bitten village in Niger.

L: By the time things get worse than some third-world dictatorship in the United States, such a person could have remitted a whole lot of cash back home.

D: And you'd have a whole lot of experiences that would give you a competitive edge back where you came from, or in the next place you go to. The one-eyed man is king in the valley of the blind. People have to lose that backward, peasant mentality that ties them to the land of their birth. Sad to say, although the average American has somewhat more knowledge of the world—mainly due to television—his psychology is just as constrained as that of some serf from central Asia or some primitive village in Africa. It's all a matter of psychology.

But if you're not poor, you want to go someplace that is safe, nice—whatever that means to you—and with a lower cost of living. As most readers know, for me that's Cafayate, Argentina, but one size does not fit all. It needs to be a place you actually enjoy spending some time, with people whose company you enjoy.

L: Fair enough. But our readers want to know if your guru sense is tingling yet, or how close you think we are to it being too late to leave—or at least too late to leave with any meaningful assets.

D: I'm a trend observer. This is one of the advantages of studying history, because it shows you that things like this rarely happen overnight. They are usually the result of trends that build over years and years, sometimes over generations. In the case of the United States, I think the trend has been downhill, in many ways, for many years. Pick a time. You could make an argument, from a moral point of view, that things started heading downhill at the time of the Spanish-American War. That was when a previously peaceful and open country first started conquering overseas lands and staking colonies. America was still in the ascent toward its peak economically, but the seeds of its own demise were already sewn, and a libertarian watching the scene might have concluded that it was time to get out of Dodge—

L: That would have been a bit early.

D: Yes, that would have been way too soon. As Adam Smith observed, there's a lot of ruin in a country.

L: On the other paw, it would have gotten you out before the War Between the States, a disaster well worth avoiding.

D: No, the Spanish-American War was in 1898.

L: Oops! Sorry, I was thinking of what Americans call the Mexican-American War, but which Mexicans call the "American Invasion"—

D: [Laughs]

L: I'm not joking. That's what they called it in the history books I was given in Mexican schools when I lived there in the 1970s. It has long seemed to me that that was an ominous turn for the worse for the

United States and a clear example of conquering a weaker neighbor purely for pillage—not just Texas, but everything from there all the way to California.

D: That's right. Davey Crockett and the boys, we love them, but in many ways they were the equivalent of today's Mexicans who want to recolonize the southwest and turn it back into part of Mexico, in what they call the *Reconquista*.

L: Indeed, but this is ancient history to most U.S. taxpayers today—I'm reminded that it's not correct in many cases to call them *Americans*.

D: Yes, just as it was a misnomer to call the people who lived in the Roman Empire after Diocletian *Romans*, because Roman citizens were once free men. After about 300 AD, most of them were bound to the land or their occupations as serfs. But the slide for Rome started at least 120 years earlier, after the death of Marcus Aurelius. Politically, the decline started with the accession of Julius Caesar 240 years before that. So, when did the slide—politically, economically, and socially—really start for the United States? When were there no more trends going up?

L: FDR? The New Deal was really a moral, economic, and political turning point.

D: You could make that argument, but the United States still grew economically, despite the roadblocks FDR threw in its path. U.S. military power and global prestige continued growing from that point, although, paradoxically, the accelerating growth of the U.S. military was directly responsible for the decline of the United States economically and in terms of personal freedom. One reason for the ascendancy of the United States after World War II was that we were the only major country in the world not physically devastated by the war.

L: Ah. Right.

D: So it seems to me that the peak of American civilization was in the 1960s. As for evidence, well, I like to put my finger on the 1959 Cadillac. Those twin bullet taillights, the opulence of it. In terms of then-current technology, things couldn't get much better.

L: "Opulence. I has it."

D: That's my favorite TV commercial! Anyway, that was the peak, in my mind. Though things continued getting better for a while, the United States started to live out of capital.

L: Had to pay for guns *and* butter.

D: That's right. The Johnson administration's so-called Great Society created vast new federal bureaucracies that promised Americans free food, shelter, medical care, education, and what-have-you. Americans became true wards of the state. But the real, final nail in the coffin for America was in 1971—

L: Nixon taking the United States off the gold standard.

D: Nixon taking the United States off the gold standard—open devaluation of the dollar, combined with wage and price controls for some months. And that was not long after the so-called Bank Secrecy Act, which abolished bank secrecy, and required the reporting of all foreign financial accounts. Nixon was, in many ways, even more of a disaster than Johnson. Republicans are usually worse than Democrats when it comes to freedom, partly because they like to couch their depredations in the rhetoric of defending the free market. While everyone understands that Democrats are socialists just under the surface, Republicans actually give capitalism a bad name. Baby Bush is a perfect, recent example.

L: But don't you worry your pretty little head about devaluation—it's just a "bugaboo"—and as long as you're not one of those unpatriotic people wanting to buy imports or vacation abroad, your dollar will be worth just as much tomorrow as it is today. The scary thing is that the Belarusian dictator Lukashenko said almost the same thing when the Belarusian ruble lost two-thirds of its forex value earlier this year, asking his countrymen why they need to go on vacation in Germany or buy German cars.

D: You see why I like to study history? It doesn't repeat, but it sure does rhyme.

L: With a vengeance.

D: So, anyway, since 1971, some things have improved largely due to technological advances, but the America That Was has been fading into the past. It was a decisive turning point. You can see that in the accelerated proliferation of undeclared wars we've had since then. I don't just mean the penny-ante invasions of Granada and Panama; the United States has always lorded it over Caribbean and Central American banana republics. Those are just sport wars. But Iraq and Afghanistan are alien cultures on the other side of the world—apart from never posing any threat to the United States. Now it looks like Iran and Pakistan are on the dance card, and they're big game. The war against Islam has started in earnest, and it's going to end badly for the United States. I explained all this at great length in the white paper, "Learn to Make Terror Your Friend," that I wrote for *The Casey Report* last month.

Domestically, saying that the United States is turning into a police state when you started this conversation was quite accurate. You can see more and more videos spreading over the Internet, not just of police brutality, but demonstrating the militarization and federalization of police, who are being inculcated with both disdain for and paranoia about ordinary citizens.

In the old days, if you were stopped for speeding, the peace officer was polite—you could get out of your car, meet the cop on neutral ground, and chat with him. You didn't have a serious problem unless you were obviously drunk or combative. Now, you don't dare make a move. You better keep your hands in plain sight on the steering wheel and be ready for a Breathalyzer test without probable cause. The law enforcement officer will stand behind you with his hand on his gun. And you're the one who'd better be polite.

L: There has been a polar reversal. The cops used to address citizens as sir or ma'am. Now, the correct response in a traffic stop is: "Yes, sir! I would love to inspect the bottom of your boot, sir!"

D: That's right. My friend Marc Victor gives out magnetized business cards. People ask, "Why?" He answers that it's so clients can put them on the bottom of their cars or refrigerators, so they can see it when the cops throw them to the ground.

L: Marc's a good man. There's a handy video on Marc's website, offering advice on what to do if you're pulled over by the police in a traffic stop.

D: A good public service announcement. At any rate, I think there's no question that the United States has turned the corner on every basis: politically, socially, morally, and now, economically.

L: Okay, but, Doug, you said that in 1979, too. The question is, how do we know when the door is going to close?

D: Well, sometimes I feel a little like the boy who cried wolf. But Roman writers like Tacitus and Sallust saw where Rome was going before it got completely out of control. Should they have said nothing, for fear of being too early? Here in the United States, it should have gone over the edge back in the 1980s, but we got lucky. There was still a lot of forward momentum, which can last for decades when you're speaking of civilizations. There was the computer productivity boom. The Soviet Union collapsed, China liberalized, and Communism was discredited everywhere except on U.S. college campuses. The end of the Cold War opened up vast areas of the world to the global market. And most surprising of all, Volker tightened up the money supply and interest rates went high, causing people to save money and stop borrowing to consume.

L: That's not happening this time.

D: No. We got lucky back then. Since the 1990s we've had a long and totally phony, debt-driven boom that's now come to an end. I feel very confident that there's no way out this time. There are huge distortions and misallocations of capital that have been cranked into the system for two decades. And not just in the United States this time, but in Europe, China, Japan, and elsewhere.

The United States is very clearly on the decline. The fact that in spite of bankrupting military expenditures to no gain for the American people, those in power are talking overtly and aggressively about attacking more countries—Iran and Pakistan in particular—is extremely grave. The fact that they attacked Libya—which, incidentally, is going to turn into a total disaster, a civil war that will last for years—shows it's not stopping. Sure, Obama brought troops home from Iraq—another disaster that's going to remain a disaster for years to come—but at the same time he put a company of combat troops in Uganda, of all places, and Marines in Australia, to provoke the Chinese.

Back home, I've read reports that people are being stopped for carrying gold coins out of the United States, in Houston in particular. Now we have authorization of the military to detain U.S. citizens, on U.S. soil, with no trail, and indefinitely, on the verge of becoming law. And Predator Drones have been used to hunt down farmers on their own ranches.

I could go on and on. This is not like spotting early signs of decay in America's expansionist wars of the nineteenth century or things getting worse with FDR. Most people can't see it with all the noise and confusion, but we've reached the edge of the precipice.

L: Don't worry about exactly where the edge is, just assume it's there and take appropriate action?

D: Yes. It really is there. It's a clear and present danger. But most Americans are as oblivious as most Germans were in the 1930s. In fact, most of them support what's going on, just as most Germans supported their government in the 1930s and 1940s.

L: So, don't worry about figuring out exactly when the gates will shut. Assume they are shutting now?

D: That's right. One should be actively and vigorously looking to expatriate assets, cash, and even one's self. A prudent person will always be diversified politically and internationally.

L: What about people who have jobs they can't continue doing from abroad and who need the income?

D: They should still prepare, as best they can, to be ready to go on a vacation when things get hot—a vacation from which they might not return for a long time. All that needs happen, with the hysteria that's building in the United States, is for a major terrorist incident—real or imagined—to occur. Homeland Security will lock the country down. I hate to admit it, but I'm almost starting to credit the stories about those FEMA camps.

Look, I know it sounds extreme, and the comparison to pre–World War II Germany has been made many times, but it bears repeating. Germany was the most literate, civilized, and even mellow, in some ways, country in Europe. It was much admired all around the world—a nation of shopkeepers, small farmers, and scholars. But the whole character of the place started changing in 1933, and it just got worse and worse. By the end of 1939, if you weren't out, you were done.

L: [Pauses] Well, not a cheerful thought. Actions to take?

D: Things we've said before: Set up foreign bank accounts in places you like to travel, while you can. Set up vault arrangements for physical precious metals outside the United States. Buy foreign real estate that you'd like to own, because it can't be forcibly repatriated. Offshore asset protection trusts are a good idea too. Become an International Man. Let me emphasize that U.S. taxpayers should stay within all U.S.

laws, because the consequences of breaking them are unbelievably draconian.

Generally, one simply must internationalize one's assets. The biggest danger investors face, by far, is not market risk—huge as that will be—but political risk. The only way to insulate yourself from such risk is to diversify yourself politically and geographically.

L: Right then. Words to the wise. Thanks for your insight.

D: You're welcome. Most won't, but I just hope readers listen.

Part Four

YOU AND ME AND THE OTHER 8 BILLION

Chapter 29

Doug Casey on the Royal Wedding

June 15, 2011

Louis: Hola Doug, what's on your mind this week? The woes of the Middle East, since you're on your way there?

Doug: I'm "wheels up" tomorrow evening for something of a whirlwind visit to Israel, Egypt, Lebanon, and Dubai. So that's on my mind. But at the moment, I want to talk about the disgraceful spectacle of the royal wedding, before everyone forgets about it.

L: You mean that cleric who did cartwheels down the aisle after the ceremony? I thought it was rather amusing, myself.

D: Well, it's nice to see the thing treated with the lack of respect it deserves, but that's entirely too rare. The whole thing makes me roll my eyes. It's an affront to the human spirit. It's degrading, the way the masses fawn over these so-called royals, as though they were superior beings. Royalty have claimed to be superior for centuries. They're not superior. In fact, they're unworthy of respect.

L: Gee Doug, you're beating around the bush again.

D: It's important to call a spade a spade, to say the emperor has no clothes, as in the old fairy tale. It's maddening and disappointing to see how people are awed by pomp and circumstance. There are estimates that a billion people around the world took time out of their lives to watch two people they don't know, and have no meaningful connection with, make promises to each other they probably won't keep. Didn't they learn anything from the union of jug-eared Charles with dim-witted Diana? Why are royals still put on pedestals? This is the twenty-first century, for crying out loud. It's disgusting to see people go all gaga and woozy in the knees because these descendants of gangsters celebrated a perfectly ordinary event at huge public expense. I'd much rather watch the excellent merengue-dancing dog than a dozen royal weddings.

L: It is a bit odd, now that you mention it. I'm not sure that one-sixth of the planet watched the wedding—even later on the Internet—but a lot sure did. People don't generally believe kings are anything special anymore, and yet these folks were treated as though they were. I was vaguely aware this was going on, but it didn't even occur to me to watch it. I'm reminded of Howard Roark, when he's confronted alone one night by his would-be nemesis, Ellsworth Toohey. Toohey tells him they are alone and challenges Roark to say what he really thinks of Toohey, and Roark answers, "But I don't think of you," and walks away.

D: Rand was a genius. She understood that one shouldn't clutter one's mind with the frivolous affairs of nonentities.

L: But really, why should we even spend a single second talking about the wedding of two people who mean nothing to us?

D: We shouldn't. It's no more important than the marriage of a couple of actors in Hollywood, or Bollywood, for that matter. But the social phenomenon means something, although I think coverage should have been consigned to the pages of supermarket tabloids, not the major media. The sad fact is that most people will pay lip service to royals and treat them with deference. That's why we should talk about it.

L: Okay, but let me play devil's advocate for a bit. This particular prince seems relatively decent, as royals go. No major scandals yet. Seems to be conducting himself honorably as a soldier. Maybe he's not such a bad fellow, and people could have reasons other than idolizing aristocracy for caring about his wedding.

D: He also plays a good game of <u>polo</u>, which inclines me towards him. Well, individually, some royals are decent human beings. You can't hold it against someone, just because he was born in a castle, any more than if he was born in a trailer park.

But being treated like royalty has to be a corrupting influence. It tilts the odds against a person, as do the negative effects of inbreeding on people who've mated within such a narrow gene pool for hundreds of years. If one stripped them of their silks and jewels, and put them in a lineup, the royals would more closely resemble people who have been trapped in an isolated hollow in Appalachia for many generations—something you'd see in that movie *Deliverance*—than they would normal people. But that's not my problem with royals. What I object to is the very concept of royalty itself.

L: That should be obvious, but spell it out for us, Doug. Why?

D: Royals, historically, are basically no more than successful thugs— people with no distinction other than being exceptionally ruthless and effective at seizing power and subduing others with it. The first king in the world was probably an unusually crafty leader of a particularly strong band of thieves who attacked and subdued a more peaceful tribe of early farmers. Instead of just killing the men and children and enslaving the women, he offered them a deal: "You give me and my men the best huts, the prettiest girls, and feed us, and we'll let you all live and keep farming—we'll even defend you against other thugs like us, if each family gives us a son to train as fighters."

Throughout the millennia since then, it's been the same raw deal. Most of the time it was simply naked "might makes right" thinking; Genghis Khan didn't bother with any excuses. Rulers in more recent times have made up different excuses for wielding power, like the "divine right of kings." In the modern world, there's the myth of the "social contract" and the widespread belief that government— democratic government—is necessary for social order and prosperity. It's all anti-rational myth.

None of these ideas are correct; they are nothing more than a collection of lies that rulers and their lackeys fabricate to keep the people docile under their yoke. As bad as monarchy is, though, in some ways democracy is an even worse system. Democracy is really just a sanitized version of mob rule, which is potentially even more dangerous and destructive. At least the monarchs had some incentive to care for the people they ruled, in the same way a rancher cares for the animals he owns; they're worth much more to him alive than dead.

But I digress. We can talk about the false religion of democracy another time. The point is that people should not bow down and worship the progeny of successful criminals and gangsters. I'm inclined to agree with Diderot, who said men would never be free until the last king was strangled with the entrails of the last priest.

L: I wonder if he would state that differently these days, since the clergy don't tend to prop up rulers the way they used to. Today, he might say "last president" and "last reporter." But you know what strikes me as being most strange about royals? It's the way they are regarded so positively in modern countries that still have them, even by people who should abhor the very concept of some men ruling over others. In England, for a particularly relevant example, I've found that even libertarians like the royals. They seem to find them endearing, like a batty old aunt who drools occasionally and smells of mothballs, but is harmless.

D: I know what you mean, even though I don't understand it. It's one thing to worship a sports hero, who is at least worthy of admiration for being supremely competent at some difficult task. Or to love certain actors or actresses who seem to have the beauty of the gods and play the roles of such admirable beings. Or a singer who makes you feel good. Or even your plumber or dentist, if you like, for being honorable and productive tradespeople who do valuable work. But royals don't do anything qua royals but parade around as though they were elevated beings of some sort. Their very existence—and the flaunting of their aristocracy in the media—is demeaning to all people. Their elevation above others, due to the successful criminals in their family trees, is a moral inversion of the most grotesque sort.

People who grovel before royals suffer from a form of what's known as the *Stockholm Syndrome*: The adoration some victims come to feel for those who oppress them. It speaks very poorly of the common man, actually.

L: I don't disagree, but people love having heroes, and they seem to need to believe in positive myths—fairy tales—to boost morale. Is there any point in criticizing them for their choices of myths and heroes?

D: Yes. Ideas have consequences. Worshiping someone like Tiger Woods may set you up for disappointment if you talk yourself into thinking of him as a perfect being, but that's about all the harm it can do. At least Tiger has demonstrated genuine ability in his chosen field, and is a self-made man, whatever his personal flaws. Allowing yourself to participate, however remotely, in the myth of aristocracy is dangerous to you and everyone else on this planet.

We may not convince many people who don't see things the way we do. But there are those who do believe it is wrong for some men to rule over others and just haven't thought about this. I encourage them to work to extinguish the demented and destructive myth of hereditary superiority of some people over others. Royals are not quaint reminders of beautiful fairy tales, but nothing more than the overrated descendants of thugs.

L: I won't argue with that, but is it necessarily so? There are many historical kings who are revered, all around the world. Didn't some of those men, and the few women among them, do some good for their people? Like Moses leading his people out of slavery?

D: When we're talking about classes of people there are exceptions to the rule here and there, but they are the exceptions, not the rule. To the victors go the spoils—and the writing of the histories. So of course royals have usually gotten great press; it has historically been very dangerous to tell the truth about them. We read about some great kings who united their people and defeated their foreign enemies, like Alexander the Great. But that just means that Alexander killed his local rivals and set out to plunder others around him, just like any successful gang member might in Los Angeles today. The fact that Alexander built great cities and monuments, encouraged scholarship and learning, and was more enlightened than many of his rivals doesn't mean that he had the right to kill all the people he killed to build his empire.

I can't think of a single dynasty that was put in place due to the acts of a heroic liberator. As soon as a supposed liberator sets himself up as the new king, he then ceases to be a liberator. And if he's the very rare "real McCoy," a real liberator who walks away from power, then there's no dynasty; his line does not become "royal blood." These things are, if not mutually exclusive, then at least in oppositional tension. For every Cincinnatus, there are a dozen Tamerlanes.

L: What about the merchant princes who rose to power in Renaissance Italy, like the Medici?

D: The Medici were not official royalty in the Republic of Florence, but four of them became popes, who certainly counted as rulers back then, and the family eventually did become royalty—rulers of the Duchy of Florence. The merchant princes originally created value by trade in those days, but it seems as if things always degrade over time. Just like in the United States. We used to have merchant princes— Carnegie, Mellon, Vanderbilt, Astor—who wielded a lot of power because they created a lot of value. They were a natural aristocracy, a meritocracy. They've been replaced by political hacks—Bushes, Clintons, Obamas—who create nothing and wield much more power.

L: Hm. Okay then. Why do you suppose we even have these fairy tales of beautiful and noble princesses and handsome princes who marry and become benevolent rulers under whom the people prosper? The reality is that princes were privileged brutes who were taught to rule over others, and princesses were poker chits, given away as sexual slaves to seal treaties and other deals. Love would have been as rare among them as a snowflake in the inner circles of hell, and nobility simply the public facade given to the naked thirst for ever-expanding power and dominion over others. At any given time and place, the poor suckers staggering under the weight of their so-called betters must have seen the ugly truth for what it is. How could fairy tales that fly in the face of such overwhelming reality ever get started?

D: That's a great question. Maybe for the same reason people like to believe in heaven and angels. Maybe because Hitler was correct when he observed that a big lie is easier to sell than a little lie. Those princes probably inspired mainly pure terror and loathing—or greed and ambition—among the women unfortunate enough to cross their paths. The princesses were locked up in iron chastity belts of such cruel designs that they made their status as sexual prisoners quite clear. The castles were not gleaming white Camelots, but dirty, smelly, filthy places full of political conniving above and prisoners in chains below, from which heavily armed and armored groups of men would sally forth not to slay dragons, but to intimidate the peasants into submission.

But then, neither do I understand how people today all around the world can believe that their soldiers are brave and honest and incapable of any wrongdoing, while everybody else's soldiers are vile and destined to defeat. And "our" politicians are honest and have the public's interests at heart, while "their" leaders are evil and conniving scum. Well, I guess they're half right on that one, anyway. All of these things fly in the face of daily experience, and yet the myths persist. It's totally perverse.

L: I've never understood that either. Sure, you grow up with a certain indoctrination; I can see why young schoolchildren would tend to see their president as a heroic figure. But as one grows older and the facts of reality clash with the myths we are taught, one stops believing in them—such as Santa Claus. Why then do so many of us persist in believing in the goodness of a political class that is caught red-handed in one lie, crime, or hypocrisy after another, on a daily basis? Or, perhaps more accurately, how is it that people can face the failure of individual political heroes time after time and not question the system that spawns them, or the myths that enable that system? The worship of royals just seems like a particularly egregious case of this general syndrome.

D: That is a really tough question, and it's one we probably won't find an answer to today. Many Russians to this day think Stalin was a hero. Many Chinese to this day apotheosize Mao. We could say it's an aspect of human mass psychology, but that just puts a label on it, doesn't explain the reasons why it happens.

Here's another question: Are Americans really that different from the Chinese or the Russians?

What I do know is that this syndrome of worshiping and following leaders has enabled the worst atrocities in history.

L: Understood. Hm. Well, I can't imagine what it would be, but are there any investment implications to the colossal waste of time and money this royal wedding has foisted on the struggling British economy?

D: Well, as you know, I like to look on the bright side of things.

L: There's a bright side?

D: I think so. The world used to be totally run by royals. Now there are very few places that even have royals, and those places don't really let them run the show; they are kept on as figureheads, with no real say in steering the ship of state. So, you could say mankind has mostly progressed beyond the belief in hereditary superiority. As we touched on above, I'm not sure that democracy is much better than monarchy—if one man rules me or a bunch of men rule me, I'm still going to object to being ruled. I'm hopeful that the march of progress, especially technological progress, will eventually lead to a society in which people rule themselves.

People often seem to think we're professional prophets of doom and gloom around here at Casey Research, but long term, we're actually extremely optimistic. Many of the great problems that confound the world today will be solved in the future. The longest-term trend of them all—one I am betting on personally—is the ascent of man.

L: And the ascent of man requires humans to grow up and stop believing in fairy tales, from Santa to royalty—and eventually to the nation-state itself. A positive note. But how do you play that?

D: It's not something you can speculate on short term. But if you believe in progress—the ascent of man—your personal and financial planning can't be stuck in the way the world is today. You have to look forward to how it is going to be and plan accordingly. At the current rate of progress in medical technology, for instance, I think 40-year-olds should have 100-year plans, at the least.

No one should be spending down his or her wealth. Everyone not on their deathbeds should be considering what to do if they live a very long time to come. In my view, that makes it important to have a substantial and strategically deployed speculative component to one's investments. And that strategy should not put all one's eggs in one basket, no matter how appealing it may look, like the precious metals look to me today. Going long on energy, short on government bonds, long on powerful, proven new technologies—strategies of that sort are vital to anyone planning to be around for years to come.

L: You're being polite and not pushing our products, but I have to mention that this is—not coincidentally—exactly what we focus on here at Casey Research. Well, thanks for another interesting conversation.

D: My pleasure.

L: 'Til next time.

Chapter 30

Doug Casey on Gay Marriage

June 30, 2011

Louis: So, what's on your mind this week?

Doug: Another subject likely to piss off a fair number of our readers: gay marriage. New York just became the sixth state to legalize same-sex marriages and will begin issuing licenses next month. Some people have asked if I think this is good or bad. My view is that marriage is a contract between two people, so I don't see why the state should have any involvement in the matter at all. A marriage needs the state like a fish needs a bicycle.

L: A good anarchist answer, but in today's world people involve the state in enforcing their contracts all the time. So it matters to them if they want to enter into this particular type of contract and the state won't recognize it.

D: Yes, that's likely the real issue here. It's not so much about being able to love and live with whomever you want—a man and a man, a woman and a woman, or for that matter, any number of men and women together—but about benefits, particularly those administered by the state. A lot of people want spousal social security benefits, for instance. Fortunately, over the last 50 years, most laws about cohabitation, sodomy, adultery, and such have been either overturned or rendered dead letters and unenforceable. So now it's mainly a question of gaining legal recognition of a relationship for the purpose of benefits.

L: Assuming that's correct, is there any reason such people should not have the same benefits others get? If your life partner is dying in a hospital, but they won't let you in because the state doesn't recognize your right to be there, that's not good.

D: No. It's none of the state's business. But such things can be handled by other means—powers of attorney, insurance contracts, living wills, and accepted social mores. There is no need for laws about these things. Laws are not incarnate wisdom, after all. They are much more likely only an incarnation of current fashion, or monetary interests, or the psychological aberrations of the legislators who pass them.

L: What about children? If there are children involved one way or another, and there's a divorce between life partners not recognized by the state, that could get pretty messy.

D: Yes, and almost any kind of legislative knavery can be justified in most people's minds if it's "for the children." Involving the state to defend the children makes about as much sense as involving a particularly stupid and unpredictable *Tyrannosaurus rex* to defend the children. It's a sign of how degraded our culture has become that people look to an instrument of institutionalized coercion as the first solution to any problem. People's private lives should be their private business. If the state is to exist at all, my view is that it should exist strictly to defend people against aggression. That could be argued to imply the core state functions of police, military, and courts. But it does not imply any laws regarding how people conduct their lives together in marriage.

L: And if the state were not involved, then fewer people would feel that they are involved in something they disapprove of. If marriage was an entirely private affair, it would be no one's business but those directly involved. When the state gets involved, the issue becomes more contentious, with those opposed wanting to ban it, and those in favor wanting it recognized. Get the state out, and that whole battle goes away.

D: True. To me, it's a sign of a serious character flaw when somebody says, "There ought to be a law!" MYOB—mind your own business. Getting a bunch of busybodies who hang out in state legislatures involved in such a private affair is ridiculous, on the face of it—worse, actually, since most of these types conflate religious beliefs with <u>ethics</u>. The situation is worst in the Muslim world, most particularly in Saudi Arabia, but it's bad enough right here in the United States.

L: I agree, but just to play devil's advocate for a moment, what about the people who say that MYOB isn't good enough in this case, because gay, lesbian, or multiple-partner marriages are a sin? They don't want to live in an openly sinful environment. They don't want their children to see openly gay couples walking down the street, holding hands, and so on.

D: Well, first we have to analyze this concept of "sin," which seems peculiar to the three popular Abrahamic religions. Personally, I don't acknowledge the popular concept of sin, although this isn't the time to explore that. Perhaps in the weeks to come.

For the moment, it's enough to note that those openly homosexual couples walking down the street are not aggressing against anyone. So using any kind of force against them, whether direct or delegated to men in uniform, is totally unjustified. Moreover, why pick on this particular sin as one that must be hidden? If you believe in sin, there are all sorts of sins going on all the time, all around us—it's on TV 24/7. If one doesn't like it, one should simply avert one's eyes, and encourage one's children to do the same.

The law is often used to make everyone act—or not act—a certain way. No wonder the law is disregarded, or even held in contempt, by significant parts of society. You're asking for trouble—guaranteed—once laws relate to anything beyond protecting people and their property from aggression.

If the law could make puppets out of men, the Soviets would have succeeded. But even if it were possible, it'd be evil to enslave people to your vision of how they should be.

If you really want to insulate your children from certain things, you could move to, or create, a community of people who all agree with your values. Fundamentalist Christians, for example, could move to communities so overwhelmingly conservative that liberals or homosexuals wouldn't dream of living there.

L: What if they don't want to move?

D: Then they should stop whining about seeing what they don't want to see. The quirky mores of San Francisco, or The Village in New York, are what give them their charm. The quirky values of small towns in the heartland give them a different type of charm. *Vive la différence*. It's strictly a matter of taste, not ethics. And how stupid is it to try to legislate taste? If you're not willing to become a dictator and impose your morals on everyone, then choose to be with those who agree with you most. And if you do want to become a dictator, then accept the fact that you have chosen a path of coercion that usually ends with a bullet with your name on it. Delegating coercion to the legislature does not change its basic nature.

L: When it comes to forcing others to do what you want, the ballot box is just an indirect form of the cartridge box.

I remember speaking with a conservative man in Utah who objected to the sale or rental of X-rated videos in local shops. This would lead to spreading moral decay, and someday a prostitute might approach his son on the streets of Salt Lake City. My answer was, "How have you educated your son? If he'd say no, then what's the worry? If he'd say yes, then the prostitute is not the problem."

D: Good point. People who want to legislate these things are, in fact, admitting that they're moral failures—and usually hypocrites as well. It's no mere coincidence, I'd say, that it's most often Bible-thumping Republicans who get outed for being gay. But further, if you'd had that conversation with that Mormon chap before Utah banned polygamy, he would have been the deviant, according to the larger society. "I'm a freedom fighter, you're a rebel, he's a terrorist." Any laws other than those dealing with aggression are completely capricious and arbitrary.

L: There you touch on something I've long argued is very important: Giving the state the power to force other people to do things, even if it's to do things your way, is very dangerous. We're not talking about stopping murder, theft, and other forms of aggression, but actively forcing others to conform to your views, even when they do not aggress upon you. If you give the state that power, it then has the power to force you to do things other people's ways, if those others gain power.

This is why we have separation of church and state: No matter who wins an election, everyone can practice their religion—or lack thereof—as they see fit. The exact same principle applies in other areas of life, including sexual orientation and lifestyle choices. It's just that certain choices have been so unpopular for so long, people have not seen this issue clearly for what it is. They've been intellectually careless, failing to stand for something on principle because it was more comfortable for them. But that sloth may come back to haunt them, as the population shifts and its dominant values shift with it.

D: Exactly. There are people who say that marriage can only exist between one man and one woman. That excludes life partnerships between men and men, and women and women—but it also excludes marriages between multiple spouses, which is perfectly acceptable in many societies, including Islamic ones—at least if it's between a man and several women. The way things are going, most of Europe—and maybe North America too—could become Muslim continents in the next 100 years.

So if you're going to wish for a government strong enough to enforce majority social mores, beware of what you wish for: You may get it.

L: I'm on your side there, but again, we don't live in an anarcho-libertarian society. People's gender, sexual orientation and proclivities, marital arrangements, and such should all be private affairs, but they are not. There are laws against many people's peaceful, consensual choices in many states. Sodomy, for example. Polygamy. Polyamory in general. So what about those who see the passage of such laws as a way to force society to respect their right to be left alone to do as they please? It would be hard, for example, to prosecute someone for sodomy in a state that has a gay marriage law—or one that has law reciprocity with a state that does.

D: Well then, the proper legislative agenda is to repeal all laws that interfere with people's peaceful and private choices. That would be a start. If homosexuals use the power of the state as a bludgeon to try to force others to accept their ways, they are no better than the moral majority types who want to make laws to promote their agendas. I hate busybodies, regardless of their sexual preferences.

L: Good answer. Okay then, what about investment implications? Buy stock in a company that makes condoms?

D: I think the condom boom peaked in the 1980s, so probably not. People will have sex with whomever they please, regardless of the law. So—ethics aside—it's just an immense waste of time and resources when the state tries to enforce the preferences of some people on other people. It makes society materially poorer, as well as morally more corrupt. They stupidly say it will make society more harmonious, when it actually leads to nothing but resentment and hostility.

There are, as readers of these conversations may have noted, a lot more reasons to be pessimistic over the next few years than to be optimistic. But the liberalization of the marriage laws we're now seeing is definitely one cause for optimism. It clears away some state-created distortions in an area of society. Now, if we could do that completely, in all areas of society, it would likely usher in a period of unparalleled peace, prosperity, and happiness. So let's hope that the legalization of gay marriage in New York is a straw in the wind.

L: Very well. I wonder if we'll get more e-mail about gay marriage than we got about our failure to love Bitcoin.

D: I guess we're about to find out.

L: Right then. Thanks for your thoughts. We'll talk next week.

D: My pleasure.

Chapter 31

Doug Casey on
Self-Immolation—
Individual
and National

July 13, 2011

Louis: Labas, "Dougas," as we might say in Lithuania—sure is beautiful here! It's 11:30 P.M. and the sun is below the horizon, but the sky is still smoldering. Where are you, and what's on your mind this week?

Doug: It's afternoon here in Aspen, a nice little communist town in the Rockies. From here the world seems to be turning as usual, but that's only because the place is full of people who are so rich that they're largely insulated from the real world, as are the parasites who live off them. We'll have to talk about the politics and sociology of Aspen sometime. But out in the real world, the engines are grinding toward a halt on the American *Titanic*—but it's still moving, so everyone thinks everything is fine. There are signs that the 2008 iceberg was

bigger than the crew is telling us, however, for anyone paying attention. Did you hear about that man who set himself on fire in front of
a courthouse in New Hampshire?

L: I did, but only through e-mail from friends.

D: Yes, the same with me; we have the same friends. It's truly shocking
that a story like this got absolutely zero major media coverage, even
though it went out on AP. In Tunisia, a fruit and vegetable street
vendor sets himself on fire to protest his government making his life
impossible, and it sparks a revolution that doesn't even stop at his
country's borders. Something similar happens in the United States
and no one even hears about it—at least not this time. In February
2010, there was a guy who crashed his plane into an IRS office; that
did make the national news. But perhaps since then the word has
gone out that these things shouldn't be reported for fear of encouraging others, "national security," or whatnot.

L: Thomas Ball wasn't a fruit vendor, but a divorced man who apparently felt that the court system had put him in an impossible situation.
[Ball's last statement is available online.] I'm not a conspiracy theo-
rist, but it defies belief that every single major news editor across the
country decided on his own that such a striking story wasn't news.

D: I know. Not a lot surprises me anymore, but this truly is shocking.
In my entire life I can only remember two previous instances of
self-immolation. The first was that of Buddhist monks during the
Vietnam War. I didn't know what to make of it at the time, but it sure
caught everyone's attention.

L: Why did they do it? U.S. troops on the temple steps?

D: No, they were protesting the rule of Ngo Diem in the south, who
was Catholic and giving them a hard time. The United States, of
course, was supporting the terminally corrupt Diem regime. When,
I'd like to know, has the United States ever supported anybody but
the worst criminal available in third-world countries? The second
instance was the one in Tunisia earlier this year that touched off the
Arab Spring—which is far from over, by the way. Thomas Ball is the
first case of it in U.S. history—first one I've ever heard of, at any
rate—and it received no press whatsoever, outside of acknowledg-
ment in the local papers. The Internet picked it up, of course, but
to me it seems extraordinarily serious that an event like this can

transpire and not even get noticed. Instead, the headlines were dedicated to such urgent matters as that stupid congresscreature, Weiner.

L: So, are you saying that the powers that be censored the story?

D: If they didn't, it's certainly further proof of how degraded society has become in the United States that something like this could go unnoticed. It's appalling—disgusting, actually. And scary, on a couple of levels.

But get this: When I was in Dubai a couple of weeks ago, a guide I'd hired to show me around had heard of the event. It was big news there that everyone heard about—it was in all the papers. So you could make the argument that the average Arab may know more about what's happening in the U.S. than the average American does. That's a turnaround.

L: What were you doing in Dubai?

D: It had been a while, and I wanted to see how things had changed since the crisis. I also went to Israel, Egypt, and Lebanon. I'll have some articles on my findings in the Middle East in the next few issues of *The Casey Report*. Obviously, the area being prime oil hunting ground, I was thinking about energy-related speculations a great deal. In practical terms, energy really means oil, coal, gas, and nuclear—green energy is nice, but hydrocarbons and nuclear are the only forms of mass power that can satisfy any need, anywhere, anytime. Most particularly oil. Developments in oil affect the Middle East, and developments in the Middle East affect oil.

L: Hm. Speaking of nuclear, we haven't talked about that since our conversation on Fukushima, and there's been time for new market trends to become visible. What do you think?

D: Well, as we speak, I see that the price of uranium is $54.25 per pound. It was about $70 before Fukushima, dropped to about this level, bounced back to the high $50s, and is now fluctuating in the low $50s, so it's definitely cheaper than it was before. But it was over $140 a pound in 2007, so it's much cheaper than it has already been in this cycle. On the other hand, it's still roughly six times what it was at the end of the 1990s, when it bottomed around $9. That's pretty good performance for a commodity. Still, I've got to say that I think it has a lot of upside yet ahead, although keeping track of prices in dollar terms is becoming ever more tricky, as the dollar itself fluctuates wildly—mostly down—and the official CPI statistics become ever more unreliable.

The reason I'm still bullish on uranium is because, as we said before—and Fukushima notwithstanding—nuclear power is still the cleanest, safest, and cheapest type of mass power generation available. I find it quite ludicrous that the Germans have announced that they will phase out all of their nuclear plants over the next decade. Where are they going to get the power to replace the approximately 22 percent they get from nuclear now? Windmills aren't going to do it. Solar doesn't have a prayer in northern Europe. Are they going to burn more coal? That'd be great for their environment.

L: Aside from pumping sulfur into the air, coal plants emit C-14 too, and that's radioactive. Nukes emit less. Maybe they plan to wear thicker coats and eat more cold food?

D: There's a lot of radioactive material released from burning coal, including uranium. Geothermal would be nice, but Germany is not Iceland. Maybe they think they can burn more natural gas, but that's a greenhouse issue—although the whole greenhouse gas/global warming hysteria has always impressed me as something in between a political scam, a fraud, and a new age religion. But we covered that in a prior conversation; no need to beat a dead horse. Anyway, it seems to me that the global warming hysteria actually peaked a few years ago, and will soon be just another idiotic embarrassment everyone will be anxious to forget. Especially when another hysteria catches their attention.

L: The Russians would love to see the Germans burning more natural gas.

D: Of course. And they wouldn't be shy about demanding political concessions as well as higher prices when they can shut off the pipelines to Europe in the middle of the winter. The Germans will get what they deserve. But then, most everybody eventually does. I've got no sympathy for them; stupidity is its own reward.

L: That would literally be a cold war. No need for ballistic missiles. Looks like national self-immolation on the part of the Germans.

D: Right—the German reaction is clearly political grandstanding pandering to hysteria. I wouldn't count on the policy ever being carried through to completion, and wouldn't be the least bit surprised to see it reversed after the first winter when there's not enough power to go around. They really have no other practical alternative, though they might try to finesse it by importing electricity from France, which produces over 75 percent of its power from nukes.

Meanwhile, that hysteria is certainly going to slow down nuclear power in the United States, but as we said in our conversation after the disaster in Japan, world demographic trends leave no choice but to employ more nuclear power. That makes the current relatively low prices an opportunity.

L: In that context, we should probably mention that there was a flood in the U.S. midwest, and the Fort Calhoun nuclear power plant in Nebraska was flooded. A dike surrounding the plant was even breached, but there appears to be no sign of danger yet. Granted, the plant was shut down for maintenance at the time of the flood, but still, the thing seems to be taking the abuse as designed.

D: That's right, and it bears reiterating that at this point, all of these operating plants are basically 40-year-old technology. Because of the hysteria and resultant government regulations, newer, better, and even safer designs have not been implemented. Almost all the reactors in use today are what are known as *Generation 2*. But there are probably two dozen Gen 3 and 3-plus designs that could be deployed; and in a few years, there will be Gen 4 units available. Some of these designs are extraordinary—from 10 to 50 megawatts, self-contained, with almost no moving parts, extremely small, low cost, and capable of being buried for a decade, until they need refueling.

L: So, buy uranium and uranium exploration stocks?

D: That's one way to play it, and we do have a lot of exposure to uranium's upside in our portfolio. Another, more ground-floor way to play it might be to look into thorium plays. As I understand it, thorium—element 90 on the periodic table—is actually better for power generation than uranium or plutonium. Nuclear scientists originally proposed it for power generation, but governments opted for uranium because it coincided with their weapons programs. As usual, government interference takes us down the wrong path.

L: As usual. So, there's an opportunity to invest in nuclear while it's unpopular, and while it's unpopular, that's bullish for hydrocarbons.

D: Right. I subscribe to the peak oil theory. By that I do not mean that the world is running out of oil, but that the easy availability of conventional sweet, light crude is in decline. There's plenty more oil to be found, but it's a more expensive to process, heavy oil. Or it's shale oil, or comes from tar sands, or it's deep under the ocean, which has its own environmental issues and is neither cheap nor easy to produce.

Peak oil is a geological concept. It basically holds that all the low-hanging fruit has been picked. Now, philosophically, it rubs me the wrong way, in that I have total confidence that human ingenuity will find scores of ways to produce new hydrocarbon fuels—and lots of totally new energy sources in addition. Furthermore, the higher oil prices go, the more will be found, and the more it will be economized. So, in a free-market world, oil is a non-problem.

But we don't currently live in that kind of world. In the meantime—let's say the next 10 to 20 years—oil is an issue, for simple geological reasons. And also because, even though consumption has been basically flat in the advanced world for decades, consumption is going to grow radically in "Chindia" and the rest of the developing world. The biggest problem though is likely political, especially because of the increased political risk in the Middle East, where most of the world's oil reserves are. You've got to be bullish on oil.

L: Even with the stuff at $100 a barrel?

D: Yes. I believe the odds favor it going to $200, even $250 a barrel before too long. I say that despite the fact I'm much more comfortable buying things when they're manifestly cheap, and nobody wants them. But at the same time, it's important to see the trend, and make the trend your friend. And I see no reason to believe this one is anywhere near an end.

L: Okay. But you're also famous for predicting the coming—now started—Greater Depression. In a major, global economic reversal, wouldn't energy consumption decrease, and hence prices drop?

D: That's certainly a possibility, but China, India, and the rest of the third world are marching, increasingly, to the beats of their own drums these days. The Greater Depression will definitely affect them adversely, but the enormous growth that has already gone on there won't stop, despite the fact China has misallocated gigantic amounts of money in property. There could very well be a real revolution there in the next 10 years. People forget that during one of the most turbulent periods in history, 1914 to 1946—including, among other disasters, World War I, the Great Depression, and World War II—the world economy expanded by something like 1.8 percent annually. That trend will continue at one level or another, even if there's a truly massive upset in the global economy, which I fully expect. The countries of the world will compete in using more oil; China will greatly increase its imports. India even more so. The price will necessarily rise.

So, sure, there could be a dip, especially if there's a big financial crash, but that would not change the major underlying trend. Long-term energy demand is not dictated by speculators or other financial factors; at heart it's based on demographic and technological trends, and those are not going to change easily nor soon. Oil, in particular, supplies very dense and convenient energy. It will be superseded, but not soon.

L: So if oil and gas stocks retreat on bad news, back up the truck for more?

D: Exactly. And it seems to me that in today's world, in which nothing is cheap, one thing that is relatively cheap and a good value is natural gas. The reason it's cheap is that previous high prices spurred technological developments, such as horizontal drilling and hydro-fracking, that have made huge resources of shale gas economic. This vast increase in supply has made natural gas cheaper, and the time to buy commodities is when they are cheap. You have to be a contrarian, buy what's unpopular, and sell when it's the flavor of the day. It's like my friend Rick Rule says: You're either a contrarian or a victim. That's natural gas right now: It's cheaper, in BTUs per dollar, compared to oil, than it's been for a very long time.

L: But there's some risk, too, especially with scare stories circulating about fracking causing gas leaks and problems on the surface. A political response could crush whole swathes of gas companies.

D: That's true, and it would be true even if the scare weren't completely unfounded hysteria, as I suspect it is. It's mostly the same people who are so hysterically anti-nuclear who are anti–new natural gas technologies. These stories about flames coming out of your water faucet have nothing to do with fracking. First, it's freakishly rare. Second, it can and does happen naturally, for the same reason you see oil (and gas) coming to the surface all over the world, or even marsh gas bubbling up from swamps. Fracking generally occurs thousands of feet under ground. Drinking water tables are close to the surface. It theoretically can have an effect, but as a practical matter does not. But I don't want to get into a discussion of that here. Marin Katusa has covered that ground, from all points of view, as you can see here.

The technophobes of the world are a costly nuisance to everybody. But the good news is that they only drive prices up more, much to the benefit of the companies which are not affected. So, the way to play this is not with any kind of blanket approach, but with well-selected companies that should do well, based on where and how they produce their natural gas.

L: Very good. And this time I don't have to ask you about investment implications.

D: Great. I love being off the hook. We'll leave it at that, then. Talk to you next week.

L: Sure, Doug, thanks for the insights.

D: My pleasure.

Chapter 32

Doug Casey on Cashless Societies

March 7, 2012

Louis: Doug, we've had a lot of questions from readers about the apparent push governments are making to go to paperless currency—all electronic, no cash. Do you think that's likely, and what would be the implications?

Doug: I think it's probably inevitable. It's not just cash, but the whole world is becoming increasingly digital. Credit cards already work very well all around the world, and everyone in the world, it seems, will soon have a smartphone—or at least everyone who might have any cash.

But it's not just a question of evolving technology. Governments hate cash for lots of reasons, starting with the fact it costs a couple of cents to print a piece of paper currency, and they have to be replaced quite often. As the United States has destroyed the value of the dollar, they've had to take the copper out of pennies, and soon they'll take the nickel out of nickels. Furthermore, with modern technology, counterfeiters—including unfriendly foreign governments—can turn out U.S. currency that's almost indistinguishable from the real thing. And the stuff takes up a lot of space if it's enough to be of value. So sure, governments would like to get rid of tangible currency. They'd like to see all money kept in banks, which are today no more than arms of the state. But it's not so simple: Increasing numbers of people trust neither banks, most of which are insolvent, or currencies, most of which are on their way to their intrinsic values.

L: Hm. On the technology front, when I was in central Africa a few weeks ago, plastic money was accepted happily everywhere I went—Rwanda, Burundi, the DRC, and Kenya—though not by street vendors yet. And I had access to the Internet everywhere I went, even in the middle of the jungle.

D: Yes, the move toward digital currencies is already happening, and not just as a result of government efforts. Remember Bitcoin. And, as you know, I'm a big fan of Goldmoney.com, which is leading the way to a sound digital currency. Although Goldmoney.com has bowed to government pressure and has suspended its service allowing customers to transfer funds among one another, it's another sign of the times.

L: Yes, and Goldmoney.com is not the first attempt, nor will it be the last. We should mention to new readers that you are an investor in Goldmoney.com.

D: The world's going to digital currencies is in part a good thing, because it's convenient. But it's definitely a double-edged sword, because of government involvement in the field. If it were a strictly market phenomenon, I'd have no problem with it. It'd be just another choice. But if the state runs it, it would reduce people's choices—and privacy. But that's entirely apart from the fact that government—and I know this assertion will be shocking to most readers—has no business creating currency or minting money. Money, of all things, should be a purely market phenomenon. Government, as an institution, inevitably and necessarily corrupts everything it touches. Money is far too important to be left to the tender mercies of the state.

L: Sure. A completely digital currency would be an unlimited license to print and spend. Need to give people more welfare? Just tap a few keys, and it appears in their bank accounts. Need to buy more missiles? Just a few more taps on the keyboard. But the privacy issue is even scarier: Digital money would seem like Big Brother's dream come true. They wouldn't even have to send their minions out to go through people's trash. They could see everything anyone ever spent money on and where they were physically when they did it, search for activity nearby, and much more, just by having computers report the details of people's accounts.

D: Exactly. They would justify it with a host of phony excuses ranging from the so-called War on Terrorism to the so-called War on Drugs. Maybe they'll tie it in to their disastrously failed War on Poverty. As the war on Islam heats up, one front will be an attack on the excellent Muslim *hawala* system, which allows cheap and reliable transfer of money between countries; that system, which is kind of a private SWIFT network, is excellent for evading FX controls. Ironically, Islamic countries are some of the very worst perpetrators of currency controls.

L: Maybe that's why the informal network exists in the first place? But yes, they gotta stop those evil money launderers from washing their money and hanging it out to dry.

D: Don't get me started on "money laundering." It's a completely artificial crime. It wasn't even heard of 20 years ago, because the "crime" didn't exist. Now, everyone speaks of it as though it were a real crime, like murder. It's ridiculous, and further proof of the totally degraded state of the average person worldwide, absolutely including U.S. citizens—what we used to call Americans. The government proclaims something as a law, and "sheeple" robotically assume it's part of the cosmic firmament. If an official tells them to do or not to do something, they roll over on their backs like whipped dogs and wet themselves out of fear. The War on Drugs may be where "money laundering" originated as a crime, but today it has a lot more to do with something infinitely more important to the state: the war on tax evasion.

Incidentally, not that a U.S. citizen can open an account with a Swiss bank anyway any longer—except with at least seven figures and loads of paperwork—but now the policy in Switzerland is to insist that clients prove that their funds are all tax paid. The situation is out of control. And the world's governments are increasingly working together to make sure no one slips through the net.

L: Gotta keep the cattle in line.

D: That's right; the United States has sent swarms of agents all around the world to bully and cajole bureaucrats in other countries into giving them access to bank account information and to impose income taxes in places that didn't have them. In Uruguay, where I was last week, for example, there was no income tax two years ago. Now there is. And they're trying to do the same thing in Paraguay. That's about the last personal-income-tax holdout among the larger countries of the world.

L: When I was in Paraguay last, they had passed an income-tax law, but it was being blocked from implementation by the legislature itself, on procedural grounds. I was told that since all of the legislators are deeply corrupted, none of them wants to have to account for their income, and that's why the measure will never be implemented. "Never" seems a bit optimistic, but it reminds me of your call to make corruption your friend. At any rate, why would the U.S. government care if other countries have income taxes—so they can have tax treaties with them?

D: I'm sure that's part of it. A bigger part may be that countries with high tax burdens want so-called tax harmonization, so it's less tempting to businesses and individuals to leave their borders and go where they can benefit from a lower tax burden—or pay no taxes at all. Governments all around the world, in spite of their differences, share a concern about their income streams, especially since most of them are absolutely bankrupt now, and their bureaucracies work together closely when it suits them. For example, the reason why you get asked if you are carrying more than $10,000 in cash on you when you board an international flight these days, even in a tiny African or South American country, is that it's an OECD standard that's been enthusiastically encouraged. When it first started, it was only $3,000, but that generated too much work for them, so they raised it to $10,000. But all the bad ideas in the world now seem to be coming out of the United States.

   You know, up until the Bank Secrecy Act of 1971, Americans didn't have to report foreign bank accounts or brokerage accounts. Reporting income generated by such accounts was required, but reporting the existence of the accounts themselves was not required.

The rules and reporting requirements have now become so draconian that most foreign banks don't even want to see a U.S. taxpayer darken their door, let alone open an account for one. It's a cancer, spreading out from the United States.

L: So, is this trend inevitable? At some point will Big Brother know everything about all transactions?

D: Yes. And if they can't get everything they want from you off your cell phone, which will probably also become your wallet with a digital credit card app at some point in the near future, they will be able to monitor everything physically via the swarms of tiny spy drones they will flood the skies with. Technology will soon make this cheap as dirt, and computational power is increasing rapidly to the point where it will be possible to process all the images.

L: Only if the people don't divulge everything they are doing and whom they are doing it with on Facebook and Twitter.

D: Ah, yes, Facebook, the CIA's most successful covert op. I idiotically opened a Facebook account some years back because someone convinced me it would be a good way to keep in touch with old school friends I'd lost touch with. Now I get scores of people who want to friend me every month, and I know very, very few of them. It will be one-stop shopping for Homeland Security to round up the usual suspects when they feel the time is right. I hate Facebook and never use it for anything. I wonder how many of my Facebook friends are actually government stooges out looking for somebody to railroad.

L: A sobering thought.

D: I have to say that the prognosis for privacy is very grim. The only possible saving grace I can see is that the snoops may end up with information overload, most of it worthless or irrelevant. That's what seriously impeded the East German and Romanian secret police. But with computer technology getting better and better, there's not much reason to believe Homeland Security will be buried the way the Stasi was with its primitive technology.

I really see no way to stop this trend, nor hide from it—at least in the United States or Europe. There's one thing, however, we can hope for: the coming collapse of the modern nation-state. This will happen, sooner or later, in Europe and North America, at least. This is a possible bright side of the building worldwide financial collapse:

It might bring down Big Brother, although it's more likely, I'm afraid, that he'll redouble his efforts to control everything. Unfortunately, the immediate aftermath of that collapse is likely to be very unpleasant, especially for those in the most developed and powerful countries.

The best way to insulate yourself from this, therefore, is to live in a country whose government doesn't have the power, financial resources, or technical ability to do these things. As per our last conversation, Africa might be a good place to get out of harm's way, but it's a bit too far off the beaten path for my taste and has way too many problems. That's why I like Latin America.

L: What about the hope that if people get pushed too far, they may rebel? Everyone has things they don't want made public, even those with absolutely nothing nefarious about them. A total lack of privacy would seem intolerable, after some—probably short—period of time. As Princess Leia told Governor Tarkin in the original *Star Wars* movie: The tighter they squeeze their fist, the more people will slip through their fingers. Or maybe not. It is, frankly, very dismaying to me that the Big Brother concept has been turned into a "reality" TV show.

D: People may think it's funny now, or even an egalitarian ideal to live in a society in which no one has any secrets, but that won't last. If only in relation to currency controls—what we started out talking about—I think there's something to your *Star Wars* quote. The more total the monitoring and control the state achieves over the legal economy, the more it will push people into the black market. We saw that in Soviet times. Stringent and very intrusive state monitoring, compulsion, and punishment only made the informal market flourish all the more. I'm sure this will happen. Even North Korea has an active black market. But I don't like that term. What's called "the black market" is really the free market; it's heroic. The legal market—with all its taxes and regulations—is actually the one in need of either radical reform or abolition.

L: But the monitoring beyond finance—your drone swarms—might make noncompliance too risky for most people to try.

D: True. And maybe the United States will get not just 10 percent of the population hooked on stuff like Prozac, but 20 or 50 percent. As Aldous Huxley pointed out in *Brave New World*, it's much easier to control zombies. That's another reason why I think that hope for the future rests in what are today derided as corrupt third-world countries.

If you're going to have a ridiculous number of impossible laws, corruption is a good thing. Increasingly, what matters is not the number or even nature of laws on the books in the place you live, but the amount of actual control the state has over private individuals. Corruption subverts idiotic laws; it's the next best thing to abolishing them.

L: I've often said that on paper, the United States is freer than Mexico, but in fact, Mexico has become much freer than the United States, in spite of its legally powerful socialist government. The average Mexican considers tax evasion to be a universal given, but U.S. taxpayers fear their government—a letter from the IRS can cause instant weight loss.

D: It's certainly true that in Argentina, where I'm building a new home, people don't fear their government. Well, not in the police-state sense, anyway; they see it as more of a nuisance. It's probably more accurate to say they are resigned to their government destroying the economy periodically than to say they actively fear it. If I get pulled over for speeding in Argentina—which itself would be highly unusual—I feel that I have nothing to fear at all, whereas back in the United States, I could end up getting tased, have my car taken, and do jail time for saying or doing the wrong thing, even without harming anyone. Any contact with the police in the United States brings an increasing risk of a lethal outcome these days. I understand that there are about 40,000 SWAT raids on real and imagined targets every year, and the number is growing fast.

Another contrast: In Argentina, most people despise the police and military, whereas in the United States, they are apotheosized. This tells you a lot about the psychological states of these populations—it's a very bad trend in the United States.

L: On the subject of Argentina, perhaps we should mention that readers who'd like to meet you could head down there for the upcoming harvest celebration.

D: Well, I'm in the middle of one right now, but another is coming up next week, and there's still time to sign up for that one. Sure—we have a lot of readers, and I've enjoyed meeting many, but it would be nice to get to know more of them. And it's a nice time to get away from the dying days of winter in the northern hemisphere and come to a place where the weather is pleasant and the wines are fantastic.

And I'm really tickled with our world-class gym, spa, and all the rest of it.

L: Very well. Investment implications?

D: Well, this highlights the importance of owning gold, but not for invest- ment purposes or even for the financial prudence we've spoken of before, but for a different kind of prudence: privacy—and even freedom.

  One thing that has changed since we started having these conver- sations—back when gold was trading at about $600 per ounce—is that having approached $2,000 per ounce, and being likely to surpass that level soon, governments are going to start clamping down on gold more and more. Back when gold was under $300 an ounce, it wasn't convenient to carry large nominal sums in gold—it was too bulky, too heavy. A roll of $100 bills was less trouble. But now you can hide $20,000 in one hand using gold. This has not gone unno- ticed by the bad guys, and customs and immigrations forms of several countries have started asking not only if you are carrying more than $10,000 in cash, but specifically gold. Incidentally, to keep up with this type of thing, I urge readers to sign up at International Man, which has a great, free daily letter.

L: I agree; it's an excellent publication. That's an interesting admission for Big Brother to make, asking people to declare cash and gold; in effect, it admits gold's value as money. But okay, if the state achieves total monitoring and control of the legal economy, and the informal economy becomes much larger, would that not greatly increase the demand for gold? The black market is, as you say, a free—if somewhat chaotic—market, so, according to you and Aristotle, would not gold emerge as the money of choice in that market? And would that not add to the speculative reason for owning gold in addition to the rea- sons of prudence?

D: Yes, and yes. Other subtrends speculators might look for, within the overall trend of digitalization of our world, would lie in various new technologies this will make possible. Many of them would be very positive and profitable for those who deploy them commercially first. This is the sort of thing Alex Daley keeps tabs on in our "Casey Extraordinary Technology" letter.

L: That reminds me of what you said about our phones becoming our wallets. You already don't really need a physical card to make most revolving credit purchases, just the information on the account. Not only do we buy all sorts of thing online these days with this information, but there are chips that transmit gas card info to gas pumps so we don't even need to get our wallets out to fill up our tanks. Who knows where that will end up, but I can imagine that as phones and computers (and what used to be TVs) all merge into one technology—which already includes payment systems—money will get folded into this technology as well.

D: I fully expect that, even though I still don't own a cell phone and really loathe the things. As an individual human being, I'm going to keep on paying for things in cash for as long as I can—and to me, gold is the real cash of the world. But as a speculator, I think there's a lot of money to be made investing in the developers of these technological innovations.

L: Good luck with that fight. As Locutus of Borg said, "Resistance is futile. You will be assimilated." There are computer chips in clothing, in cars—heck, it won't be long before they're in our food and in the drinking water. Only to help doctors monitor our health, of course.

D: I know, I know. The prison planet we live on could get pretty ugly before it frees up again. I fear that before things get better, they will have to get much worse, and our world will soon come to resemble a cross between Huxley's *Brave New World* and Orwell's *1984*—or maybe *Soylent Green* if it gets really bad.

L: Another cheerful thought, Doug.

D: You know I call 'em like I see 'em. I hope many of our current readers will look into *The Casey Report* as well, if only because this month has part two of a long article that I'm rather fond of, titled "Evil, Stupidity, and the Decline of America," which examines the root causes of the pickle the West is now in.

But the greater the invasion of privacy, the greater the need for privacy there will be—and the market will respond. I doubt you'll need stolen eyeballs for retina scans, as in the movie *Minority Report*, but technologies that identify you to the monitors as a Boy Scout from Iowa (with a perfect grade-point average, totally clean driving record, and no arrests or interrogations) will certainly become available. Clean digital identities should become highly lucrative commodities, all the more so for being illegal. But, with any luck, when the revolution comes—and it will, even though it will be most unpleasant, inconvenient, and dangerous—I hope it turns out more like the revolutions in *V for Vendetta* or the American Revolution than the one in France under Robespierre. In any event, there's no doubt in my mind that things will get much worse before the world reboots and gets better again.

L: Well, that's marginally better. As has been observed before, as in the times of chattel slavery, for example, when laws become unjust, just people must become outlaws.

D: Just so. Maybe we'll all have our chance to play Robin Hood against an evil king.

L: Right then. Thanks for your thoughts. I'll have to take a closer look at our technology picks for my own investment portfolio.

D: You should. And you're welcome. Talk to you soon. In the meantime, live, and be well.

L: Until next time.

Part Five

WRESTLING FOR COUNTRIES

Chapter 33

Doug Casey on the U.S. Constitution

April 4, 2012

Louis: Doug, we got a lot of mail last week. I screwed up—I was thinking of the much-abused "general welfare" clause in the preamble to the U.S. Constitution when I said the "interstate commerce" clause was in the preamble. The power to regulate commerce between the states is indeed granted to the federal government in Article I, Section 8. Both the interstate commerce clause and the general welfare clause have been greatly abused, and I simply crossed those wires in my mind. I apologize to our readers for the error.

Doug: I didn't catch it either. It pays to research everything, as opposed to relying on memory. But we're not writing dissertations; we're having informal conversations.

That said, I think the essential point we were making remains sound. If you look at that section of the Constitution, which lists powers given to Congress, it says: "To regulate commerce with foreign nations, and among the several States, and with the Indian tribes. . . ." This concept was aimed at a very high level, akin to dealing with foreign nations and Indian tribes. It was meant to keep the legislatures of the states from acting the way governments typically do: erecting barriers and putting on tariffs.

Also, I believe the connotation of the word "regulate" has changed considerably in the last couple of centuries; in those days it meant simply to "make regular" or to normalize. The idea, as I understand it, was to ensure a level playing field between the states, since some of the states had sweetheart deals with some states and trade barriers with yet others, greatly complicating business concerning them all. Over the years, this has devolved into a blanket power to control every minute detail of any good or service that might cross state lines—or might not even do that, but could affect prices in other states simply by existing wherever it is. What was a very reasonable intent has opened Pandora's box.

L: I agree, but nevertheless, I misspoke and stand corrected. That said, we've threatened to talk about the Constitution many times. Since we've started, maybe we should go ahead and discuss the U.S. Constitution.

D: Good idea. I confess I knew this was coming up—I saw the mail too—so I just now read the Constitution again. This is actually something I recommend to everyone. Unfortunately, the Constitution is now a dead letter, but reading it is instructive in a number of ways, and it only takes about 10 minutes. One should know the law of the land, even if it no longer applies.

That will probably be enough for one conversation, but we should probably also take up the amendments, especially the Bill of Rights, in a future conversation, and then maybe another on the Declaration of Independence—another short document everyone should read.

L: Well, some might argue that since the Constitution was ratified with the Bill of Rights attached, they really ought to be considered together, but I'd certainly agree that the later amendments, like the ones establishing and repealing Prohibition, should be a separate conversation.

D: Thank heaven for the Bill of Rights; it slowed the descent of the United States considerably, while it was still taken seriously. So, where to begin?

L: How about with the fact that there wasn't supposed to be a constitution? The Continental Congress authorized delegates to gather to amend and improve on the Articles of Confederation, not to replace them with a new form of government.

D: I've read that James Madison of Virginia showed up with a document called the "Virginia Plan," bearing close resemblance to the current Constitution, except that it clearly described a single, national government. That didn't sit too well with the more independent-minded delegates, so they struck the words "national government" and replaced them with "United States," which went over a lot better.

Now, I wasn't there—and the convention was held behind closed doors—so I hope readers will give me a little wiggle room if they read a book that tells a different story, but my impression has long been that the adoption of the Constitution was actually something of a coup. It replaced a confederation of separate governments with a single super-government. Many people didn't realize this at the time, or they would have objected. The War Between the States demonstrated the reality of the matter, when people did object.

L: I think I've read the same books you have. Or maybe I'm just remembering our conversation on the Civil War.

D: People often gush about what a wonderful thing the Constitution is, but I've always suspected that U.S. and world history would be different—and better—if those delegates had done as they were told and just smoothed over the rough spots in the Articles rather than replaced them with the Constitution. Greater independence among the states could have led to more innovation, and I doubt there would have been the unpleasantness of 1861 to 1865. People with differing ethical values and economic interests would not have been forced to obey the same laws.

L: Perhaps. But they did, and we're stuck with the Constitution we have, for now.

D: For now. Sometimes I think those who've called for a new constitutional convention are on to something, because the one we have now has fallen into almost complete disuse. People talk as though it were carved into the sacred bedrock of the universe, but few people have actually read it, and most of those who have seem to spend their time trying to figure out ways to get out of the clear and simple rules it set out, rather than abide by it. People talk about how it should be a "living document" that evolves with the times. But those people almost always want to abolish what few limitations there are on the government. They want to change the actual working parts of the Constitution, the ones that define and shape the government, not the tedious pages with "Robert's Rules of Order" type stuff governing how motions are passed in Congress and the like. Curiously, this trivia—about how the president of the Senate is elected and so forth—is the only part of the Constitution that the government still adheres to. It follows the trivia fastidiously but disregards the important parts that designate what the government may and may not do.

L: Ah, the irony. But a constitutional convention is a terrible idea, Doug; you know that if we had one now, we wouldn't get anything like enumerated and restricted powers or the Bill of Rights. The average "educated" person in the United States has been taught that the Great Depression proved that capitalism doesn't work; and the average couch potato believes that work is a tedious imposition to be avoided, rather than a virtue. If a new constitution were drafted today, we'd get unlimited and expansive powers and a Bill of Entitlements.

D: [Sighs] You're absolutely right. All institutions—countries, companies, clubs, whatever—inevitably degrade and become corrupt over time. That's one reason why revolutions occur in countries.

But okay, let's look at the one we've got. Some things stand out. Let's start with the item you tripped over, the power given to Congress to regulate commerce with foreign nations, Indian tribes, and between the states. That was a problematical idea from the get-go. As we talked about last week, there should be separation of economy and state for the same reason we have separation of church and state. And there should be a separation of state and education, and everything else that might be provided by society. Otherwise the state will insinuate itself and eventually try to usurp the whole area. Even though the founders' idea of "regulate" was very different from the current one of total control, it left the door open to misinterpretation. And now corporatists, lobbyists, bureaucrats, and influence-peddlers completely control the coercive power of the state and use it to destroy their competition and enrich themselves.

L: As opposed to beating the competition in a fair contest in the marketplace.

D: Yes. We're told competition is supposed to be "fair" not "cutthroat," although both terms are ridiculous misnomers. But Article I, Section 8 is full of things that have been perverted or really shouldn't be there to start with. It says the Congress has the power to coin money and regulate its value, as well as establish weights and measures. Any sensible person could have told the guys who wrote this that that's like asking the fox to guard the henhouse. Money is a market phenomenon that's quite capable of orderly evolution in a free-market environment. Governments are not necessary to establish money and should never be trusted with a monopoly power over money—when they have it, they *always* abuse it and debase the currency. It happened in ancient Rome and has happened again and again throughout history; it's the easiest, but also the most destructive, way for the state to get revenue.

L: Fine, but you're an anarchist, and the writers of the Constitution were not. They were practical men of their day, trying to set up a system they thought would work. Keeping the state's grubby hands off the money supply was not an idea they would have been familiar with.

D: Not really. Bank notes back then were issued by private companies—banks, gold- and silversmiths, and such. They issued notes stating that so-and-so had X amount of gold or silver on deposit. Many people used all sorts of gold and silver not issued by nor regulated by their local governments for money. If memory serves, in the original colonies that formed the United States of America, Spanish pieces of eight were among the most common items used for money.

The framers of the Constitution should have known better. And maybe they did; the Constitution gives Congress the power to coin money, but it doesn't forbid anyone else from doing the same thing. So anyone could have gone into the business of minting coins for use as means of exchange and stores of value. The market would decide which were the most reliable.

L: I wonder when and how competing with the government on that front became a crime.

D: I'm not sure it is, even today. What the government has done to people who've issued private money in recent times, like the creators of the Liberty Dollar, is to prosecute them for counterfeiting, which *is* spelled out as a crime in the Constitution—but only if you counterfeit the currency of the United States. During the War Between the States, a printer in Philadelphia hit upon the idea of counterfeiting Confederate currency and made a huge amount of money for himself. He was never prosecuted. Washington overlooked it because it aided its war effort. But by late in 1863, it was no longer even worth the man's effort because the Confederate dollar had lost so much value, due mostly to the foolish policies of the Confederate government in Richmond. I suspect that was a major, but generally overlooked, contributing factor to the collapse of the South.

L: I've long thought the North's victory was largely economic, not military. "Unconditional Surrender" Grant's bloody march into Virginia was an insanely expensive way to beat Lee. Anyway, you may be right about counterfeiting, but everyone has gotten the message: Money is the state's turf, and woe unto ye if you trespass.

D: Yes, we live on a prison planet. Trapped here by the aberrations of human psychology.

L: So, what else would you list among Doug Casey's top 10 gripes with the U.S. Constitution?

D: The provision to establish post offices and post roads. The post office is a paragon of inefficiency and bad service, was never necessary as a government function, and absolutely should never have been a monopoly. And the first roads in America were private toll roads.

L: I remember reading that Lysander Spooner competed with the U.S. Post Office in the 1840s, and did a better job at lower cost until the government shut him down.

D: Once again, the power to establish post offices and post roads is given, but the authority to crush private competition is not. The first power was later interpreted to include the second, and so it's been with everything in the Constitution ever since it was written. Things like this and the power to coin money were the camel's nose under the tent flap; now the state camel has filled the tent, and there's hardly any room for individual freedom.

L: Okay, what else?

D: The item setting up copyrights and patents was, at least arguably, another mistake along these lines, and for the same reasons. As a writer who wants to benefit from the effort I put into using words to communicate information, I'm a bit ambivalent about that, but I don't see how it's possible for anyone to own an idea, and I'm sure getting the government involved is a bad move.

L: We published a conversation with our friend Paul Rosenberg on the subject of intellectual property. His conclusion was that the state's involvement has become useless anyway. All creators can do now is adapt to the marketplace.

D: It's interesting to me that in spite of all the hand-wringing on this subject, the ongoing demise of patents and copyrights has not stopped inventors from inventing, nor musicians or writers from creating. In fact, wikis and open-source projects have created many valuable things. Patents, copyrights, and trademarks really just turned into a bonanza for lawyers. I do want to benefit from my intellectual work, but I suspect Paul is right; all we can do is adapt.

It's also interesting to me that aside from counterfeiting, which we've already mentioned, there are only two other crimes mentioned in the Constitution. One is piracy, and the other is treason. Today, nobody knows for sure how many crimes there are on the books, but it's thought that there are over 5,000 crimes defined in federal law. I've read that the average U.S. citizen breaks three federal laws every day, intentionally or otherwise. And now many federal agencies have armed—sometimes heavily armed—branches that round up people and prosecute them for these so-called crimes.

I suppose I could live with just three federal laws—piracy, counterfeiting, and treason would be easy to remember, at least.

L: But counterfeiting wouldn't be a federal crime if we got the government out of the money business, as you suggest.

D: That's right, and piracy could be handled by letters of marque and reprisal, as it was in the old days.

L: What about treason?

D: Well, you could look at that as the state's right to self-defense—but let me just ask: When the state becomes unjust, what is a just man or woman to do?

L: On an ethical plane, the answer is clear, but on a practical plane, that's a tough one.

D: Indeed. And working against the interests of the state, overthrowing the government, or killing the ruler—all of which can be called treason—may actually be working for the benefit of society. What about treasonous people in Nazi Germany or Soviet Russia? I'd call them heroes.

Another thing worth covering is the power to declare war. The authors of the Constitution were rightly worried about leaders with the power of kings to plunge nations into war for personal or imagined grievances, so they gave the power to declare war to Congress. But like everything remotely sensible about the Constitution, that too has been set aside. The United States has had numerous wars, one after the other, for at least the last seven decades, but the last time Congress actually declared war was World War II.

L: Really? I thought Korea was declared.

D: No, that was a "police action." Technically, it was a UN police action against North Korea, although in reality it was a war between the United States and China. At any rate, it's just another example of how thoroughly ignored the Constitution is in the United States. The president can now unilaterally send U.S. troops anywhere to do almost anything. In fact, he can do almost anything, period—at least if media lapdogs are able to justify and rationalize it.

L: Wasn't it Henry Kissinger who said that doing something illegal was no problem and that doing something unconstitutional just took a little longer?

D: "The illegal we do immediately, the unconstitutional takes a little longer." You've got to admit Henry is a clever guy. Come the day I write an obit for him, perhaps I'll subtitle it "Comedian and War Criminal."

L: Okay, okay, I get the picture. I don't think we need to go through every clause to see how far the United States has fallen from the America That Was. That prompts me to say to those who think this conversation shows that we hate America that just the opposite is true. Personally, I love the idea that was America, and I still love the land of America, from sea to shining sea. What I loathe and despise is the corruption being visited upon her by the maggots in Washington, DC, who've been gutting all that is good and noble about her.

At any rate, we've been saying for a long time that all is not well in Mudville. Are there any practical implications to this conversation? Investment implications?

D: It's yet another sign that the United States has gone way beyond the point of no return. You can't make a sensible investment in a country which doesn't have the rule of law; you can only speculate—which is to say, try to capitalize on politically caused distortions in the market. There's no way the U.S. federal government can or will return to observing the Constitution; it's just something it pays lip service to—and then only rarely. When you're on a slippery slope that's rapidly turning vertical, it's no longer a question of *if* there will be a painful stop at the bottom, only when.

L: Does your guru sense give you any feeling for how close we are to that crash?

D: You know I don't like to predict "what" and "when" at the same time, but I can't make myself believe it can be put off too much longer—a couple of years at most. And it could still quite possibly happen this year.

L: In which case we invest for crisis, as you've been saying all along.

D: Yet another reason, yes. We're headed for a genuinely historic time of troubles.

L: Roger that. Until next week, then.

D: Travel safe. Personally, I dread and despise the interrogation and searching one gets from ICE when entering the United States. But I suppose it's no more degrading than the grope from the TSA. No problem though—it must be somewhere in the Constitution. I better read it again.

L: Sure, Doug, it's right next to the clause granting everyone free health care, free education, and a free lunch.

Chapter 34

Doug Casey on Immigration

May 19, 2010

Louis: So, Doug, a while back there was a big furor among many people, including some of your libertarian friends, about the new immigration law—or anti-illegal-immigration law—passed by the state of Arizona. We had other fish to fry at the time, and then the markets got all jittery, but I know you have thoughts on the subject of immigration, so let 'er rip—what do you make of all this?

Doug: I think it's incumbent upon a free person to go anywhere he or she wants.

L: And that they have every right to do so, without restriction?

D: Absolutely. Everyone should be able to travel, whether they're coming or going, without the approval of a state. As I'm sure you're aware, it was only 100 years ago that almost anybody, from almost anywhere, could go almost anywhere else, without a passport.

L: The good old days.

D: At least from that point of view. In a free society, all property is privately owned. Immigrants, like other travelers, would only have to make sure they have a place to lay their heads down at night. And don't trespass on others property.

L: Some people might argue that it was different back then because travel was long, arduous, and expensive, so you wouldn't get masses of poor and poorly educated people flooding into rich countries the way you would today. The world is a different and far more dangerous place today, and such idealistic policies from the past are no longer workable.

D: Well, they would be wrong. Anyone who thinks the world was a safer place back in the U.S. Civil War era, or when the Indians were watching the Europeans arrive, or during the crusades, or during the Black Death, or during the rise of Rome, or during the last ice age . . . well, ignorant is about the best that can be said for them. And as for the poor masses, that's exactly what America came to be filled with, in wave after wave.

For example, in the 1840s and 1850s, there were the starving and penniless from Ireland fleeing the potato famine. Over the centuries, most of the immigrants to the new world were not rich adventurers on holiday, coming over to see the exotic flora and fauna. They were typically the most persecuted and impoverished people from all over Europe. These were desperate and sometimes dangerous people, fighting for survival. The ones who did so successfully were among the most resourceful, driven, and creative—in other words, just the sort of people who can add value to an economy.

So no, that thinking is just plain wrong and wrong-headed. It's always been the poor, the hungry, huddled masses.

L: As Emma Lazarus's famous poem about the Statue of Liberty goes: "Give me your tired, your poor, Your huddled masses yearning to breathe free, The wretched refuse of your teeming shore. Send these, the homeless, tempest-tost to me, I lift my lamp beside the golden door!"

You know, I shouldn't be surprised—because, as you like to point out, after hydrogen, stupidity is the most common thing in the universe—but it somehow always does manage to surprise me when I run into obstinate anti-immigrant bigotry. This entire country was built by immigrants. We're *all* immigrants. Even the "native" Americans are just older immigrants. How can any American possibly be so blind as to fail to see the hypocrisy of being against immigration?

D: Just so. You know, that poem also says: "Keep ancient lands, your storied pomp!" I've always rather liked that line, because it's quite anti-elitist. It's truly a sad thing that the Statue of Liberty has become an empty symbol, as meaningless as the Declaration of Independence. It's another sign of the death of America, which has gone from being the land of the free and the home of the brave to the land of tax slaves and the home of welfare recipients. And it's precisely because it was the land of the free and brave that America was so fearless of immigrants; Americans were not afraid to work hard and compete with anyone from anywhere.

The statistics tell us that now, however, about 47 percent of Americans don't pay income tax; they look forward to April 15 as a day the government sends them money. Of course I don't believe in the income tax—or any other taxes, for that matter. But the United States, like Europe, has turned into a place where most people feel entitled to have the state—or rich people—take care of them. They certainly don't want to compete. They want free handouts and will keep voting for them, come hell or high water. Forty million Americans are on food stamps, and I promise you that number is going much higher.

L: I think they'll get both hell and high water as a result. But didn't immigrants cause some problems back then? I know there were anti-Irish sentiments, to continue with your example. "No Irish need apply," et cetera.

D: There were certainly problems. Look, life isn't just full of problems; life *is* problems. Though I'd guess that even back then, more problems were caused by the people already in America than by those arriving. But that doesn't mean the new arrivals were bad for America. Just the opposite. The kind of people who would leave wherever they were born and make their way—as long and arduous as you say—to America would have been the best class of people. They clearly had the most "get up and go."

L: Literally.

D: Yes. They were the most opportunity-seeking and generally the most freedom-loving. Those poor wretches were not a net drain, as their modern counterparts are seen today, but a huge boon to the country— and the same could be true today, if we had the right policies.

L: Well, look what Australia has built on foundations of being a prison colony. It seems pretty clear that whom you let in doesn't matter, it's what the systems in place encourage people to do once they get there that matters.

But one more challenge—some people would say that back then America had wild frontiers, beyond which anyone could go and hack a living out of the wilderness. Now the United States has no open frontier; it's a closed system with limited resources, resources newcomers may take from those already on board.

D: They're wrong too, and self-serving in their myopia. The United States still has vast, vast stretches of empty land, owned by the federal government, which could be re-opened to homesteading. And Space Ship One has shown that there is an infinite frontier opening up for those daring enough to go colonize it.

But this is the twenty-first century. Homesteading shouldn't mean hacking a farm out of the wilderness anymore, it should mean launching a technology company, or engineering some new solution to an expensive problem, or offering a valuable service to people who need it, and so forth. Space isn't the final frontier, *opportunity* is, and it's infinite. It serves no useful purpose whatsoever to try to limit people's access to opportunity—and if the United States stops the best and the brightest among us from following new opportunities here, they will do it elsewhere, and the United States will get left behind.

L: So, you don't see any problems with throwing the borders wide open today? Let anyone into the United States who wants to live the American Dream—maybe they'll bring it back to life?

D: Well, to start with, it's not America anymore, it's the United States, a welfare-warfare state that offers perverse incentives to be nonproductive and goes around the world creating enemies with an extremely aggressive foreign policy. So I expect there would indeed be problems if opening the borders were the only change made.

As long as the United States is mass-producing enemies in the Middle East and elsewhere, it does make some sense for it to try to erect walls to protect itself. Welfare is a disaster, but while the United States is handing out expensive goodies and subsidies, it makes sense for the United States to try to limit how many people it has to support. In both cases, however, the answer is to get rid of these destructive and counterproductive policies, not to close the border. If you get rid of the welfare-warfare state, you solve the perceived immigration problem. The United States needs to return to being America.

L: "Peace, commerce, and honest friendship with all nations—entangling alliances with none." But America is not the only thing that has changed over the last 100 years.

D: That's right. There are two main differences between the people who want to immigrate today and those who did so in the past. First, in those days, it was mostly Europeans, so there was less racism in the reaction to them. Today, it's not mostly Europeans, and I'm sorry to say that, regardless of what people say, I think the cold reception is very much race-driven. But racism is a fact everywhere—the Orient, Africa, Europe—everywhere. It's a holdover from primitive times. But I believe it will diminish over time, by which I mean the centuries to come.

Second, in those days, immigrants had to work and produce in order to survive. There were none of the counterproductive policies I mentioned above; no welfare, no unemployment benefits, no health care subsidies, no government housing projects, no subsidized transportation, none of these things. So immigrants had to start producing immediately and become self sustaining right away, or they'd starve. That sounds harsh to modern ears, but if they were starving where they came from and had limited opportunities, just the chance to not starve in America, with its unlimited opportunities, was an attractive prospect.

Today, immigrants are actually encouraged to explore all the wonderful benefits and services the U.S. government has to offer—and this attracts the wrong kind of person. And corrupts everyone else. It's not that poor people want to come here that's the problem today; we always had poor people wanting to come here. It's that our government handouts are attracting parasites as well as creative opportunity seekers.

L: Are you saying that some anti-immigrant feelings may have some justification?

D: Only because of the corrupting influence of the system. There's a certain atavism in the hostility toward immigrants. We believe, correctly, that America used to be in many ways better than any other country in the world. And these new people are not integrating the way past immigrants have. They come from different cultures, with different values, and they often seem to be bringing those cultures here, rather than becoming Americans—they are changing America, and that scares people. This creates resentment among people who like things the way they were, and that, while not necessarily laudable, is understandable.

But even the fear of American culture being changed wouldn't be such an issue if America hadn't ceased to be America. In the past era of "rugged individualism," immigrants *had* to integrate. They wanted to be Americans as soon as possible—that's why they came. Now the state, with services in several languages and all its "safety nets" makes that optional—even subtly encourages them not to, for the sake of "diversity."

L: And of course no one wants to give up their old ways if they don't have to.

D: Exactly. Even though perhaps well intended, the hate crime laws that punish boorish behavior toward people who are different have the unintended consequence of further reducing the incentive to integrate.

L: Hm. But if the America we knew and loved no longer exists, there's the question of what immigrants would be integrating into today.

D: At this point, they'd be trying to integrate into a militarized welfare system, in which everyone is trying to live at the expense of everyone else. And that's exactly the problem.

As I've said before, America was a beautiful idea, but pandering politicians and social engineers have killed it. Instead, we have the United States, which is just a country, like any other in the club of 200 or so states that are nothing more than protection rackets in terminal decline. The racket is done—the system doesn't work anymore, and I believe that the nation-state as we know it will cease to exist as a meaningful player within the next generation or two.

And that's a good thing. Because of technology, almost everyone can go almost anywhere they like, and the result will be new groupings of people based on common values, not the random and meaningless groupings we have today, based on where people are born. I believe these new forms of social organization that will replace today's governments will be more stable, productive, and valuable to their members (who will be able to shop for the ones they deem most advantageous), so I'm in favor of making that transition happen as fast and easily as possible. Open borders would help with that.

L: So, the basic answer to those who fear open borders is that free immigration is not the problem, the problem is the welfare-warfare system.

D: Right. It's the government of the United States that is creating the problems that a lot of individual citizens resent. It's rather inchoate anger, in most cases, but they do sense that something is wrong. Unfortunately, they don't understand the causes, so they blame the immigrants, while they should be blaming their rulers and tossing them out of office.

L: Okay, but that's the ideal answer. Realistically, it's hard to imagine a sudden burst of reason in Washington causing the federal government to roll back its counterproductive welfare and warfare policies and to open the borders to the most creative, driven, and entrepreneurial people around the world.

D: Yes, that's completely out of the question. They may make noises about national security in a world awash in terrorism, et cetera, but the truth is that every politician knows that opening the borders would allow a huge influx of relatively cheap and competent labor into the U.S. market. That would break the rice bowls of too many fat, overpaid U.S. laborers who think they have a birthright to $30, $50, or $70 per hour jobs. It's not going to happen, not by vote of the parasitical/political class that rules the world today.

However, an equalization of wage levels around the world *will* happen, in time, as a result of economic trends that can't be stopped. The Chinese fellow who works for $2 a day, doing the same thing a U.S. worker does for $20 per hour now, may soon be making $10 per hour—and so will the American. But the Chinese fellow might actually be better off than the U.S. worker at that time, because he won't be burdened with the monstrous tax and regulatory burden of his U.S. counterpart.

L: And he won't see anything wrong with working more than 40 hours a week.

D: Nor would he dream of taking sick days and three weeks of paid vacation. The Chinese guy will simply work harder than his U.S. counterpart.

L: That might change as the playing field levels. But the bottom line here is that you're saying that people can be as closed-minded as they want, close the borders entirely, keep those different-looking people out—but you can't keep the jobs in. Even if the U.S. adopts a law preventing companies from employing the cheapest labor available on the global market, that will just ensure that U.S. companies will be replaced by more nimble international competitors. It's going to happen, regardless of what anyone wants, says, or votes for.

D: And, perversely, the more political action the U.S. takes to stop it from happening, the more certain the outcome is. It *will* happen.

L: I love the irony; the market will level the playing field, elevating the world's poorest, most needy people—and it will do so where decades of wrong-headed and destructive foreign aid have failed.

D: Yes, and at that point, when opportunity abounds around the world, the nation-state as we know it will have <u>no credible value to offer people</u>, and it too will go into the dustbin of history.

And it's already started. I happen to be speaking to you from Washington, DC, and last night I went to the Tyson's Corner shopping center.

L: I remember when that was a gas station out in the middle of nowhere.

D: I do too. It's gigantic now. So, my wife and I were people watching. We didn't do anything resembling scientific research, but we did consciously try to quantify what we were seeing. Looking at the people working in the shops, I would say that about 80 percent of them were discernibly foreigners. And then we counted people riding the escalator from the first to the second floor, and we could immediately see that about 50 percent of the shoppers were discernibly foreigners.

L: What do you conclude from that?

D: That all these immigration laws do is raise the cost of entry. And what that does is discourage the sort of entrepreneurial middle-class people who'd have the easiest time contributing positively to the U.S. economy the moment they got here. Those people will go elsewhere, where there's less state interference with opportunity, leaving more of the welfare-seekers who sneak in illegally. It's completely perverse.

L: Any other comments on the Arizona law specifically?

D: Well, you know governments are always passing reams and reams of stupid laws. It's what they do. I don't believe stopping immigration is a legitimate function of government. If I did believe government was necessary, I'd restrict it to protecting life, liberty, and property via police, courts, and military. But most people see the state as a magical cornucopia that will give them anything they want as long as they vote for it, and, more frighteningly, as a Big Brother that will make everyone play nice with them.

L: Heh. Yes, people forget that a government powerful enough to compel others to do what they want is powerful enough to compel them to do what others want. Big Brother . . . doesn't anyone read anymore?

D: I don't know; perhaps they just talk on their cell phones and watch reality TV. But it's pretty alarming. These attitudes are sending what's left of America down the wrong path fast. And as the economic situation winds down, *Boobus Americanus* is going to blame the immigrants. That's bad enough, but for readers of this column, the more serious consequence will be that they will blame the emigrants as well. It's a double-edged sword that cuts the wrong way, both ways.

L: Emigrants—those bastards. Why won't they stay here and let us tax them more so they can pay for us to live beyond our means? Where's their patriotism? Traitors. I bet they don't even like baseball and apple pie!

D: The only good news about that is that wealthier people are generally welcome in other countries. So, for many reasons we've talked about before, it's important to diversify your assets out of the United States, or wherever your home country is, and start looking for places where you'll be more welcome.

L: Makes me wonder why any smart person would want to immigrate to the United States. I guess they still see it as America.

D: Well, most of those who do come here to study go back where they came from. It's mostly Asians, who go to U.S. universities for higher degrees in advanced sciences and the like (while their U.S. counterparts are taking courses like gender studies and sociology), and then take that knowledge home. They can see that the United States still has more capital, but it's on a curve going down, while other places are on a curve going up—which is a much smarter place to build an enterprise. And they can feel that immigrants are not welcome in this country anymore.

L: That would seem to have investment implications. Would you rather place bets in Shanghai than Wall Street?

D: I'm not inclined toward stocks anywhere right now. I hate to employ an overused phrase, but it's perfectly apt to say that we're facing a perfect storm. This and many other trends we've discussed—just about every trend I can see—they all point to very dire consequences for the United States, making conventional U.S.-centered investment strategies very risky. It's not just stormy weather but a class-five hurricane on the horizon, and this attitude toward immigrants is one strong sign of our times. Not good.

L: It's gone way beyond straws in the wind; we've got whole hay bales blowing by. And they say, "Short Wall Street!"

D: That's right. Short Wall Street. Short the dollar *and* the euro—paper currencies in general. Short bonds. Get more of your cash out of the United States before they ratchet up the currency controls. Go long on the precious metals, quality energy plays, and certain agricultural commodities, especially productive land. It's the same thing we've been saying all along in these conversations, only it's getting more urgent.

It's just amazing. You'd think that people could see this train wreck coming and try to prevent it, or at least get out of the way. Instead, they're asking the government to throw more coal into the boiler, as the locomotive heads toward the tracks dangling over the edge of the cliff.

L: Right then. Off I go—got some hatches to batten down.

D: You do that, and we'll talk again soon.

Chapter 35

Doug Casey:
War Is Coming

August 4, 2010

Louis: Doug, last time we conversed, you said: "Let's talk about what Clausewitz called 'the extension of politics' next time—I think the odds are increasing that we may see war rear its ugly head again soon."

There's been a lot in the news lately about Israel blockading the Gaza strip and about the potential for the Middle East to boil over. Is that what you had in mind?

Doug: I just got back from a trip to the Middle East—Iraq, actually. There's a feature article on what I found there in this month's _The Casey Report_. Doing country studies has long been a specialty of mine, and I've got to say that most of what most people think they know about the place just ain't so. But yes, I do think there is a very significant chance that we are headed for something that might vaguely resemble World War III.

L: That's going to be a pretty shocking statement to a lot of people—too much cognitive dissonance for most to let themselves think

311

about it. Many readers might say that folks in the Middle East have been squabbling for years without the world going up in flames. Did you have a guru moment while there? Why now?

D: Well, people, especially Americans, forget that war, far from being an alien experience only read about in books, is actually a common-place occurrence. Major powers have had major wars periodically, continually throughout history. There's no reason to imagine man-kind has kicked the habit. It may not be the conflagration people once expected from a conflict between the United States and the Soviet Union, but it could still happen, and I suspect that the Middle East, Israel in particular, will be the epicenter.

One thing that drew my attention to this possibility again at this time is not what's going on in Gaza, but a friend of mine who had just been to a conference with an ex-director of the CIA, some high FBI officials, a whole bunch of defense department wonks, and simi-lar types from Israel. He reports that all those spooks and military types really think Israel is going to attack Iran. The situation looks very serious to them. And one of Obama's top military advisors has just said the United States itself has plans formulated, and they would be put into effect should the Iranians be proved to have nukes.

You add that to all you see in the news, including Iran's new reactor plans and so forth, and we could be pretty close to the edge.

L: So, if Israel attacks Iran, presumably to prevent Iran from becoming a nuclear power, I can see the region going up in flames, but how does that become World War III? I don't think the United States, Russia, and China are bound by treaty to enter the fray.

D: It may not. But the logic goes like this: Israel is just a tiny sliver of a country, about the size of New Jersey. It's the kind of place that would be totally wiped out with just two or three nukes. And due to the nature of the place, those weapons could be delivered by yacht, or a cargo ship, or an airliner, or even a truck, for that matter. So Israel is very concerned about any hostile countries gaining nuclear capability—any of them that could produce just two or three such weapons could completely obliterate all of Israel. The spooks at the conference my friend went to all thought Israel would simply not allow any of its hostile neighbors to achieve that capability.

L: Okay, but isn't "military intelligence" usually an oxymoron? They got 9/11 completely wrong (unless you believe the conspiracy theories).

D: It usually is. With failures like Pearl Harbor, the Chinese invasion of Korea, the Cuban missile crisis, and the Tet offensive to its credit. I've long held the president of the United States would do just as well reading the *New York Times* for intelligence. And the fact that the United States now has a literal army of people in intelligence—about 854,000 with Top Secret clearances, according to a recent *Washington Post* series—doesn't mean the situation is going to get better. It means it's going to get worse, because none of these people know who's on first, and they all have competing agendas.

The U.S. government is far more out of control and byzantine than the Byzantines themselves could even have imagined.

Of course some of those guys are very good at what they do. But people rise in bureaucracies because of political infighting skills, not competence. What's needed for sound decisions is a wise man in command, not hundreds of thousands of bureaucrats. And we don't have a wise man in command, we have a glib ward healer from Chicago. If anything, he may be worse than Bush, which I didn't think was possible.

But to get back to Iran: It's important to recognize what has happened before. People forget that back in 1981, Israel bombed the Osirak nuclear reactor in central Iraq, just weeks before it was to be loaded with fuel. And in 2007, they did the same with Syria's secret al-Kibar reactor.

But Iran is much further away, and they are building their reactors in hardened facilities—the jets that bombed Osirak barely had enough fuel to make it back to Israel—so Israel will probably need some help if it's going to pull it off this time. And since Israel is practically the fifty-first U.S. state, the feeling is that the United States would get sucked into helping them. Or, even if the United States doesn't help, it would still be blamed for not having kept its dog on a leash.

This is all compounded by the fact that the United States has been engaged in an unspoken war on Islam for close to three decades now, although it's styled the War on Terror.

L: And if the United States gets dragged into it, it becomes World War III. I get it. It's interesting that Iran actually attacked the Iraqi reactor first, for much the same reason Israel did. Even more striking to me is that the UN boldly responded to Israel's actions with . . . strong words. And those words included the assertion that self-defense did not justify preemptive strikes, but that's exactly the excuse the United States used when its turn came to bomb Iraq.

D: I know, you can't make this stuff up. Although Iran attacked the Osirak during the nasty war between Saddam and the Ayatollah, shortly after the Shah fell in 1981. But these things do happen. They can be hard to predict. Still, the evidence is building; the latest press reports have a new carrier group joining the U.S. Fifth Fleet in the Persian Gulf. It's the type of thing that's considered provocative by a neutral observer.

But the fact is that nuclear weapons have been around now for over 60 years. The technology for making them is well known and getting cheaper, easier, and better all the time. North Korea can make them; even a rich individual can. But why not buy them from a Pakistani general or even a Russian supply sergeant? Rogue regimes now recognize, based on Saddam's experience, that having some nukes is the best way to prevent an invasion by the United States, or someone else. Therefore, they *will* proliferate.

L: I wonder how the peace activists who voted for Obama feel about that. Pretty scary stuff.

D: It is. You know, historically, the United States typically picks entirely too many fights with little nothing nowhere countries—rabbit- and squirrel-size game in Central America or the Caribbean. All it's ever done is foster the next generation of rebels; at best, it puts in a right-wing strong man who's recognized as a stooge and who makes the United States a lot of new enemies.

Anyway, Iraq was a country with only 20 million people, and even Vietnam was not a large country at the time—and desperately poor. But Iran is genuine big game.

L: I just looked it up in the CIA World Factbook, and they say it has 67 million people as of an estimate last month, and is the nineteenth largest country in the world.

D: Yes. It's a theocratic police state, with a highly regulated, state-managed economy. Everything is either subsidized or price controlled. The government gets 80 percent of its income from oil, but the fields are so badly run that production is going into decline. The fact is, if the United States just waits, economic collapse or revolt from the kids, or both, will bring the regime down. Instead, the United States may act as a catalyst to unify the people behind their goofy government. It's completely perverse.

If this spins out of control, it could do some very, very serious damage. It's not like the Iranian army isn't expecting something. They're an old civilization, they're not stupid, and I'm sure they have contingency plans if they're attacked.

L: I see. But even if the United States is drawn in, that makes the conflict one of global scope, but it doesn't really plunge most of the world into war. I doubt China or Russia would attack the United States in retaliation. But I could see Muslim countries around the world deciding to go to war. This could become an open war on Islam—is that what you mean by World War III?

D: Well, let's just suppose that Israel, or Israel and the United States, attack Iran before Iran can become a nuclear power. Now, what would the Iranians do? They could do nothing, which is what the Iraqis and the Syrians did when Israel bombed them.

L: Somehow, that doesn't seem likely. They are a proud people. And their military had to have learned some lessons from the Iraqi experience with the United States.

D: I agree. A likely response would be to close the Strait of Hormuz, by way of punishing America through a denial of a large part of its oil supply. About 40 percent of all seaborne oil shipments pass through that strait—20 percent of *all* the global oil supply. Its closure would be a major disruption to the whole world.

Of course, Obama would thump on his chest and say that Iran can't be allowed to close international waters. Iran would likely say, "We just did. What do you expect after launching an unprovoked attack?"

It's well known that sea-skimming missiles go 2,000 miles per hour. They have hundreds of them, maybe thousands, and they can be launched from small, fast boats. Even in the United States' own war games conducted a few years ago, the U.S. Navy lost against these things. If the United States tries to open the Strait of Hormuz by force against Iran, I think it's likely that most of the fleet will soon be turned into an artificial reef that divers in future decades will explore with morbid fascination. Militaries always fight the last war, and that's precisely what the United States is doing with its carriers and B-2s.

L: Here's a map. And then what?

D: Remember that World War I started with the assassination of one archduke. These things are chaotic and unpredictable, but one thing leads to another, drawing all sorts of parties into the fight as it spins out of control. The trouble is that the ante has gone up considerably since those days. The only way to win a game with nuclear weapons is not to play.

L: What if everyone who could help Israel attack Iran realizes this and refuses to help? Does peace have a chance?

D: Anything's possible, but this is not the only flashpoint. The war in Iraq could heat up in all sorts of ways. Pakistan could boil over. There are probably 50 other combinations that could be as serious as the U.S. and Israel picking a fight with Iran. The global stage is a powder keg with many fuses. The situation with Israel is just one of them.

L: But that's long been the case. What makes it more likely to blow now?

D: The economic crisis is just getting going. It's important to remember that the whole world has been in a long boom, punctuated by relatively minor recessions, since 1946. What's happening now is not just another cyclical recession. As it gets worse, and I'm quite confident it will, people will look for others to blame, and politicians will look for distractions to appease the masses. These factors are actively fanning the flames.

L: Nothing like a good war to distract people from their own misery— and their own responsibility for their individual circumstances.

D: That's right, at least until their house gets blown up or their son gets killed. Nothing like a good foreign war against an invariably evil and subhuman enemy to distract people from local problems. And, of course, there are actually fools out there that believe war stimulates economies.

L: Yes. Can't tell you how many times I've heard that World War II ended the Great Depression—they told me so in school, so it must be so. Alas, the dumb masses.

D: Indeed. If that were true, the best prescription for prosperity would be to make every city look like Berlin in 1945, so the economy would be restimulated as the starving masses rebuilt them with their bare hands. But I do think the conflict between Israel and Iran has high odds of happening. Whatever they say about peaceful uses—and, actually, Iran should have a massive nuclear program since it beats burning valuable oil for electricity—Iran is going to develop nuclear weapons. North Korea has shown that it's the best thing they can do to protect themselves from the bigger kids on the block. And of course Israel can't let them do that. These countries are on a clear collision course.

L: Grim. I don't often wish you were wrong, but I do on this one. But it is what it is. Investment implications, beyond the obvious bet on soaring energy prices?

D: I have to say I have a problem with recommending many investments right now. As a speculator, I really only like to do things when they look very, very cheap, or very, very expensive. At which point I'll go long or short, respectively. I don't like even-odds bets or a level playing field. I only go for deals that seem, to me, to offer large returns for low risk. It should be as Warren Buffett said: a ball game with no called strikes, so you just wait and wait for the right ball to come over the plate. And, unfortunately, almost everything in the world looks expensive to me today.

I've said this before, but it bears repeating: It's odd, prices being relative, for *everything* to be expensive. It's a metaphysical impossibility—but there just aren't any real bargains out there. We are in an investment Twilight Zone, where governments the world over are creating trillions of new currency units, and there's still little or no evidence of higher prices. It's a very dangerous time; we're in the eye of the hurricane.

That preamble said, even with oil at a not-particularly-cheap $80/barrel, it is one of the cheaper commodities around and would look like a screaming bargain should the United States go to war with Iran. But even without that, for other reasons ranging from the geological to the political, there are many factors that could push oil prices up, and not many that would push them down radically, from here.

I wouldn't bet on natural gas, because that's a local market, and not so much uranium, though that will make a comeback too, because it's the safest, cleanest, and cheapest type of mass power we have, and that will win out in the end. So, it's oil, and, self-serving as I know it sounds, I have to say that the best investment strategist in the business is Marin Katusa, editor of *Casey's Energy Report*. And let me say it again, gold is still in a definite bull trend.

L: Roger that. Well, thanks for another stimulating, if gloomy, conversation.

D: We could talk about lighter stuff, and sometimes we do, but this trend has become clearer in my mind of late, and I think people should consider it. Unlike the title of that idiotic book written a while ago, this isn't *The End of History*. Regrettably, we're very much a part of it.

Chapter 36

Doug Casey on Revolution in Egypt and Beyond

February 2, 2011

Louis: Doug, there are flames going up in the Middle East, something you've long said was in the cards, but it's not between Israel and its neighbors. The revolutionary spirit sparked in Tunisia seems to have spread to Egypt, the largest Arab nation and a major U.S. ally, greatly destabilizing an already shaky region. The whole world suddenly seems in greater peril. What do you make of this?

Doug: Well, I think it's about time—in fact, way past time. Revolution in the Middle East is long overdue.

L: [Chokes on tea, starts mopping keyboard with napkin.] Care to elaborate?

D: I'm not saying I favor the unpleasantness and inconvenience for so many people that comes with such events, but this upheaval is long overdue. These Arab countries have long been the most repressive places in the world, with the possible exception of the despotisms in Africa, to their south. It's very good to see these regimes being overthrown. And the revolution—hopefully that's what it is—is internally generated. It's not the product of an invasion by foreign troops from an alien culture, which is what happened in Iraq and Afghanistan. Regime change in that whole part of the world is inevitable, necessary, and salubrious. The problematic question is: What are the old regimes going to be replaced with?

L: Fair enough. Let's take this one piece at a time. I think I know what you'll say, but do you think this is a fire that's going to spread, or were Tunisia and Egypt just particularly rickety?

D: I think it is going to spread, and I'll tell you why.

First, these regimes are not the only highly repressive ones. Every regime in the Arab world—in fact every regime in the Muslim world—is corrupt, backward, and repressive.

Second, with the communications and travel revolutions of the last few decades, the people in these places know they've been getting a raw deal and suffering a lower standard of living than much of the rest of the world. It was one thing, in the old days, to live from hand to mouth and get beaten by the police if you stepped out of line. People thought that was the natural order. But now they can see people in the west live vastly better, and they aren't going to take it any more.

Third, with Facebook, Twitter, cell phones, text messaging, and so forth, people can actually organize action on a massive scale far easier than ever before.

So a broad revolution in the Muslim world has been inevitable for a couple of decades. I suspect it's now imminent.

L: I remember reading that a major factor in the Soviets losing control was the fax machine, which enabled a primitive form of what you're talking about. It's interesting that the Egyptian authorities tried to prevent losing control by shutting down Twitter and other social networks. It didn't work. I just heard a news story saying that some 2 billion people across the planet are now on the Internet in one form or another. I don't think one-third of the planet's population has even been literate at any past point in history, let alone actively participating in a language-driven system of information exchange. We've said before that the Internet is the most revolutionary thing to come along since the printing press; now we're seeing that this is literally true.

D: Yes, you can download the "Flash-Mobs for Dummies" app right now. And there's no way to stuff the genie back in the bottle. Technology is everywhere the friend of the common man, starting with fire and the wheel. But political and religious elites—the Atillas and the witch doctors of the world—always try to keep the genie in the bottle. The printing press, gunpowder, the automobile, the computer—the elites have always hated these things, and don't want the common man to have them. Radical new technologies always work to overturn the status quo.

L: So, where do you think the next place will be where the people decide they've had enough?

D: Could be anywhere. Of course we can't be sure this revolution will succeed—maybe it will be a false start, like the aborted insurrections in Europe in 1848. But I think it's more likely to catch fire, like the wars of liberation in South America in the 1820s.

The trouble is that there are all kinds of revolutions—as different as the Russian revolution of 1917 was from the one of 1989. I think this one is likely to be more like the latter: pro-freedom. We're watching chaos theory in action. It could appear in Pakistan, a perennial candidate, partly because it isn't even a real country—just a hodge-podge put together by an imperial power. Algeria and Libya are two more highly repressive regimes that deserve to go. Saudi Arabia is probably the biggest risk. This is not a Middle Eastern problem, but could quickly become a worldwide conflagration, especially if a keystone like Saudi Arabia falls.

L: I could see Saudi Arabia going next; it's hardly a bastion of freedom and respect for human rights.

D: Far from it; it's a medieval theocracy/kleptocracy. And yet, the "talking heads" on TV are not praising the people for throwing off their chains. The reason is that most of these horrible, repressive governments are all U.S. puppets. They are stooges, getting anywhere from tens of millions of dollars to billions of dollars per year, in the case of Egypt, in direct support from the United States.

L: Rape and pillage all you want, we'll support you as long as you're a good ally.

D: Right. But aside from being grossly unethical, this is a short-sighted policy. In the minds of millions of people all around the world, it associates the United States with repression, rather than freedom, which is what the United States should, and once did, stand for, back when it was America. And unfortunately, people conflate America with the U.S. government, even though they're totally different things—antithetical things, actually. I remember years ago walking down the street in Cairo, and a kid of about 15 yells at me, "Damned American." I'd never done anything to him. But the U.S. government had obviously done something to make him feel that way. If I'd thought of it, I would have said, "Hey kid, I've got nothing to do with your secret police—I'm on your side." But it wasn't the place for a philosophical discussion.

L: It's Orwellian; the "land of the free and the home of the brave" is the supporter of tin-plated despots around the world.

D: I know—it's totally perverse. We supply their arms. When a protestor picks up a can of teargas, its label reads: Made in USA. They see U.S. military equipment being used against them. The U.S. government is supporting all these disgusting despots, making enemies of billions of people, turning the U.S. into a police state, and bankrupting the American economy. They're truly multitalented. But, the average American sees the government as a friend and protector. It's funny— the average Arab may actually be much more politically hip and realistic, and desirous of liberty, than the average American. Maybe someday they'll send their CIA and military over here to bring us freedom.

L: "Underprivileged dictators of the world: Apply here for financial aid!"

D: That's what it amounts to. And it's all free. The Federal Reserve can create as many trillions of dollars as anyone needs.

L: The amazing thing is that all these bright boys in Washington never seem to get a clue. They supported murderous dictators in Latin America until they got thrown out. They supported the Shah of Iran until he got thrown out. They supported Saddam Hussein, and then ended up turning on him themselves. And they still support some of the most brutal regimes in the world today, sowing the seeds of even more suspicion and hatred. How can they be so blind?

D: They never learn at all. And the worst part of it is that there's no need to—nor benefit in—having any involvement whatsoever in any of these places. It's both unnecessary and counterproductive to American interests; it only benefits the people who live within the DC beltway, and those who slop at the same trough. You can't impose a new social order on a people from the outside. And even if you could—whoever you put in office, there's going to be some group or another that's going to object, dig in, and hate you for it to boot. You create more future conflict and enemies for yourself. All these idiots blathering on about what "we" should do should just mind their own business.

L: If only the would-be "nation builders" would remember Jefferson's mandate: "Peace, commerce and honest friendship with all nations; entangling alliances with none."

D: Better watch out—quoting Jefferson can get you on the terrorist watch list these days. But you know I'm an optimist, and the good news is that all of this is coming to an end. Whatever happens is going to happen, and there won't be much the United States can do about it, because all this nation-building nonsense is horrifically expensive and the United States is already tapped out trying to rebuild Iraq and Afghanistan—not to mention Detroit and New Orleans. It's game over for Mubarak, and close to game over for the U.S. empire.

The U.S. government is bankrupt, and will be increasingly immobilized. In a few years, they'll be completely unable to meddle anywhere, because there simply won't be any money to pay for it. The Fed's own projections say the entire budget will be consumed by Social Security, Medicare, Medicaid, and interest on the debt, with no money even for the military, unless something is done soon. There is no politically feasible way to cut spending on those programs. Does that mean the U.S. Navy will wind up rotting at the dock, like the Soviet Navy? It will be interesting to see. Either the roughly $1.5 trillion for "defense" goes, or the $1.5 trillion for Social Security, Medicare, and such goes, or interest on the national debt goes, or the scores of federal agencies go.

At this point, the U.S. budget is like Wile E. Coyote after he's run off the edge of a cliff. His legs are still windmilling in the air, but he doesn't realize it yet.

Sometimes things need to get worse before they can get better. It almost certainly means that in the not-too-distant future, U.S. foreign interventions are going to be scaled way back, or stop entirely, because they simply won't be possible anymore. That will be a good thing for backward countries all over the world.

L: Okay, back to the Middle East, which is looking more and more like the Muddled East, do you think there's any chance this could blow over and die down?

D: These things are chaotic over the short run, but I'd say no. I think the cat's out of the bag, for the reasons we discussed earlier. I have not been spending much time there lately, so all I know is all anyone knows—if you can say they know anything at all from watching TV and reading the papers. One interesting thing about Egypt, in particular, is that no one really knows that much about the "Muslim Brotherhood"—what they actually believe, how powerful they are, and what they'd actually do if they take over.

I think back to the French Revolution. It was, initially, an excellent thing; they got rid of a tyrant and the entire old regime—a big plus. But what replaced it? First they got Robespierre and his Committee of Public Safety, the Jacobins and La Terreur, then they got Napoleon, who was another kind of disaster. The same thing could happen in the Middle East.

Nobody appreciates a busybody. Especially one who's consistently backed repressive criminals for decades. The best thing the United States could do at this point would be to butt out completely.

L: I'm not going to hold my breath for that.

D: I'm glad, because good analysts are hard to find. I've said for years that the way to defuse and start unwinding the war with Islam is to listen to what Bin Laden said was upsetting those people so much. We should get our troops out of their holy land, stop setting up brutal puppet regimes, and stop supporting Israel. If we did that, and sincerely apologized for our destructive actions and the criminal actions our tax dollars have paid for, a lot of those people would cool off and go back to herding goats, looking for oil, making shish kebabs, or some other pursuit of happiness.

L: We should not have to say this—and I know you won't try to justify your remarks—but some people are so touchy on this subject, so let me stress that you are not singling Israel out for harsh treatment. You would have the U.S. government stop supporting all government overseas, including Israel's Arab neighbors, as well as Israel itself. The point is not to take the Arab world's side against Israel, but to let the Israelis and the Arabs work out their own problems.

D: Of course. Israel and all countries should be treated the same—free trade and no military involvement, as you and Mr. Jefferson said. It's really that simple. I went into a lot of detail on Israel in the April 2002 issue of *International Speculator*. And I wrote an analysis of Islam in the July 2001 issue of IS. Never let it be said that I shy from controversy.

L: Perish the thought. Hm. You're saying there's no reason for this fire to be contained in the Middle East—I wonder if there's any reason for this fire to be contained by religion or culture. I'm remembering the mass protests I got caught up in Belarus, just a few weeks ago, which is about as far from the Muslim world as you can get. I have to wonder if Lukashenko, the Belarusian dictator, is watching what's happening in Tunisia and Egypt and wondering how close he came to being forced to flee the country. If the military had switched sides on December 19, as they appear to have just done in Cairo, he'd be toast. I have to wonder if people suffering under other highly repressive regimes around the world are watching and wondering if their time has come to reach for freedom. Could it be that we're seeing another "shot heard 'round the world" today?

D: I think the chances are excellent. Whatever happens, I'm convinced that the next five years are going to be among the most interesting in history, from about every point of view. At some point it should get interesting enough for me to jump in to the Egyptian, Tunisian, Pakistani, and Iraqi stock markets with both feet.

L: Interesting in the Chinese sense of the word.

D: Yes. Particularly interesting is the risk of twenty-first century Robespierres. The problem is that all these people still think in terms of government by nation-state. In that regard, unfortunately, what's happening is not really revolutionary; changing one ruler for another doesn't get to the root problem of the rule of some people by others.

Egypt is a perfect example. The government there serves absolutely no useful purpose whatsoever. It has done nothing but repress the people, act as a vehicle for theft by those in power, and hold the place back for decades. It's likely that whoever replaces Mubarak is just going to have his own goofy ideas of what the government should *do*, instead of just getting the government out of the way.

You know how it is: It's the most cunning, ruthless, and polished liars—the ones who can persuade the most people to support them by promising to take from others—who get elected. Dictatorship is no answer, but absolutely neither is democracy.

Over the long term—the entire span of history—humanity has gone from a state of 100 percent plunder by rulers to now only about 50 percent plunder. The long-term trend is, therefore, good—but I don't see any reason why we should take a cosmic leap forward just now, as nice as that would be.

L: Sounds like you've been listening to that song by The Who, "Won't Get Fooled Again."

D: Does seem appropriate. Behind the scenes, the United States is certainly going to be agitating for another repressive stooge, such as it always picks. Since World War II—or really, since the days of Teddy Roosevelt—when has the United States not picked the most repressive toady? And while the United States won't have much power around the world in a few years, because of the economic problems it's going to have, it's pretty powerful now, and it will be pushing in that direction.

L: Well, instead of a freer world, would you say this new revolutionary fervor is going to end up a big step backward, setting the stage for worse repression and more war?

D: It's entirely possible, but I'm not going to make that prediction. Remember the French Revolution. Remember Rome: They assassinated Caligula, but then got Claudius; they killed him and ended up with Nero. And after Nero, they had a bloody civil war, in the Year of Four Emperors.

L: Well, Nero, I've read, at least had the grace to kill himself. Okay— investment implications seem pretty clear; oil just shot up over $100 a barrel.

D: Yes indeed. I think the commodity bull market is likely to stay intact, and this instability is bullish for energy prices—good news for companies not operating in the Middle East or other areas at high risk.

Sustained higher oil prices are also very bullish for alternative energies, especially alternatives to light sweet crude, including heavy oil, oil sands, and shale oil. All of these are abundant in the Americas, and some even in Europe. These are the kinds of opportunities we specialize in, in our energy newsletters.

On the other hand, this is very bearish for the economies directly affected. The top revenue industry in Egypt, for example, is tourism, and tourism there has dropped to zero. That's going to be devastating and make it all the harder for the place to get better.

L: So, bearish on the region, but bullish on commodities.

D: Yes, but looking ahead for the bright side: Once places like Egypt bottom out, there could be some real bargains to be had there. There could be fantastic deals on prime real estate in Cairo and Tunis, and the local stock exchanges could become a gold mine, for those daring enough to buy when no one else will. Too early now, but the time could be coming.

L: One more question. A lot of people are probably wondering what you think of the changing odds for open warfare in the Middle East? If pro-Israel stooges get replaced by people whose sentiments more closely reflect those of the Arab masses—who are no fans of Israel—doesn't that bring the area that much closer to a shooting match?

D: Well, it's anyone's bet, but these people have been having wars with each other for the last 5,000 years—I see no reason for them to stop now. And as close to the edge as the poor people in these repressive Arabic countries live, and with the economic outlook looking so grim, anything could happen. Even with Israel's nuclear deterrent, *anything* could happen.

L: That's a very sobering thought. If the oil fields of the Middle East turn into large glass bowls, that will have obvious and dramatic consequences for energy prices—but what if this all blows over instead of blowing up? Could oil prices retreat, hurting those who buy in now?

D: I think oil prices will go up anyway. There are new technologies on the horizon that could all but eliminate the use of oil as an energy source, but that's years away. Based on the fundamentals that underlie the commodity, I expect steadily rising prices for years to come, with fluctuations along the way, of course. Everything we see says that trend is very solid, so on top of that, political turmoil is just a bonus.

L: Okay then. Not exactly pleasant thoughts, but important ones. Thanks for your insight.

D: You're welcome. I feel insulated from the turmoil, here in Argentina. But only a plane ride away if I want to smell tear gas in the morning. 'Til next week.

L: *Hasta la proxima.*

Chapter 37

Doug Casey: Something Wicked This Way Comes

February 23, 2011

Louis: Doug, a couple weeks ago we talked about mass riots spreading beyond the Middle East, and you were right. Yemen, Bahrain, and Libya—hundreds reported dead in Tripoli. But I see on Google News that some very brave individuals have organized protests in Moscow and Beijing. And now we have tens of thousands protesting in Madison, Wisconsin, citing the successful uprising in Egypt. There are counter-protesters in Wisconsin, fears of violence, talk of the governor calling up the National Guard. Is the spirit of revolution in the air?

Doug: On a deep level, there is a common thread running through these events. But, in bankrupt Wisconsin, the pro-union forces trying to hold on to artificially high wages and benefits have nothing in common with the hungry, oppressed, miserable people who took to the streets of Egypt. It's fashionable for all sorts of people with

329

a grievance to call those Egyptians "freedom fighters" and identify themselves with them. I'm a freedom-fighter, you're a rebel, he's a terrorist. The semantics are used to muddy the distinctions, not to clarify.

To a fair degree the Egyptians really are freedom fighters—they actually did oust a tyrant—but they are just going to replace the old boss with a new boss. It's not been a radical revolution, at least not so far. The odds are that the new boss will be every bit as bad as, or worse, than the old boss, regardless of whatever window dressings of reform he uses to gain international acceptance for his regime.

Back in Wisconsin, it's completely disingenuous—actually ridiculous and shameful—for unionized state employees to label themselves freedom fighters. These are the people who most directly slop at the trough at the public's expense. They're minions of the ruling class. They're not trying to overthrow an unjust situation, they're rioting to maintain it.

L: So, what's the deeper, connecting thread?

D: Economic hardship. It seems to me that the driving factor behind these protests spreading in the Arab world—and what pushed them from inevitable to imminent—was rising commodity prices, especially food prices. Food prices are also rising rapidly in the United States. Many fruits and vegetables have doubled, and bread is up 50 percent over the last year. Cotton has tripled over the last two years. That's going to make clothing more expensive. The difference is that most Americans don't live hand to mouth, not the way most Arabs do. But nonetheless, they don't like to see their standard of living drop, and they'll strike out as well. As we just discussed in January, it would be most prudent to <u>prepare for chaotic times ahead.</u>

L: Oppressed Middle Easterners take to the streets out of hunger. Wisconsin union members take to the streets because their entitlements are threatened. Both relate to the rising costs of real things resulting from the global currency crisis, which is part of the larger train wreck of the old economic world order.

D: Yes, and with modern communications, widespread public sentiment can be mobilized with speed never seen before. But you know, it's a bit similar to what happened back in the 1960s, although for different reasons. We had simultaneous riots in Europe—mostly in France, but also in Germany and Italy. In Paris, they were tearing up the cobblestone streets to throw rocks at the cops. You had the race riots in Detroit, LA, and Washington, DC, among other U.S. cities, and later, antiwar protests. At exactly the same time, you had the Red Guard and a huge conflagration in China. Three major centers of world civilization erupted in civil unrest at once. But those riots were strictly political. Today's riots are economic, and that's much more serious. Political riots are generally for sport. Economic riots are the real thing.

I've no doubt that with the economic, social, and political forces at work in the world today, we'll see more unrest—lots more. But it's going to be much more violent, and much more dangerous than it was in the 1960s, because the world is much less stable.

L: And more countries have nuclear weapons. If more U.S. puppets fall in the Middle East, that's going to be really bad for Israel, which is surrounded and outnumbered by foes who have no interest whatsoever in reaching a peaceful accommodation. If pressed hard enough, Israel could go nuclear, the threat of which has not stopped individuals from shooting rockets into their midst. I know you don't like making predictions, but does your guru sense tell you that's likely to actually happen soon?

D: Nobody knows, of course, but the odds favor new leaders in most of the Arab countries, and most of the Muslim world. Israel is opposed to any change, because they have an accommodation with the old governments. The same is true with the United States. Israel and the United States are like a nasty dog and his bad-tempered master, although I'm not sure which is which. Sometimes the master kicks the dog, sometimes the dog bites the master, but they still work together.

Anyway, now both the United States and Israel are going to have to cut new deals with new governments. I suspect the new governments will be less inclined to be U.S. stooges, and more likely to be actively anti-Israel.

Meanwhile, bankrupt state governments in the United States could precipitate chaos there, before the balloon goes up elsewhere. We are in uncharted waters, in which anything can happen—and probably will. The key is that most people in the world live on less than $3 a day, most of it goes to food, and food prices are exploding upwards. As is fuel.

L: I remember the terrible events in New Orleans when civil order broke down just a couple years ago. Most Americans seem to be ignoring that embarrassing event, and have long forgotten the Watts riots and Kent State. How do you get such people to consider the facts without sounding like Chicken Little?

D: Good question. When the going gets rough, it often turns out that civilization is really just a pretty veneer that lies on top of a fetid cesspool. The fact of the matter is that many—actually most—people suffer from serious psychological aberrations that rise to the surface if you push the right hot buttons. Losing what they have, and going hungry—especially when they see thieves like most politicians and their pals making billions—won't sit well with the masses. It's going to push a *lot* of hot buttons.

I don't like thinking about rioting and martial law and all of that unpleasantness either; people get hurt, property is destroyed, and so forth. But at this point, a good dose of that looks almost inevitable. What we've seen in Tunisia, Egypt, now Bahrain, and Libya—it's not just a flash in the pan. It's the start of something *big*.

L: It's a pity to see so much human energy being unleashed, creating powerful forces for change, at a time when it's unlikely that that power will be used for good. So few people have any grasp of basic economics—they have no idea where prosperity comes from. So few people understand that human rights are *individual* rights and that entitlements are *not* rights. These people are going to ask for Big Brother to take them in hand, and Big Brother is going to give them what they ask for, good and hard.

D: You're quite correct. The logical next step, as we mentioned before, is a new Robespierre—or a whole slew of them. But you know I always try to look at the bright side, and the good news is that a lot of despotic states are going to be overthrown. Others that are not overthrown will be discredited—also very good. This comes at a time when many of these states are on the ragged edge of collapse anyway; their days are numbered, even without this force precipitating their collapse.

Perhaps technology has advanced to the level that people will begin to see they can conduct their lives without the dead hand of the state trying to tell them what to do, and taking most of what they produce for the privilege.

L: Perhaps. The time may not be far off when the very idea of the nation-state itself will be discredited, and human society will evolve to a, hopefully, better form of organization.

D: I'd love to think so. I think that as technology continues to advance and liberate the individual, the disappearance of the state is inevitable, even if it's not imminent. But whether things get better after the crash or not, I'm increasingly convinced that what has long been inevitable for the whole world is now becoming imminent. We are in the early stages of a major upheaval. In other words, distortions in the way the world works have been built up to a level where the old order could easily collapse. I'm quite serious when I refer to the coming Greater Depression.

L: Just as we all knew the Soviet Union had to collapse from its internal problems—tyranny and economic stupidity—but weren't sure when. Now, decades of economic mismanagement and bad decision making in the global arena must eventually be liquidated. But how do you know the bill is coming due?

D: Well, timing is always the problem. If you wait long enough, absolutely everything that is possible will happen. I suppose that's why we have time itself—to keep everything from happening at once. But we have to think about what's likely in the course of a single lifetime, so we can benefit from foresight, or be punished for guessing wrongly.

Consider that several other U.S. states are looking at "union-busting" legislation such as Wisconsin's. Unions can no longer pretend to be vehicles to protect the workers; they are really nothing but cartels that reward their members at the expense of everybody else. And, unlike the federal government, the states can't just print money. They have to tax people directly to pay for things. Now they have two choices: raise taxes or default on past promises.

Raising taxes is very hard to do during a depression. People who feel their standard of living is slipping just won't stand for it. Taxes were a major cause of the French Revolution and the American Revolution.

The riots in the 1960s weren't about this type of thing—entitlements and taxes—but remember, in the 1960s, few states had sales taxes, and where there was one, it was usually only 1 percent, or 2, max. Now, sales taxes regularly run 6, 7, 8, even 10 percent. In addition, real estate taxes have gone up tremendously, as have state income taxes, of which there were also fewer back then. So these governments are already straining their ability to tax, and they know that if they raise taxes again, it will destroy much of what's left of their economies.

L: But they can't really default either—that would get the politicians thrown out of office just as quickly.

D: Default would hurt bondholders—generally older people who are very active voters. Also, pension funds, insurance companies, and banks would see a large chunk of their assets wiped out, which would be another body blow to struggling state economies. Not being able to print money, they won't be able to keep paying their debts, so they'll be forced to lay off more and more government employees. State and local governments are truly between a rock and a hard place, just like the U.S. government. But the United States has the option of destroying the currency to put off the hour of reckoning, and that's what they'll do.

L: Well, if the governments have to fire a bunch of employees, that's a good thing. But it will add to the unemployment burden, unless they scrap unemployment benefits too, which would also get the politicians tossed out of office.

D: Well, most government employees just push paper, and stop things from happening. It would be cheaper and better to pay them *not* to work, so they won't do actual damage—or give them unemployment compensation. Unfortunately, though, they'll just fire a few employees, or cut their wages and benefits a bit. What they need to do is totally abolish whole departments; each state has hundreds of them, making the lives of businessmen miserable and expensive. They won't do that, so the bureaucracy will just grow back if there is any recovery. Rather, the reduced number of employees will slow down approvals even more, slowing business even more. And that will further open the door to corruption.

Actually, it would be therapeutic to see some of them end up like Mussolini. It's certainly a good thing to see action toward recovering the money Mubarak stole. The same should be true in the United

States. Everybody in high office emerges very wealthy from a small salary; it's all stolen money.

But at this point, there is just no way out. It's like jumping off the top of a 100-story building—it's an exhilarating ride until you get to the bottom. That's exactly where, not just the United States, but the whole global economy is.

L: I guess so. You could spread your arms and try to slow the fall, or if you were an experienced sky-diver, you could try to angle your descent toward one side or the other, but it's not going to change what happens when you hit the street.

D: That's exactly right. In the real world, actions have consequences. Economic causes have effects, and the piper can only be put off from payment for so long. I don't think he can be put off any longer.

L: When, exactly, do you think the bill, and its ever-accumulating interest, will come due?

D: I'm not going to put a date on it, but it's starting. The next 10 years are going to be the most *interesting* decade in centuries. The events that are now underway—economic, <u>financial</u>, <u>social</u>, <u>technological</u>, <u>political</u>, and <u>military</u>—have the promise of being the biggest thing in a very, very long time.

L: Okay, but, with all due respect, you were full of doom and gloom back in 1980—said we were going to tip over the edge, but we didn't.

D: I was, and I did say that—and we could indeed have gone over the edge back then. It was a very close thing. Fortunately—or unfortunately, if you consider the much, much larger bill now coming due—they papered it over. And things actually got better, due to two things: one, many individuals produced more than they consumed, and saved the difference; and, two, we got many improvements in technology. But financial and economic affairs are *much* worse now than they were then.

L: You don't believe it's possible to paper it over this time? Doesn't it make you uncomfortable to say, "It really is different this time!"—at least a bit?

D: Sure it does. Famous last words. But, in fact, it really is different this time, as anyone who searches the news for phrases such as "unprecedented," "record deficit," "record bank failures," et cetera, can see. It's a judgment call, obviously. But we have to make judgments if we're going to succeed, or even survive. Sometimes you have to call for a change in a major trend, which is risky. But not nearly as risky as getting trampled by the mob after it actually changes. I'm not afraid to leave the mainstream. In fact, I far prefer it, whether I'm right or wrong.

L: How can you be so sure there's no possible way to paper this over again? Mugabe trashed his currency and is still in power. Life goes on in Zimbabwe. Couldn't multitrillion-dollar deficits become the new normal in the United States?

D: No, that's not possible. It would destroy the currency. It's bad enough when you do that in a nothing/nowhere country like Zimbabwe, where subsistence farmers can keep on scratching a living out of the dirt with sticks and stones, if they have to. But it wipes out most of the economy above the subsistence level, as just about everyone has their savings in the destroyed currency. If you do that to the Canadian dollar, say, it would be a disaster—but mainly for people who live in Canada. And plenty of Canadians have assets in other countries. But if you do it to the U.S. dollar, it wouldn't just be a disaster in the United States. The U.S. dollar is the world reserve currency. Few Americans have assets outside of the United States. Foreigners hold, maybe, 8 trillion U.S. dollars. All the central banks of the world have mostly dollars. People all over the world have dollars in their pockets and bank accounts. When Bernanke destroys the dollar, it will be a worldwide catastrophe. And that will happen all the faster if the Feds bail out the states, which is a possibility with someone like Obama in charge.

Let me reemphasize this. Almost everyone with net worth around the world tries to keep much of it in dollars. There are trillions of dollars outside the United States—far more than inside—and the people holding them are going to be impoverished. They won't be able to invest or to spend. A collapse of the dollar would lower the standard of living of a lot of people around the world, basically overnight.

This is really, *really* serious, and there's no way out. We are going to go through the meat grinder.

If we were to somehow stumble through this one—I would be fascinated to see how—and manage to move ahead in some semblance of the way things were pre-2008, I very much doubt it would last long. And I'm very sure it will just make the ultimate reckoning day that much more catastrophic.

I hate to say it, because I know the human cost will be enormous, but I think the odds greatly favor this being "it." I only hope to not be very adversely affected by it—and to have the right to say "I told you so," although it will be unwise to draw that to anyone's attention after it happens.

L: Hm. Well, even if there was some way to gain a reprieve for a few more years, it's still going to be ugly. The 70,000 people protesting in Wisconsin show that the so-called jobless recovery is a lie. Improving the bottom line by laying people off is not the same as increasing the top line, and increased government spending is not real GDP growth. Even if we manage to struggle on this way, the minimum payments now due the piper are going to keep things dicey. That means that the risk of social/political collapse remains, even if we avoid economic collapse.

Snow Crash could be starting right now.

Investment implications?

D: Nothing we haven't said before: We're headed out of the eye of the storm, so you better rig for stormy weather—the worst you've ever seen.

L: Specifically?

D: Buy gold—lots of gold, even though it's no longer cheap. To capitalize on the likely next bubble, buy gold stocks. Given the trouble in the Middle East, the right energy stocks are also good to invest in. Short anything that won't do well in economic hard times, including the whole financial sector, and the retail, consumer, and construction sectors. Use those investments to build your cash position so you're ready to take advantage of the spectacular investment opportunities all of this turmoil is going to cause.

And do not—*do not*—forget to diversify yourself out of your country of residence. If you have the means, and have not done so yet, buy a "vacation" home. Make it in some nice remote place where you'd enjoy spending time in any event, but where the people live close to the earth and don't depend on the modern global economy. Also, make it in a place where hungry masses from unsustainable cities are unlikely to show up on your doorstep.

L: And if the sky is not falling?

D: Then you still make a bundle on the volatility ahead and end up with a nice vacation home you can sell if you decide you no longer need it for insurance.

But remember, nothing lasts forever. Few governments last as long as that of the United States has, and it's showing clear signs of terminal decay. Don't kid yourself, thinking, "It could never happen here." Europeans have an advantage over Americans; they remember fighting each other much more recently, and know full well it certainly can happen there.

L: Okay, Tatich. I guess I'll add the gun shop to my stops when I head down to my local coin shop to buy gold—time to load up on ammo again.

D: Sure, why not? You can always sell it later if you don't use it. Cigarettes too, even though I know you don't smoke. And alcohol, even though I know you don't drink.

L: I'll feel like a Y2K fanatic, but I guess there's room in the attic.

D: Sounds trite, but it's better safe than sorry, and it won't hurt to prepare for the worst and hope for the best. 'Til next week then.

Chapter 38

Doug Casey on North Korea's New Kim

January 4, 2012

Louis: So, Doug, there's a new Kim in North Korea. Did you see that he apparently went to school in Switzerland, as both you and I did?

Doug: I did see that. He's supposed to be 28 or 29 years old and attended a boarding school near Bern. Bern is in the German-speaking part of the country, but very close to the French-speaking area, so he could speak both of those languages—plus English, which every educated European speaks, as well as, almost certainly, someone who went to a boarding school there. So this Kim would appear to have some sophistication. You have to assume he was sent there in order to ensure that. But Korea has always been an inward-looking place. I believe well over half of all Koreans are surnamed Kim, Lee, or Park; there aren't a lot of foreigners or outsiders. They used to call it the "Hermit Kingdom" for good reason.

L: Do you think that's significant? Could a Western education be grounds for optimism that this new Kim will allow his subjects to arise from poverty at least a little?

D: Well, there were others before him educated in the West, with no' visible positive effect—Ho Chi Min, for example.

L: Hm. I didn't know that. On the other hand, many of the rulers of Latin American countries are U.S.-educated, and, while not hardcore free-marketeers, they do tend to understand enough economics to know that nationalizing everything is a recipe for poverty, not prosperity. Mexico is a good example of this.

D: That's true, but Correa, the president of Ecuador, is a counterexample. I remember when I met with the president of Bulgaria a few years back. He'd also been educated in the United States and spoke perfect English. I'd thought we might have some common ground, but it was like fire and water. I'm not sure that there's a good correlation here, though I'm not sure anyone has done a statistical study. It's a question of the old nature versus nurture argument, where I come down very much on nature's side. In my own case, I believe I'd be exactly who I am, in terms of moral essence, regardless of the accidents of birth and upbringing. Neither can you make a silk purse out of a sow's ear. I like to offer three famous examples of criminals from classical history: Alexander had Aristotle for a tutor; Nero had Seneca; and Commodus had Marcus Aurelius. A lot of good it did them.

L: I take your meaning regarding Alexander merely being an excellent plunderer, but I suspect that most readers are used to thinking of him as "the Great," but okay. So, our conclusion for now would have to be, given the examples and counterexamples, that a Western education doesn't guarantee anything. It's unreliably neutral at best.

D: Anyway, as we discussed in our conversation on education, most of what passes for education today is just a meaningless mish-mash that no longer emphasizes the liberal arts, which originally referred to the body of knowledge a free man needed to know. And few people study the sciences, which at least tend to teach people something about how the universe really works. It seems to me that most take excruciatingly inane subjects, such as political science and gender studies.

L: Hm. So let's forget about his education. What about Kim's youth? As a simple consequence of being a relatively young man, he can't be as hidebound in last century's communist thinking as his predecessors. Any hope in that?

D: Well, I guess there's always hope. But just look at him: He's a porky little butterball. He doesn't have to be as fit as Bruce Lee or Jackie Chan, but looking like a doughball speaks of someone with no self-discipline, used to a life of indolence. It's out of step with a culture where not only is Taekwondo an obsession, but the average person is skinny as a rail. Further, he's likely to have picked up lots of bad habits from his scumbag father and his sociopathic associates. The outlook for sound judgment from the baby Kim is not encouraging.

L: What I want to know is this: How did a country that's supposed to be a communist state—founded on the core principle of worker emancipation—get turned into a hereditary kingdom? How can that make any sense whatsoever to anyone, and how could anyone stand before the people and spout the necessary bullshit without dying of embarrassment?

D: That's actually a fascinating question. The sad fact is that most people still act like chimpanzees; they just aren't happy without a chest-beating leader and a place in the pecking order that supports him. For some perverse reason, people honor hereditary royalty, even though they're almost all swine. People seem to like "strong" leadership. The Germans loved Hitler, the Russians loved Stalin, and the Chinese loved Mao. Americans idealize their worst and most warlike presidents—with Lincoln and the two Roosevelts at the head of the pantheon. So, in the world of *realpolitik*, baby Kim would be well advised to give the people what they apparently both want and deserve—good and hard.

L: Ve must haff order!

D: Yes, or God forbid, we'd have anarchy!

L: Note to readers who don't know Doug: He's being sarcastic.

D: Yes. And as we've discussed, most people conflate anarchy and chaos, even though they are actually opposites. But anyway, the human default mode seems to be to fall back upon reliance on a wise, alpha-male leader who can kiss everything and make it better. This is one of the reasons why in politics, the worst-case outcome is also the most likely outcome.

L: The vast amounts of evidence to the contrary notwithstanding.

D: Careful. You'll become as cynical as I am.

L: After the last two Kims basically plunged North Korea into a dark age, I don't understand how anyone could possibly say with a straight face that this Kim is just what the place needs.

D: Maybe that's just what you say when there's a man with a gun pointed at you, standing just off camera. Or maybe it's just the natural reaction of a jackal when it's close to a hyena. That's in addition to the fact that Korean culture is about the most groupthink-oriented in the world. And perhaps the most nationalistic. It's quite appalling; even South Korea is a place I wouldn't even consider for a second home.

L: Yes, and I have to add that I had more than a few doubts about the sincerity of the hysterical tears we saw on television upon the passing of the previous Kim.

D: Sure. But there were masses of sincere mourners in the USSR when Stalin died. As far as I'm concerned, we're dealing with a mass psychological aberration. It makes me question whether the human race isn't speciating on psychological grounds, a bit like H.G. Wells's Morlocks and Eloi. Beyond that, from a strictly economic perspective, it's a complete mystery to me where a country like North Korea—which, according to every report, has long been losing a battle with chronic malnourishment—gets the capital to build a serious arsenal of nuclear and other weapons.

L: I guess that even if you have a small GDP, if you take most of it and spend it on weapons instead of food, you'll have weapons.

D: Weapons and caviar and Johnny Walker Blue for the guys in the palaces. The weapons ensure that things stay that way. The soldiers and police are well fed, so they're happy to do as they're told, or else they'll be demoted back to being half-starved peasants. And they're deified in propaganda, just like their U.S. equivalents. The North Korean people are responsible for their own slavery. I wonder if they'd even understand it if they watched the movie *V for Vendetta*.

L: I'm sure the guys on top deserve all their perks for doing such a good job taking care of the proletariat. But anyway, does any of this matter? North Korea has a new Kim, probably just as bad as the old

Kim—does this affect the geopolitical balance of the world in any meaningful way?

D: Well, unless perhaps you happen to be South Korean, it's really not important at all. The only difference between the Kim dynasty and a gang of street thugs is that the Kims are accorded honors and standing as heads of state by the apparatchiks running other nation-states. I understand that when the last Kim died, the UN flew its flags at half-mast—one of thousands of indications of how terminally corrupt the UN is and how totally in need of abolition.

L: Part of the rules of the good old boys' club. We mustn't look too closely at the wrongdoings of other leaders, lest anyone look into our own. No matter how murderous or evil, we must give them due respect, so we get our own.

D: Yes. I'm trying to think of another example of a blatant criminal who died in office recently—seems like there are more who died after leaving office, like Pol Pot and Idi Amin. But I would assume it's SOP to do that for all heads of state.

Well, the good news is that the nation-state, as a form of social organization, is definitely on its way out. Cheap air travel, the Internet, and micromanufacturing—just to name three powerful new technologies off the top of my head—are making it increasingly easy for people to live and work where they please. That makes it increasingly difficult for industrial-era organizations like today's governments to control them, as much as most people seem to want to be controlled.

L: I tell my students that in the not-too-distant future, governments will be forced—by people voting with their feet—to stop abusing taxpayers as slaves and start competing for them as customers.

D: A big improvement, although the state is still a parasite that serves little useful purpose. You're right, and that's the good news. The bad news is that they won't go down without a fight.

L: Kaddafi showed that. He went on fighting long, long after he had lost, simply refusing to believe that he had.

D: Just so. I wonder if the UN half-masted the flags for him because he was still in office when he got what was coming to him. Maybe not.

In the current U.S. electoral campaign, it's fascinating to witness the absolutely hysterical and visceral hatred that Ron Paul is

generating from the chattering classes. And Ron is as good-tempered
and mellow a guy as you could ever hope to find in politics. I'm
afraid the transition is going to be—

L: Messy.

D: Very messy, for all of us small mammals who have to hide while the
dinosaurs are thrashing around in their death throes.

L: Sigh. So, back to North Korea. Nothing changes? No need to worry
about the new Kim going psycho and starting a nuclear war?

D: As I see it, the U.S. government is the bigger danger at this point. As
nasty a place as it is, North Korea doesn't appear to have expansionist
aims nor any interest in meddling in the affairs of other countries and
killing other peoples. Actually, I understand that the North Koreans
have been seeking a formal nonaggression pact for years—something I promise will never be reported on Fox News. Technically,
the Korean War has never ended for them; it's just been a truce since
1953. But they would like some sort of guarantee that the United
States won't attack them. Of course the average U.S. person would
react by saying, "What? That's ridiculous! Those Koreans are bloodthirsty paranoid maniacs taking orders from a crazy dictator!" And
there's a lot of truth to that belief. They certainly are paranoid—but
rightly so. The indications are that the United States would attack
them, just like Iraq, if it thought it could get away with it. The United
States has massive naval forces in the area and lots of troops and
nuclear weapons in Japan and South Korea.

L: The United States certainly has attacked or invaded plenty of other
countries that never attacked it, from Panama to Iraq.

D: Yes, and whether the rulers of such places are good people or
bad people is not the issue; the United States now provokes and
attacks on the flimsiest of pretexts, and few people anywhere dare
protest.

L: With the United States deploying ever-more-advanced technology
in military applications, I wonder if it might get to a point at which
U.S. leaders imagine that they can take out North Korea's leadership so fast there won't be enough time for the remnants to make a
nuclear response. If destroying Iraq over imaginary weapons of mass
destruction was good PR, taking out North Korea would have to
seem like great PR. And this is an election year, after all.

D: I'm sure the bright boys in Washington are actively thinking about it. But I have to step in and object to the sloppy use of the phrase "weapons of mass destruction" that we see so often in the mass media. It used to be that these things were called ABC or NBC weapons: nuclear, biological, or chemical weapons. They were just a special class of indiscriminate unconventional weapons. The only actual weapon of mass destruction among them is the nukes. If you want to talk about a real weapon of mass destruction, that would be a sweeping B-52 raid. I hate to see the nomenclature corrupted and misused in that way. It's done for political purposes, much the way the whole terrorism thing is. If you corrupt the language that describes things, you corrupt the way people think about them.

At any rate, the fact that North Korea has nuclear weapons—no matter how primitive and ineffective they might be—is a fairly good guarantee that the United States will not act preemptively. Too many missile commanders could have standing orders that could not be stopped by taking out the leadership. And that guarantees that other countries are working to acquire such weapons and gain that same protection. If Saddam had actually had nukes, the United States would never have dared to attack him. That actually encourages other regimes to go nuclear.

L: So, what happens to North Korea?

D: Frankly, I don't know, but I suspect it ends with an economic collapse.

L: But aren't they already pretty much economically collapsed?

D: Yes. It's much like the USSR that way. The USSR collapsed in 1990 because the people got news from abroad from travel, newspapers, books, and TV, while technologies like the fax and the personal computer allowed them to spread dissatisfaction. News from abroad increasingly percolates into almost every nook and cranny of the world, unless you're going to run a completely closed off and backward police state. North Korea is much, much more poor, backward, and isolated than the old Soviet Union was. But even so, people there are becoming more aware that their standard of living is lower than it is abroad, in good part because of improvements in China and word seeping in from the South. At some point, I hope a critical mass will be reached. It may take some time yet, but left to its own devices, it'll collapse, just as the Soviet Union did. North Korea is actually a non-problem; it'll take care of itself. It's a threat to no one, except maybe the South Koreans, and insofar as it's a problem at all, it's their problem, not that of the United States.

L: Well, if North Korea is largely a nonproblem, is there another conflict you see as being more important?

D: That would be Iran. The United States is beating the war drums louder and louder—has been for decades, actually. To read the popular press, it seems to be building up to a genuine crisis. This could be the year when, either by intent or by accident, the pot boils over.

L: As I said, it is an election year, after all; time to wag the dog.

D: That's right, and war is the health of the state, especially in an election year. There's also Pakistan and other potential conflicts. None of these countries are very savory; they're not beacons of freedom. But neither are they any threat whatsoever to the United States. It's actually literally insane to start a war—bankrupting the United States and turning it into a police state, pretending it's under attack. The United States has a dozen aircraft carriers poking about the world now. They are about as welcome off foreign coasts as foreign aircraft carriers would be on station off the east or west coast of the United States. The natives don't like it at all; they actively dislike it and resent it.

Not even considering the economic realities we face, which I think are going to be especially nasty, I think 2012 is going to be a particularly dangerous year, geopolitically.

L: Right, then. Investment implications?

D: Buy gold. Buy silver. Diversify your assets internationally. Nothing new to our readers. But I have to say again that the gold stocks are starting to look genuinely cheap, and I think the chances are excellent that there's going to be a real mania bubble in the gold sector. That's been in the cards for some time, but now current pricing makes them particularly attractive before what's coming next. What do you think?

L: Well, you're singing my song, of course. That's pretty much what I just wrote about for tomorrow's issue of the *International Speculator*. With the stocks cheaper and the price of the underlying commodity—gold—up, it certainly looks like a great buying opportunity. The producing miners are making bunches of money, which will catch the attention of broader markets when most other sectors are losing profitability. That will enable and encourage larger companies to go out and buy successful exploration companies, to replace depleting reserves. It all looks very good.

D: I do think that many billions—out of all the trillions of new currency units being created all around the world—are going to pile into the gold sector.

L: I hope you're right; that's the way I'm betting, both in the newsletter and with my personal investments.

D: Good for you—me too.

L: All right then, thanks for another sobering conversation.

D: My pleasure.

Chapter 39

Doug Casey on Obama's War and Your Survival

September 12, 2013

Louis: Well Doug, despite an almost universal lack of support from governments and other organizations around the world—not to mention a Russian fleet moving to position itself right in the way—Mr. Obama seems intent upon committing an act of war against the government of Syria. It's becoming harder and harder to tell the difference between Republicans and Democrats. What do you make of this?

Doug: It's completely insane. It's further proof that the U.S. government is completely out of control at this point. It's been captured by sociopaths, and the chances of a gentle reform are about as good as they were in the USSR in the 1920s, Germany in the 1930s or China in the 1950s—to use some examples of equal importance. But that's looking at the big picture. From a strictly tactical point of

349

view, it makes no sense at all to get involved militarily in yet another Middle Eastern country.

L: We should note that, unlike many pundits, you've actually been to Syria.

D: Yes. A couple of times, actually, including renting a car and driving all around the country a few years back. That hardly makes me an expert, but being on the ground doesn't hurt. We should also point out that, like most of the countries in the region, Syria isn't really a nation, in the sense of being one people living in a particular geographic area. It was artificially constructed in the boardrooms of Europe decades ago, like so many other so-called countries around the world. It's a conglomeration of numerous religious, ethnic and political groups that have very little in common except mutual longstanding grudges and hatreds, however irrational. Syria as an entity shouldn't exist—and probably won't much longer. Arbitrarily deciding to drop bombs on one portion of those groups will serve no useful purpose whatsoever.

L: It does seem crazy. I mean, you can't have a war on chemical weapons any more than you can have a war on terrorism, or a war on artillery barrages, or a war on cavalry charges, as you've said many times. Syria's chemical weapons stockpiles won't all be sitting in one place with a big bull's-eye target on it. Even if U.S. cruise missiles could hit most of the caches, who's to say dangerous amounts of nerve agents won't be released to the harm of all downwind? But aside from the pragmatic foolishness of it—even assuming Obama is right about who used chemical weapons in Syria—where does it say in the Constitution that the U.S. government is authorized to bomb dictators who massacre their own people?

D: You are right to question the so-called facts in this case. The White House asserts that 1,400 people were killed with chemical weapons used by the government of Syria. What is the proof that this is so? There is nothing but allegations and circumstantial evidence, such as the report that a rocket believed to have carried a chemical weapon was launched from a government-controlled area of Damascus to an area with a high rebel concentration. But the government has nothing to gain—and everything to lose—from doing the one thing Western governments have said they would not tolerate: use chemical weapons. On the other hand, any of the numerous rebel groups—there are many—have much to gain from having the West bomb their opponents. So a false-flag operation seems much more likely. People assume they know what's going on because they hear a newsreader blather something on TV or read something by a "reporter" who's only parroting a government press release. That's extremely naïve, in that the first casualty in war is always the truth.

L: A striking thing about this is that despite the UN saying no, NATO saying no, and visible preparations for war by the Russians, Obama seems to be in a great hurry to bomb something right away.

D: Yes; it's idiotic. The UN sent an inspection team, and the world is waiting for the report. Even if we accept the premise that the United States has the right—and U.S. taxpayers have the obligation—to punish users of chemical weapons, what's the hurry? With Obama's finger on the trigger, it's unlikely in the extreme that the government of Syria would use chemical weapons again in the near future, if it's even true that it used them in the first place. So why not let the UN commission issue its report?

How do the warmongers in the United States expect bombing some military targets can possibly solve anything? It's as if the Japanese reasoned that attacking Pearl Harbor wouldn't be an act of war, just a limited air strike, with no boots on the ground.

It's also unlikely that Assad will resign. About 15 percent of Syria's population are Alawites—his sect—as is most of the Army. If he forfeits power, these people are in for some serious payback. It's likely a battle to the finish; I don't expect him to run and hide.

L: Still, it might be a good thing if he did.

D: Maybe not; there's no evidence that any of the potential candidates to take his spot will be any better than he is. As bad as he is, some look considerably worse. In fact, if Obama, or Cameron, or Merkel, or Hollande were ruling Syria now, you can be assured they'd be doing exactly what Assad is doing to maintain power. Syria is disintegrating. It's likely to break up into several little countries, regardless of what Western powers do. That's actually the best thing that could happen—hopefully without outside intervention. If it happens with Syrian blood on American hands, that can only make things worse. Much worse. Tribal societies are especially resentful of meddling by outsiders.

This whole hysteria about chemical weapons, like so many other memes pushed by fear mongers in government, is ludicrous. If a child or other innocent bystander dies from being gassed, he or she is no more dead than if the means had been a stray bullet or a bombed building. It's considered an unconventional weapon, but so are the drones the United States has deployed all around the world—and even at home.

The hysteria is hypocritical in more ways than one. The U.S. government has used chemical weapons in foreign wars: thousands of tons of Agent Orange and napalm in Vietnam; and plenty of white phosphorus and depleted uranium in Iraq. It reputedly still has the world's largest stocks of chemical weapons. The United States supported Saddam Hussein even though it knew he was using them during the Iran-Iraq war. And the United States has used chemical weapons against its own people: the massacre at Waco, Texas, would be a prominent recent example of the United States gassing its own citizens, including women and children.

L: Yes, the hypocrisy of it is outrageous. However, back to your starting point: The insanity of it is even more striking. Even if the United States could do what Obama wants done, there is no way the result would be greater peace and stability in the Middle East—and it certainly would not reduce the amount of hatred and threats of violence directed toward Americans.

D: That's absolutely correct; it will increase them. One threat currently being circulated is that if the United States launches an attack, a counterattack will be launched worldwide, not against blameless civilian targets, but against U.S. officials, government employees, and individual military personnel. In particular, Obama, his staff, his advisors, and all of their families.

Now, on one hand, some might say that is overly nasty. On the other, it makes more sense and is much more moral to take the fight directly to the perpetrators. First, it might actually serve to discourage them and make them think twice; it could be therapeutic for them to get some of what they're giving. Second, it reduces collateral damage and hurting innocents. Third, it would not only be much more effective, but much cheaper than conventional warfare. This approach was touched upon in Tarentino's movie *Inglourious Basterds*, which centered on making the war personal for Hitler and his Nazi coterie—a far cry from taking it out on the sheep-like German people with atrocities like the Allied bombing of Dresden and Hamburg.

It will never happen—well, maybe with Putin—but if the leader of some country wants a war because he thinks the leader of another country is a criminal, let them have a cage fight, man to man. Or, if neither sociopath has the guts for that, let them have a gang war between their minions which doesn't affect civilians overly much.

We should call a spade a spade: Certainly at this point in U.S. history, the U.S. government is no more ethical than any of the other 200 governments in the world. It doesn't even observe its own Constitution. You can forget about all the noble words of Jefferson, Washington, Paine, Adams, and the other founders; those are now just meaningless window-dressing.

But in the larger scheme of things, this hullabaloo about Syria's chemical weapons is really just a sideshow. Syria will disintegrate, regardless. Egypt may not disintegrate, but it will descend into chaos when the food and oil imports stop. Libya is splintering into factions beyond counting, perhaps headed for a loose collection of warlord principalities like Somalia.

The only countries in the region that have any sort of ethnic or cultural integrity are Egypt and Saudi Arabia. Egypt, as we've already said, is bursting apart at the seams. It has absolutely no possibility of surviving as an economic entity; it survives solely on foreign aid and tourism, and those are both going away. Saudi Arabia is a medieval theocracy—it seems to me that Saudi Arabia is the real ticking time bomb and is on the verge of blowing the whole region sky high.

Of course, regardless of who's in the White House, the United States always feels compelled to go sticking its nose in these problems. At a minimum, it's going to get its nose bloodied.

The Arab Spring, I'm sorry to say, is looking more and more like it was the beginning of the Arab Meltdown, which will last for a very long time. This trend looks irreversible at this point.

L: The tragedy of that war-torn region of the world is about to be compounded. It's a terrible thing, and I don't want to make light of it, but we can't stop it—the best we can do is try to capitalize on the investment opportunities it may present. Successful investors could even help with the rebuilding, when the time is right.

D: Yes, especially in the energy sector, since this region is where most of the world's oil exports originate. Whatever happens, none of what's going on is going to make oil any cheaper—and it could make it much more expensive. It's as if the world situation was giving oil speculators a free "put," ruling out the possibility of loss. Similar to the "Bernanke Put," where his creation of trillions of dollars ruled out the possibility of losing money in stocks over the past few years.

L: What about shale oil? Some people are saying that the United States has enough that it could even become an exporter again.

D: As wonderful as shale oil is, and as abundant as it is in North America, Argentina, China, and parts of Europe as well, it is by its very nature an expensive form of oil production. It's a far cry from drilling a hole in the ground and having tens of thousands of barrels of light, sweet crude gush forth under natural pressure every day. So, even if we can exploit all the shale oil there is, that doesn't mean gasoline or heating oil will get any cheaper. And it's unlikely that we will be able to exploit all the shale oil there is; it's politically very unpopular because of the hysteria about hydraulic fracturing—fracking—of the shale. Shale oil is not a cost solution; it's an availability solution, if it's allowed to go forward.

L: I've heard of anti-fracking protests in the UK, a place that desperately needs cheaper oil. But I see your point: Even if all the obstacles can be overcome, deposits permitted for production, and the capital raised to exploit them, it will still take years to develop all these resources. And we'll be able to see it as they come online. So, for the near- to mid-term, it seems very unlikely that prices will go down and much more likely that they will go up.

D: That's the way I see it. I have not seen oil as being cheap—in the "buy low, sell high" sense—for some time. The chances are better that it's going higher than going lower at this point—but that doesn't necessarily make it a great speculation.

   In my view, a good commodity speculation, from the long side, is one that is trading way below its previous highs, even trading below production costs. Ideally, it's in a period when producers are closing down and everybody sees the investment as a dead duck. That doesn't describe oil today. That said, I'm friendly to oil because the era of finding super-giant fields of light sweet crude is over. Now all that's available is shale oil, tar sands, heavy oil, deep ocean oil, oil in very dangerous places, and the like. Plenty of oil, true—but it's expensive and inconvenient. Plus, while consumption in advanced countries is flat, it is rising and will continue to rise in the developing world—where all the people are. And the political problems in the Middle East are going to get worse, not better.

That sums up the commodity. However, there are good oil and gas companies I'm willing to bet on—that's a different question. There are thousands of oil companies, and I don't have the interest in trying to sort them out; it's a very specialized area. Marin Katusa, head of our energy team, has really developed a sixth sense regarding these things. He thinks he's figured out where the next major, world-class discovery will be made, very much ahead of the crowd. I urge those interested in this field to subscribe to his monthly newsletter, *Casey's Energy Report*.

L: Okay, that makes sense. Do you see any other investment implications to the rising tide of chaos in the Middle East?

D: Buying gold remains the single best allocation of capital I can think of today. I mean physical gold—and silver—bullion coins and bars under your direct personal control, stored in multiple locations around the world. This is for prudence. It's the single best thing you can do protect yourself against any particular government turning predatory and deciding you're the prey. You should investigate both our new Hard Assets Alliance and Goldmoney.com.

As for making money on the trend, buying stocks in companies that explore for or produce precious metals is the best way to speculate for profit. Most of them are garbage, although when the wind blows, even the turkeys will fly. It's been, believe it or not, about 17 years since we've had a screaming, runaway bull market of the type that made these stocks famous. With all the currency units that have been created since the start of the Greater Depression, the likelihood of a bubble in gold and oil and a super-bubble in the stocks of their small producers and explorers, is quite high.

L: You didn't call a bottom last month, but you did tell our readers that gold was again a compelling buy at around the $1,200 level. It may well turn out that that was the bottom after all.

D: With rare exceptions—that are mainly luck—only liars buy at the exact bottom and sell at the exact top, but I'm very happy with what

I said when we were at $1,200. Purchase of precious metals remains the most prudent thing you can do to protect your wealth, and a very reasonable speculation at this point. Gold is not the giveaway it was at $250 back in 2001, but it's very reasonable near $1,300 now. I think mining stocks have also bottomed at this point, and there are several great speculations available today. All the so-called quantitative easing—money printing—by governments around the world has created a glut of freshly printed money. This glut has yet to work its way through the global economic system. As it does, it will create the bubble in gold and the super-bubble in gold stocks I mentioned above. This remains in the future; what we've seen so far is just foreshadowing.

As a side comment, I hate to say "quantitative easing." It's a ridiculous and dishonest euphemism for printing money. Everybody uses it, parrotlike, because it's the expression the government uses. It is, however, a huge mistake to let the enemy control the language.

Anyway, in light of what we've been talking about today, I'm now seeing similar potential in junior oil stocks. On the other hand, I should caution that I'm less bullish on other industrial minerals at this time. The same factors that are bullish for oil and gold point to slowed economic activity and higher costs for many industries, which is bearish for copper, other base metals, and other industrial raw materials.

For the same reason, I have to stress again that I think equities in general are grossly overpriced. That's where all the money's going now, but all this money printing is going to destroy economies, not stimulate them, so I expect that flow to reverse. Where's the money going to go? Not real estate: It's highly vulnerable to higher interest rates, which are inevitable at this point. Plus, property is the easiest thing for bankrupt governments to tax. Gold is the only financial asset that's not someone else's liability. Plus it can be private, like cash. It's the logical destination for a lot of that money.

I hate to reinforce my reputation as a permabear, but the global economy—led by the United States, the EU, Japan, and China—is thoroughly and inextricably caught in the wringer; there is no way out except through. I am very pessimistic about this; what we saw in 2008 was just a prelude, a warmup. It's going to get very, very ugly.

L: Doug, you've told me for years that you're an optimist.

D: I am, about what philosophers call "the human condition." I'm very pessimistic about the political death spiral the world's governments have got themselves into. The most recent example of what can happen is offered by the Polish government, which has just confiscated half that country's pension accounts; that one came out of nowhere. But pension funds are sitting ducks everywhere, including the United States. It's important to remember that the prime directive of all organisms, whether amoebas, individuals, or organizations like governments, is: Survive! And they'll do anything, at any cost, to do so.

The current world order must crash—and it will—before something better can replace it. I've long said that that will be even worse than I imagine it will be, but that the future after the collapse will be even better that I *can* imagine it to be. The rapid pace of technological progress is one of the factors that inspires such optimism in me.

L: That reminds me of how you like to point out that there are more scientists and engineers working on making the world a better place today than have existed in all previous generations combined.

D: Exactly. Just today I was reading about the successful test flight of *SpaceShip Two*, Virgin Galactic's passenger spaceship. It's scheduled to begin commercial service next year. Ordinary people will be able to go to space, like tourists anywhere else. It's extraordinary. Hopefully this will show the truth of what we said about the need to abolish NASA and sell off all its assets to the private sector.

There's also the continuing success of Bitcoin, a digital currency backed by nothing and issued by no one, that you and I have criticized. Despite its obvious flaws, Bitcoin is gaining wider and wider acceptance all around the world. This is striking, because the main selling point of Bitcoin is that it is not issued by governments and is completely private. The fact that such an idea can gain traction speaks volumes about how much the world is changing.

The continuing revelations from Edward Snowden are another part of this, now that it's becoming evident to all just how far the U.S. government has insinuated its tentacles into everything everywhere, not just in the United States. I'm hopeful the stage is being set to make sure such wholesale invasions of privacy can never happen again. I don't think it will happen, but if there were a big enough backlash and the NSA were abolished, I'd like to see its big facility in Utah junked and the assets sold off, just as should happen to NASA. That's what should happen, but it won't. Fortunately it won't matter; that mammoth facility in Utah is a typical dinosaur artifact, and it will soon become as obsolete as the organization that created it.

L: We don't need to fight it—Moore's Law will take care of it?

D: Yes. Add to this 3-D printing; crowdsourcing and crowdfunding; social networks that cut across borders, languages, cultures, time zones, and laws—many of the things we talked about in our <u>conversation on technology</u>—and you can see that government systems set up in the Industrial Age are dinosaurs on their last gasps. These sorts of technologies are making work itself transportable and life more individualized—independent of the nation-state. More powerful than the ballot box will be the shoebox, as people vote with their feet. Soon governments will be forced to woo taxpayers, treating them like highly desirable, wealthy tourists, instead of being able to cage them like slaves. I don't see governments as necessary, of course, but most people still do. Governments will, however, be forced to be more constrained in the post–Greater Depression future.

The bad news is that as the dinosaur thrashes around in its death throes, it can and will do a lot of harm. The good news is that once it's gone, our world will be a much freer, healthier, and wealthier place. I'm really looking forward to it.

L: I worry about that dinosaur. We talked about Cyprus seizing private individuals' savings, but that was a small, obscure country. Poland, as you mentioned, is a much bigger country. I'm afraid that's the sort of thing more and more cash-strapped governments around the world will be doing.

D: All the more reason all of our readers should redouble their efforts to internationalize their lives and their assets. Wherever you live, you should get your money out of your country, before the country gets money out of you. For more on this there's no better source than our free <u>International Man</u> website.

L: Very well, I know that tune. Thanks for another stimulating conversation.

D: My pleasure. Until next time.

Chapter 40

Doug Casey on the Fourth of July

July 6, 2011

Louis: *Hola*, Doug. You know I'm not the angry type; I don't tend to walk around with a chip on my shoulder. Still, I find myself irritated around this time of year, as person after person wishes me a happy "Fourth of July"—as though the passage of the fourth day of this or any month had any significance whatsoever. It's *Independence Day*. Successful rebellion against tyranny is what all the fireworks are about, not just some random long weekend that gives people more time to drink beer and distract themselves from maxed-out credit cards with fireworks. What do you make of this annual showcase of doublethink?

Doug: I totally agree with you. One particular irony is that real fireworks are basically illegal these days. We are supposed to be celebrating the fact that individual farmers, coopers, and carpenters had the firepower to throw off their government—in a society that now disallows the average individual to own more than sparklers.

L: Well, there are loopholes. I buy my fireworks on an Indian reservation. Mostly high-lofting mortars, the biggest I can get. I've got a half-kilo "cake" type firework here.

D: Really? That's great! I wonder if you could hit anything with those mortars. When I was a kid, we'd make real mortars by dropping a big firecracker down a pipe planted in the ground, and then dropping a marble with another big firecracker glued to it down the pipe. Primitive, and a bit risky, but fun practical science for any grade-school kid.

L: Hm. I'm not sure I could hit anything if I tried. These are pretty hefty for civilian use; the launch tubes are not the usual cardboard, but some sort of tough resin polymer, and the mortar rounds weigh between five and six ounces. But there are no fins on the rounds, and the launch tubes are not rifled, so I doubt they'd be very accurate. In my younger days, I might have done some tests to see what I could blow up with one, but my little ones get such a kick out of seeing them go off in the sky, that's where they've all gone.

But I take your point. It is ironic that I have to find a scrap of land populated by the descendants of the people who lived here first to buy supplies—all made in China—to celebrate the imaginary freedom of the descendants of those who crushed them and took their land.

D: The sad history of American Indians is a topic we can get into another time. It's the imaginary freedom you mention that I'd like people to think about now, as they decide whether to celebrate Independence Day, or the fourth of July.

L: What percentage of U.S. citizens even think about the meaning of Independence Day on the fourth of July?

D: Whatever it is, I would say it's smaller than the percentage of so-called Americans who've actually read the Declaration of Independence.

L: That's not many.

D: The correct statistical term is "teeny-weeny." And sadly, in a country where you can't even light a sparkler 364 days a year without the neighbors calling a SWAT team in on you, the chances of the people rising up as commemorated on July 4 are trivial to nonexistent. It's a pity how the political class can lord it over the serfs, because the serfs are still well fed.

L: Setting us up for a long "history of repeated injuries and usurpations."

D: That is, after all, what the state does for a living, including the one in the United States. We should talk about that. There are a number of points in the original "Unanimous Declaration of the thirteen united States of America" [capitalization, including "united," as in the original] that are worth thinking about today. I strongly recommend reading the whole thing to all our readers, and all people around the world; it takes no more than 10 minutes. Despite the fact that everyone has heard of the Declaration, and despite the fact that it contains very important ideas, almost nobody has actually read it, including the pompous talking heads who pontificate in the media about "America's birthday." Regrettably, America has largely ceased to exist, having been replaced by the United States.

L: Or the United State. I'm with you on this one: The Declaration of Independence is a good read, and many, if not most, of Jefferson's grievances against old King George are just as applicable to the U.S. government today. Let's talk specifics.

D: Specifics are critical, as is precision in defining words and ideas; it's part of what differentiates intelligent discourse from a rant. Let me start off by saying that the Declaration adopted by the Continental Congress on July 4, 1776, is not perfect. Right off the bat, the Declaration says: "When in the course of human events, it becomes necessary for one people to dissolve the political bands which have connected them with another. . . ." But the American states were not one people—anything but. Different religions, different languages, different traditions, different customs—and that's just among the European inhabitants.

When the American Revolution started, it was in many ways a civil war as well. As it turns out, only about a third of the European population of the colonies actually wanted to sever their connection to the crown of England. It was rather bold for the men who assembled themselves in congress to presume to speak for "the people" and set them on such a dangerous and costly course—that of war. It was a huge arrogance, and an object lesson exploding the myth that the so-called representatives of the people actually represent the will of the people. A lot of black slaves, and even Indians, enlisted with the British against the Americans.

L: I've read that too. And many of the loyal British subjects who did not want to partake of rebellion found themselves surrounded by enemies and eventually on foreign soil in their own homes. A good bunch of them ended up moving to what became Toronto, and the Queen of England is still nominally the Canadian head of state.

D: That likely wouldn't be the case if Benedict Arnold had succeeded at the first U.S. invasion of Canada, in 1775. But British sympathizers had to leave under very . . . unpleasant circumstances, not the least of which being leaving their property behind. It could have worked out worse for them, of course—look what happened a few years later with the French revolution. Maybe we should talk about that, come *quatorze juillet*. But the point is that the Declaration was not quite as unanimous as many would like to believe. I say that in the interest of intellectual honesty, even though I'm a big fan of the sentiments in the Declaration.

L: Fair enough. I also think it's important because people who speak of "unifying" the country today—who imagine they can get everyone working together under some brave new banner—are dreaming. It's just as crazy a dream as the Soviets had, when they imagined their next five-year plan would unite all the workers to pull unanimously in one direction.

D: I'm congenitally suspicious of anybody who wants to "unite" people. Most often they're collectivists who want everybody to follow the party line, become lemmings, and drink the Kool-Aid. Horrible busybodies.

Anyway, the next famous line I think is particularly worth looking at is that of the unalienable rights: "Life, Liberty and the pursuit of Happiness." I note that in the "Individual Declaration of Independence" you wrote in 1996, you amended it to: "Life, Liberty, and the Pursuit of Property and Happiness." We should link to your Declaration, so people can see what I'm talking about. I wish the original had the same emphasis on property you put in.

L: Well, I should explain that I declared independence from the United States approximately 15 years ago because I'd had enough of the long history of abuses and usurpations of the day—particularly the Waco massacre. As you note in your first point, I didn't think my fellow Americans would unite as one people to oppose murder and mayhem paid for with tax money extracted from us by force. I also did not—and do not—believe it was necessary for me to wait for or have anyone else's approval. I did not apply for citizenship elsewhere. So, in my view, I am not a U.S. citizen; I am a sovereign individual.

This may seem rather fantastic, in the literal sense of the word, to most people. I'm aware that the U.S. government never replied to nor acknowledged the Declaration I published—with the same sincerity and perhaps more honesty than the Continental Congress published its Declaration. Uncle Sam still considers me a tax slave, along with the rest of the herd. But to me it was more than symbolic: It cleared any mental clutter that might have prevented me from my pursuit of life, liberty, property, and happiness. It opened the door for me to become an International Man.

D: I congratulate you on being ahead of the curve on that. Although, I suspect that if you sent it to them today—now that the ridiculous Forever War on Terror has been declared and the Department of Homeland Security established—you might have to deal with a dawn raid on your house. The Declaration of Independence has become a piece of subversive and seditious literature, and those who take it seriously . . . should be careful.

L: Thanks, but now back to your point. It is my understanding that Jefferson actually did originally write "Life, Liberty, and the Pursuit of Property." But, as you say, there was not unanimity on the idea of declaring independence, and the declaration was amended a lot before it eventually passed. For some reason that escapes me at the moment, the pursuit of property was changed to the pursuit of happiness. I also understand that Jefferson had originally included language that would have freed the slaves, but that was struck to gain the votes of the southern states, and that Jefferson predicted there would be trouble over the issue within 100 years—just about the time when the War Between the States erupted.

D: I didn't know that.

L: You still don't; you just have my assertion. But 1776, the play, has an entertaining and educational telling of the story. At any rate, I got my idea for the pursuit of property—an essential human right—from Jefferson.

D: Well said. A pity they removed it; just goes to show there were cracks in the Liberty Bell before it had been rung.

L: Okay, what next?

D: The part where it says that, "whenever any Form of Government becomes destructive of these ends, it is the Right of the People to alter or to abolish it. . . ." We've talked about the War Between the States already, but I think it's worth pointing out that this language basically guaranteed the right of the southern states to withdraw from the union. It just goes to how the Declaration had become a dead letter long before today. Most of what the colonists complained the king was doing is now being done—and to a vastly greater degree—by the U.S. government.

L: I see it that way, too. Southerners did not march under the banner of ensuring the survival of slavery, but "states' rights." That term has negative associations these days, but at the time, those states thought of themselves as independent countries that had a right—guaranteed in the founding documents of the union—to leave that union when they no longer saw it to be to their benefit.

D: Yes. I don't recall how Lincoln, who was a good rhetorician, finessed that point.

L: I think that just like a politician today; he largely ignored it. I don't think anyone could logically get out of it. Instead, the argument was that "a house divided cannot stand." And that European powers would take advantage of a divided America and attack.

D: Irrelevant to the point, and wrong to boot. At any rate, I think it's worth reiterating that when the cost of participating in any society exceeds the benefits of belonging to that society, people have the right to remove themselves. That can be individually, as you did—if only in principle and theory—or in groups. But in the latter case, I'd say it has to be truly unanimous for all members of a group. No one should be forced to be part of a union they object to.

L: That's probably going to sound logical, but impractical to many people. Perhaps we should refer them to our conversation on anarchy.

D: It's a pity that the words "principles" and "politics" sound contradictory when used in the same sentence. The next bit I think is worth another look states: "mankind are more disposed to suffer, while evils are sufferable, than to right themselves by abolishing the forms to which they are accustomed." It's like the old saw: "Better the devil you know than the one you don't." People know that things can always be worse, and as bad as the situation is in the United States today, it's definitely true that it could be worse.

L: It hasn't gotten to the point where we would be arrested for having this conversation.

D: Yes, but for how long? Maybe we should talk faster. At any rate, people in the United States still enjoy a relatively high standard of living, even if that's largely because they're living off of capital and debt. It's enjoyable living in a paradise, even if it's a fool's paradise. So of course they are reluctant to see serious change. Things might get worse.

L: I've never taken that part of the Declaration to have been an argument. I don't think Jefferson thought there shouldn't be change more often; his writings show that he expected tyranny to grow back and have to be overthrown frequently. I see it as a psychological observation on his part; it's just the way people are that they will put up with a great deal of injustice—until it becomes unbearable for a critical mass among the population. The status quo has momentum, and there are psychological reasons for this. A revolution or big social change generates a lot of costs and uncertainties, both of which people avoid. Real change comes at such a high price, people put it off as long as they can.

D: Agreed. I think that's a correct statement of fact in the Declaration, and I'm afraid it's bearish for the United States, because it seems pretty clear that as bad as things are for many people, we have not yet gotten to the point where a large fraction of the population would actually consider overthrowing the government by force. Things will have to get much worse before they can get better. That's what Lenin meant when he said "The worse it gets, the better it gets," although his intentions were not good. But that's further proof of how dangerous revolutions are.

L: As long as the rent-to-own furniture fills the living room, *American Idol* remains on the flat screen, and the minimum payments on the credit cards cover this weekend's fun, why should we expect the masses to get out on the street and face real danger? The gilding has not yet come off the bars on the cage.

D: Yes, well, we'll see how things look in a few years when a majority of the population can't make its minimum payments and has to confront the grim reality of downsizing its lifestyle. We should come back to this at the beginning of July in 2014. I've got a feeling we're going to look back at July 4, 2011, as the good old days.

L: I'll try to remember that—if we're still having these conversations.

D: A foreboding thought. So next we come to the long list of grievances the colonials had against King George. As written, some of them are just issues of the day, such as the rather quaint one accusing the king of "bring(ing) on the inhabitants of our frontiers, the merciless Indian Savages, whose known rule of warfare, is an undistinguished destruction of all ages, sexes and conditions." But most of them really ring a bell. It's striking how applicable they still are today. Or are again today, if you update them for modern times, as you did in your Individual Declaration of Independence.

L: For example?

D: If you change "He" for King George to "It" for the U.S. government, you get things like:

"It has endeavored to prevent the population of these States; for that purpose obstructing the Laws for Naturalization of Foreigners; refusing to pass others to encourage their migrations hither. . . ."

As we discussed in our conversation on <u>immigration</u>, that's certainly still true today. But this isn't a good example because, I fear, most voters in the United States are anti-immigration and want to bar the doors. So, a better example would be:

"It has made Judges dependent on its Will alone, for the tenure of their offices, and the amount and payment of their salaries."

The federal judiciary system today is thoroughly corrupt—perhaps even more so than the King's judges were in 1776. The U.S. government employs both judges and prosecutors; that's a clear conflict of interest right there. Federal judges—prominently including those on the Supreme Court—are appointed, not elected. That makes it almost impossible to hold them accountable for their decisions. And they're all employees of the state—even the elected ones. Prosecutors are also state employees; they get promoted and further their political careers by securing convictions. The incentive in this system is not to secure justice, but to secure convictions. And the police are also state employees, of course. When the government is the plaintiff, prosecutor, and judge, defendants are at a huge disadvantage, as they were back in King George's day.

L: Can you back that up?

D: I don't have current stats, but last I saw, the conviction rate in federal cases was over 90 percent—an accuracy rate that defies belief for an organization that can't even deliver the mail reliably. Grand juries are a sham; it's no joke that a DA can get them to indict a ham sandwich. And our attorneys general have been a parade of goons for years: Ashcroft, Reno, Holder—these people could have worked quite happily in Auschwitz.

It is very, very dangerous that the government—not private citizens against one another—now brings the majority of the cases filed in court. Especially since, if memory serves, the only two crimes enumerated in the Constitution are treason and counterfeiting. But that's a subject for another day.

One more thing I would add: There is private arbitration in the United States. It's much cheaper, faster, and more ethical than the government system. I strongly encourage people to put "consent to arbitration" clauses in their contracts and use the private systems for justice.

L: They could start by looking up the American Arbitration Association. Okay, any more examples?

D: Yes; see if this sounds familiar:

"He has erected a multitude of New Offices, and sent hither swarms of Officers to harrass [sic] our people, and eat out their substance."

It's particularly egregious to see ourselves back in this same pickle. We have a largely unauthorized and unaccountable fourth branch of government in all the alphabet soup agencies: ATF, FBI, DEA (now DHS), DOL, DOA, DOE, DOC, IRS, FDA, SEC, and on and on. These parasites literally swarm over the countryside, making it all but impossible for an honest man to earn a living off the sweat of his brow.

L: It's sad, really. I realize that 235 years is a long time, but it's amazing that the descendants of people who rose up against their government over a three pence per pound tea tax, or whatever it was, exactly, now submit to 30 percent life-confiscation (taxes)—or even 63.4 percent life-confiscation, if you go by "cost of government." Who are these people? How can they celebrate "the fourth of July" without an inkling of how deeply they betray the revolution they toast?

D: Well, lapdogs are descended from wolves. I suppose they imagine themselves as sons of wolves, not lapdogs, even though they've actually evolved into a different species—as have Americans.

L: [Sighs] Ouch. My take is that generations of propaganda and government schooling have destroyed the average U.S. citizen's ability to engage in real, critical thinking and inculcated a culture of dependence and entitlement. Maybe not a separate species, but this is not a problem that can be fixed in a day, nor with the simple turning of a new page. It would take a lot of re-education, deprogramming, or maybe just generations of facing harsh economic realities to really regain the independent American spirit that made America great.

D: Let me stand corrected. Lapdogs are only a different breed, not a different species. Released from captivity, their descendants would revert to type—if you assume they survived long enough to do so. People have been taught to be good little cogs in the wheel. They call it being patriotic. And I agree with you that there's no quick fix for generations of cultural decay; there is no political solution. It doesn't matter who gets elected today; no one who can get elected could do what needs to be done. Even having a revolution today wouldn't fix anything; given what the average citizen feels, thinks, and believes, we'd only end up with something worse.

L: We'd get Robespierre, not Jefferson.

D: Yes. That's why, I'm sorry to say, I fear any radical change in the United States at this point. Does that make me a conservative? Anyway, next we have:

"It has kept among us, in times of peace, Standing Armies without the Consent of our legislatures."

And, among other related items:

"It has affected to render the Military independent of and superior to the Civil power."

Today, we have a vast and powerful military-industrial complex—not just militarily powerful, but sociopolitically dominant. Not only do we get treated to one counterproductive—and unconstitutional, if anyone cares—war after another, we get to pay $5,000 for military toilet seats and similar abuses that contribute to the bankruptcy of the nation. We get roughly 1,000 U.S. military camps overseas, plus all those at home. The economies of whole counties rely on U.S. military bases, just as others rely on prisons. We also get increased hatred of Americans among the survivors of our foreign military adventures. Perhaps most dangerous of all, we get hordes of ex-military types who've become inured to a life of slavery and violence entering our police forces. These people have become a force unto themselves now, both dangerous and unnecessary, as we discussed in our conversation on the military. "Keeping the peace" has been transformed into "law enforcement"; this is turning the United States into a police state.

L: Where you can get thrown to the floor and hauled off to the slammer for quietly dancing with your girlfriend in front of Thomas Jefferson's statue.

D: Or any of the other things David Galland mentioned in closing his *Daily Dispatch* Friday. And here's one more:

"It has combined with others to subject us to a jurisdiction foreign to our constitution, and unacknowledged by our laws; giving his Assent to their Acts of pretended Legislation. . . ."

Sounds to me just like the UN and all the U.S. treaties that subject U.S. citizens to foreign powers and interests.

Then there's:

"For cutting off our Trade with all parts of the world. . . ."

We have tomes and tomes of regulations, as well as import and export duties and such things that have the same effect, and ever-tighter currency controls, as we've warned readers.

And this:

"For imposing Taxes on us without our Consent. . . ."

Well, I sure haven't consented to any taxes. We could do a book on that one.

L: Heh. Let's see the IRS dismiss its armed branch and end its draconian punishments, then see how many people pay and how voluntary the federal income tax is.

D: In my dreams. Another:

"For transporting us beyond Seas to be tried for pretended offences. . . ."

Sounds like taking U.S. citizens to Guantanamo Bay and calling them "enemy combatants" so as to avoid the U.S. Constitution and any established law. Or, much worse, executing people based on suspicion alone. The Orwellian "PATRIOT Act" comes to mind.

One more:

"For depriving us in many cases, of the benefits of Trial by Jury. . . ."

In the U.S. today, juries are absolutely denied the right to determine the justice of the law. In the past it was understood that they had not only the right but the duty to seek justice, not just to enforce laws as instructed by some judge. But we've talked about <u>fully informed juries</u> before. I consider this an unconscionable usurpation.

That's enough of that; all of these things are unconscionable, even though they're passively, supinely, accepted by the whipped lapdogs that Americans have devolved into. I think our readers will get the picture: The current government of these forcibly united states is much, much more dangerous and capricious than the monarchy our ancestors rebelled against.

But there's one more thing in the Declaration's closing thoughts particularly worth noting:

"A Prince whose character is thus marked by every act which may define a Tyrant, is unfit to be the ruler of a free people."

That certainly describes the situation in the United States today. The government is not the friend of the people, nor their protector, nor their benefactor. The government is the single greatest threat to an individual's life, liberty, property, and even his pursuit of happiness. It's unworthy of the support people give it. It's an entity with a life of its own.

L: Strong words.

D: I'm not saying we ought to have a revolution, because as I said before, in the current cultural and intellectual environment, we'd just end up with something worse. But the fact that the fire is worse does not make the frying pan a good place to be. This is why the U.S. government doesn't have to worry about me becoming a rebel nor fomenting a revolution; I truly believe it would only make matters worse.

It's also why I've chosen to step aside from the coming troubles. It's not that I don't care about America—I loved the America that was—but that I don't think risking life and limb will do the kind of good it did our forefathers. And I would encourage our readers, who are smart enough to see what's coming, not to fall prey to misguided ideas of patriotism. We have no moral obligation to rescue those who try to vote themselves free lunches at our expense.

L: Has it ever crossed your mind that, particularly in a so-called democracy, people may actually get the government they deserve?

D: Yes, indeed it has. On a philosophical plane I've always believed that, with a few random exceptions, everyone gets what they deserve. Actions have consequences. It's as simple as that. Cause has effect, what goes around comes around, and you generally reap what you sow. The residents of the United States broadly accept all kinds of unsound, unwholesome notions. Reality is going to reward them with a lower standard of living, and a lot less respect from other people. The universe isn't malevolent, but it is disinterested. Residents of the United States will find that they've forfeited the right to consider themselves some kind of chosen people.

L: Okay then. Investment implications?

D: Well, as I've been saying, the more free and unregulated an economy, the more it's possible to invest—that is, to allocate capital so as to increase wealth. But as the government grows in scope and power, the economy becomes less stable and you have to switch to <u>speculating</u> on the outcomes of government distortions in the economy. That's the kind of economy we're looking at for some time. Most unfortunate. But we needn't be adversely affected.

L: No particular Independence Day plays, I suppose.

D: No. This is just a public service announcement. Word to the wise. Instead of wearing red, white, and blue, people should wear black on the fourth of July, to mourn the passing of the spirit of independence that was once America's greatest virtue and driving force.

L: Okay then, thanks for another somber, but, I believe, important set of ideas.

D: You're welcome. Enjoy your mortars! I hope the police don't mistake them for IEDs.

L: Me too!

Afterword

Dear Reader:

    In the introduction, I described this book as a set of keys for speculating successfully in today's exceptionally troubled environment. Now that you've had a chance to rummage through our intellectual toolbox, I hope you've not only grasped the method, but you are already seeing ways to apply it to your own finances and life.

    This is important. Doug's method is to look at the world in the light of realistic general principles and then to think about the specifics of what he sees. In applying this method, each reader will have to start with his own understanding of how the world really works. While part of the reason we assembled this book is to entertain and enlighten, our more important goal is to enable you to take action that will benefit you financially, and perhaps in other ways as well.

    We would like nothing better than for you to put the book down and call your travel agent to arrange for a visit to whatever destination you judge is a good place to start internationalizing your life. Or make that call to your broker to discuss ways of implementing Doug's financial recommendations that still apply today. Or just hop online, to further educate yourself in whatever you need to understand to be able to take the actions Doug is pointing toward.

Do it today.

Don't wait.

Don't let the ideas cool off.

Don't let the urge to take action fade away, lest when you remember it, it's too late.

I sincerely and urgently recommend that you take this seriously; as bad as the coming economic upheavals will be for those who are caught unaware, they will carry a special sting for those who understood and saw the trouble coming but did nothing.

If you're just not sure where to start, I humbly suggest that you include the offerings of Casey Research in your continuing education. Specifically, for those who like Doug's style of investing and are just starting out, I recommend our flagship service, *The Casey Report.*

In *The Casey Report,* Doug and his team accurately predicted and alerted subscribers early about:

- The meteoric rise of gold in the early 2000s
- The bursting of the housing bubble in 2007
- The financial crash in 2008

Subscribers to *The Casey Report* have profited handsomely from this foresight and from the Report's practical advice in applying it. In addition, they have been well protected from the volatile market swings of recent years; optimal diversification is one of *The Casey Report*'s focal points. From physical metals, to easy and practical ways to hold foreign currencies, to high-yielding stocks, to emerging-market funds, you'll find all the tools for perfect portfolio allocation. And you can try *The Casey Report* with no risk to you.

No hard feelings if you choose not to, of course—there is plenty of help available to you from other sources. The important thing is that before you turn this last page and put the book down, you make a commitment to yourself that you will take action based upon whatever conclusions you have drawn for yourself after thinking over what we've had to say.

Thank you for reading, and may you not only survive, but thrive, during the greater depression to come.

Sincerely,

Terry Coxon

About the Authors

Doug Casey is a highly respected author, publisher, and professional investor. Doug literally wrote the book on profiting from periods of economic turmoil: His book, *Crisis Investing,* spent multiple weeks as number one on the *New York Times* bestseller list and became the best-selling financial book of 1980, with 438,640 copies sold—surpassing big-caliber names, like *Free to Choose* by Milton Friedman, *The Real War* by Richard Nixon, and *Cosmos* by Carl Sagan.

Doug broke the record with his next book, *Strategic Investing*, by receiving the largest advance ever paid for a financial book at the time. Interestingly enough, Doug's book, *The International Man,* was the most sold book in the history of Rhodesia.

He has been a featured guest on hundreds of radio and TV shows, including those of David Letterman, Merv Griffin, Charlie Rose, Phil Donahue, Regis Philbin, and Maury Povich, as well as NBC News and CNN. Doug has also been featured in periodicals such as *Time, Forbes, People*, and the *Washington Post*.

Doug is the founding Chairman of Casey Research, an investment research publisher that helps self-directed investors earn superior returns by taking advantage of market dislocations.

Louis James, senior editor, Metals Division, Casey Research. Louis travels the world, visiting highly prospective geological targets, grilling management and company geologists, and interviewing natives. His background in physics, economics, and technical writing prepared him well for his role as senior editor of the *International Speculator* and *Casey Investment Alert*. Wherever he is, Louis is on the lookout for the next double-your-money winner.

Terry Coxon, president, Passport Financial. Terry Coxon is the author of *Keep What You Earn* and *Using Warrants* and the co-author (with Harry Browne) of *Inflation-Proofing Your Investments*. He edited *Harry Browne's Special Reports* for its 23 years of publication and all of Harry Browne's investment books since 1974.

Terry was the founder and for 22 years the president of the Permanent Portfolio Fund, a mutual fund that invests in precious metals as well as stocks and bonds.

Index